WORD CARVING

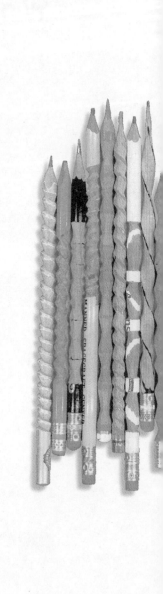

WORD CARVING

The Craft of Literary Journalism

Edited by Moira Farr and Ian Pearson

THE BANFF CENTRE
PRESS

All the essays in this book were written and published with a generous contribution from a fund established by Maclean Hunter and Alberta Advanced Education to support The Banff Centre's Creative Non-Fiction and Cultural Journalism program.

National Library of Canada Cataloguing in Publication
Main entry under title:

Word carving : the craft of literary journalism / edited by Moira Farr and Ian Pearson.

ISBN 1-894773-02-0

1. Canadian essays (English)—21st century.★ I. Farr, Moira, 1958-
II. Pearson, Ian, 1954- III. Banff Centre for the Arts.
PS8373.W67 2003   C814'.608   C2003-910774-4
PR9197.7.W67 2003

Book design by Warren Clark
Copyediting by Maureen Nicholson
Proofreading by Vivian Elias
Printed and bound in Canada by Houghton Boston, Saskatoon, SK.
Cover artwork by Peter Schuyff (see acknowledgements for details)

The Banff Centre Press gratefully acknowledges the Canada Council for the Arts for its support of our publishing program.

BANFF CENTRE PRESS
Box 1020
Banff, AB T1L 1H5
www.banffcentre.ca/press

The Canada Council | Le Conseil des Arts
for the Arts | du Canada

THE BANFF CENTRE

Acknowledgements

The editors gratefully acknowledge the editing contributions of Don Obe (for Douglas Bell's "The Accidental Course of My Illness") and Mark Abley (for Camilla Gibbs' "Foreigners"). We would also like to thank Carol Holmes and Kathy Morrison for their tireless devotion to the program, Lauri Seidlitz and Karen Buttner for the editing and management finesse they have put into this volume, and Alberto Ruy-Sánchez for all the warmth, wisdom, and magic he has brought to his role as chair.

The publisher would like to thank Peter Schuyff for the permission to use the cover artwork, titled *Sans Papier*. Schuyff is a Canadian visual artist based in New York. He created the piece at The Banff Centre in 2002.

Contents

MOIRA FARR AND IAN PEARSON

Preface

WRITERS CRAVE TIME AND SPACE ABOVE ALL ELSE. Fewer and fewer magazines grant writers these basic creative necessities, which is why The Banff Centre's Creative Non-Fiction and Cultural Journalism program has become such an important refuge for good writing. Founded in 1989 with generous endowments from Maclean Hunter and the Government of Alberta, the program selects eight writers a year (chosen from a highly competitive field). The writers have a month to work on a longer article in close consultation with an editor and in intensive workshops with their peers. They have the luxury of working in the gorgeously secluded Leighton Studios, another form of blessed space. For a month, they experience a nurturing mix of solitude and fellowship that can be rare in writers' lives. Most of all, they have an opportunity to push their writing to its limits, as Alberto Ruy-Sánchez explains in his introduction.

The twelve writers here reach those limits with diverse styles and challenging subjects. Katherine Ashenburg explores her favourite nurse novels, touching on the sensual pleasures of reading and how books mark us in childhood, indelibly shaping our identities. Douglas Bell illuminates the profound impact a devastating childhood accident has had on his life and his relationship with his mother. Ted Bishop finds that his twin obsessions — riding motorcycles and cruising literary archives — are surprisingly intertwined. A-A Farman-Farmaian tosses out most preconceived ideas about "home" and finds his own place in the wider world. Alyse Frampton's portrait of her eccentric father shows how misguided ideologies can squander a fortune and fracture a family (and still leave room for love). Through friendship with a "foreigner," Camilla Gibb unravels her own foreignness. Matthew Hart's intricate deconstruction of a notorious Irish art heist shows how theft brought new meaning to a priceless Vermeer. Johanna Keller's memoir of her relationship with the renowned pianist Samuel Sanders, Itzhak Perlman's beloved accompanist, becomes a cultural ghost story. Chris Koentges takes a wild, youthful road trip into the heart of American culture at its most gloriously tacky and marginal and comes home with a one of a kind meditation on innocence and experience as his souvenir. Anita Lahey examines the lost art of the eulogy and finds the power of words in the face of death. Philip Marchand recounts his formative years in a 1960s therapeutic community and shows the contradictions between personal growth and self-involvement. And Ellen Vanstone hilariously reveals the strange undercurrent of sexuality at a conservative national newspaper, wickedly satirizing its politics in the process.

All these writers dig deep into themselves and their subject matter, offering their final original creations for readers to savour. We have been privileged to work with these gifted people as they used their time and space in Banff to explore their thoughts and shape their stories — to carve their words into finely crafted works of writerly art.

April 2003

ALBERTO RUY-SÁNCHEZ

(TRANSLATED BY RHONDA DAHL BUCHANAN)

Introduction:
The Rituals of Writing

ALTHOUGH I UNDERSTAND WHY IT HAPPENS, I'M ALWAYS amazed that people consider the customs and beliefs of their culture to be universal. For example, many Mexicans are certain that people eat corn tortillas in every country of the world, just as they do in Mexico, and that *mole* and other regional delights form part of the daily diet everywhere. Similarly, many Americans believe the best way to travel is to stay in hotels where the rooms and amenities are exactly the same, and the best way to eat is to buy hamburgers in restaurant chains whose goal is for each food product to taste exactly the same in every city in the world. This North American dream of sameness now dominates many cultures throughout the world.

In much the same way, Anglo-Saxon culture has upheld, as if it were a universal truth, the distinction between fiction and non-fiction, which seems strange to many of us from other cultures. In Europe, and throughout much of Latin America, the distinction is viewed differently. It surprises us that in bookstores in the United States, Canada, and some other countries, volumes are arranged according to literary genre, whereas in European bookstores the topic and the author are the determining factors. In Europe, the books of brilliant literary essayists, such as Roger Caillois, Maurice

Blanchot, and Roland Barthes, appear in the same section and on the same shelf as the narrative works of Marcel Proust, Gustave Flaubert, and André Gide.

Both the essay and the novel bear the unique mark of the writer. Given that the author of a non-fiction work is an active participant in the writing, it would never occur to those outside the Anglo-Saxon culture that the author's presence is transparent or invisible. Indeed, the presence of the author is what enhances an essay. It is precisely the author's perception of reality that transforms the essay into a valuable work of research, reflection, and creative experience destined for a community of readers. Likewise, it would never occur to most non-Anglo-Saxon readers that either genre is more capable of expressing the truth than the other simply because of its generic classification.

For a long time, novels have been viewed as intense investigations of reality. No one assumes that the plot of a novel by Marcel Proust documents historical events, nor would anyone deny that Proust's fiction is a document of great historical value reflecting the desires and attitudes of his time. The portrait of French society in *Remembrance of Things Past* is indispensable for historians who consider themselves serious scholars of the period and believe that history is much more than a parade of dates, battles, and governments. Each novel may be regarded as a testimonial document of the century in which it was written. In it lie the dreams of the period as well as its creative energy, attitudes, ethnography, and passions.

The novel and poetry continue to exist because these genres possess instruments for penetrating certain dimensions of reality that other disciplines, such as psychoanalysis or sociology, cannot explore as profoundly. Literature speaks to us about some aspects of reality that can only be grasped through fiction. And moreover, only literature offers us one of the greatest pleasures of life — the pleasure of understanding in a way that engages all the senses without subordinating them to the hierarchy of a rational argument whose logic goes to the point to avoid poetic or narrative digressions, which may be viewed as irrational or too fictional.

Given the controversial nature of the distinction between fiction and non-fiction, the significance of the unorthodox form of writing known as creative non-fiction may be understood in terms of culture, in the most ethnographic sense of the word; that is, as a phenomenon in which writing forms part of a Protestant cultural ritual based on the fetishistic cult of the word as truth. The distinction between fiction and non-fiction has religious origins stemming from the relationship that certain founding communities established with the truth, as set forth in the Bible. What we are experiencing today is an echo of that belief in the truth as it is revealed in sacred texts and the consequential condemnation of those texts that stray from the true word. The reverence for non-fiction is a direct descendant of the Protestant Reformation. It is a modern concept linked to the culture that dominates how we live today under capitalism, as Max Weber explains in his classic *The Protestant Ethic and the Spirit of Capitalism*. The religious dimension has become tacit, but we still continue to embrace it in the act of classifying some books as more "truthful" than others.

Evidence of this cultural and historical phenomenon may be seen in the fact that those cultures whose development strayed completely from the Reformation, following instead the path of the Counter-Reformation, do not embrace the traditional distinction between fiction and non-fiction. This is true of the Spanish culture, and also to a large extent Hispanic American cultures, whose ways of perceiving the world may be characterized as baroque rather than modern. Their literature is also baroque, faithful to their search for multiple truths, including the sensorial truths expressed in an artistic or well-crafted form.

The heterodox introduction of cultural journalism or the personal essay, or creative non-fiction (whatever you wish to call this amphibious adventure that strives for respect), implies certain challenges to the traditional practice of writing today. Let us call these challenges our ethnographic tools for writing creative non-fiction.

The first of those useful principles involves a greater presence of the author in the work. This is why the word *personal* has been placed next to *essay;* in other cultures, the second term is already understood as representing a deeply personal act of writing, which eliminates the need to modify the expression. In the traditional Protestant way of thinking, the author introduces subjectivity, the supposed enemy of the truth.

In creative writing, the presence of the author and the author's subjectivity are not only a necessity, but also an act of honesty. Moreover, the *I* who writes, although that presence appears invisible, impartial, and objective, can be identified by the perceptive reader as one more character in the story being told. That character may be one who conceals or one who reveals himself or herself; a character who pretends to have no passions or one who recognizes them and allows others to see and judge them if necessary. A writer who is aware that the *I* who writes is always a character, whether implicit or explicit, will have a greater command over the final form of the tale or essay. A fundamental mask is lifted with this recognition.

Another ethnographic principle that serves the author of creative non-fiction is the ability to see himself or herself as a tribal storyteller, no longer as the symbolic prototype of the priest or the preacher, as was the case of the traditional conception, but rather as the ritual figure of the storyteller. The narrator's purpose is not solely to entertain, nor to distract the mind from the lively centre of community life. Although selected narrative techniques capture the attention of an audience, the narrator tells stories that in a direct or indirect manner speak about the vibrant life of the tribe: daily conflicts and celebrations, but also mythical origins and the destiny of the clan, the essence of life. A storyteller always speaks about that which constitutes the essence of life for the community or some sector of it.

Let us consider another ethnographic principle: writing is a ritual. The idea is not to create a mirror of words or a superficial reflection of life, unless the ritual involves those powerful, enchanted mirrors that reflect reality without masks, revealing many of its profound virtues and defects. The content that surpasses the superficial aspects of reality is what makes this narrative act transcendental in the end. For this reason, writing is a ritual. Moreover, in ethnographic terms, this magical written mirror should be an object whose beautiful and aesthetically strong form is an expression of the implicit powers of the ritual act in which it is incorporated.

To write is to create a ritualistic object — the text — with a mighty expressive force in its form. It is the creation of something that other cultures, or our own, may consider a work of art.

For all these reasons, I have conceived my work as chair of the Creative Non-Fiction and Cultural Journalism Program at The Banff Centre as an eminently ethnographic adventure.

The first time I was invited to chair this program, in 1999, I was asked to introduce my point of view as a foreign author and editor into the group discussions of particular projects. I was given the task of examining, from a different cultural perspective, the topics that concerned the writers, especially how they approached those topics. I have proceeded under the assumption that the type of creative work this program seeks (that which is rooted in a vital and intense investigation, often with ties to journalism), is precisely the type of writing that surpasses the traditional and cultural norms of what is considered non-fiction. During the month-long program, the writers receive no exact instructions regarding what should or should not be done. They are not asked to conform to certain strict rules of writing, but rather to adopt some loose guidelines for living and working together. They also attend a series of four conferences, one each week, in which distinguished practitioners of creative and documentary writing speak to us about their work, providing lessons in an indirect way.

Of primary importance is the intense exchange of ideas between the writers and their editors, and between the writers and the group, which takes place during discussions of the major themes intrinsic to each text. Every session teaches us that entire books could be written based on the group's interest in each other's work, the individual approaches to each topic, their experiences and research, and much more. The goal is to provide an incentive to the writers that will enable them to enhance their own creativity and ability to communicate, beginning with the communication with that small community of writers who come together for one month. Each year the program includes eight writers, two brilliant experienced editors, Ian Pearson and Moira Farr, and one chairperson, who together form an ephemeral, communal nucleus, which often runs the risk of not being so ephemeral, persisting as a long-distance network.

We also hope to invigorate ourselves culturally and professionally through each individual presence, a mutual enrichment that rarely occurs among a group of writers, the majority of whom are established authors with important published works. Nevertheless, another challenge for the group is that the month of writing in Banff becomes a unique experience that changes, slightly or profoundly, how each writer views the major theme of his or her work. On certain occasions the experience has transformed how the writers see their craft, their relationship with writing, and through this, their relationship with the social and cultural surroundings.

When a member of the group presents a work that stimulates us, the most intimate obsessions of that author begin to inhabit our beings and grow within us. We learn from our experiences with the other members of the group. We also share a privileged environment in the mountains that offers intense contact with nature. The eleven-member group benefits from the administrative organization in Banff, which provides all the necessary infrastructure to allow the writers to dedicate themselves to their work. The Department of Writing and Publishing, as well as the entire administration of The Banff Centre, takes care of and protects us, allowing our work to go on uninterrupted. For each writer, the cabins in the woods — the Leighton Studios — are an inspirational space, practically a dream come true.

In addition, there is the extended community of the other artists who work in Banff at the same time. Musicians, dancers, photographers, painters, sculptors, potters, installationists, techno artists, and actors — all form an interesting community during the month. And these artists, with their specialties, choose the extent to which they wish to socialize during their stay in Banff. All must measure to what degree their experiences will be enriched or dispersed.

Without realizing it, many of the artists in Banff walk down parallel paths that suddenly converge. This has been the case with Peter Schuyff, a visual artist who enjoys international renown and who has visited in Banff at the same time as several of our groups of writers. Coincidence has become confluence: Schuyff's sculptures made of carved pencils grace the cover of this book. For me, they seem like visual echoes of ancient rituals, micro-totems of the rituals of writing from imaginary civilizations. They lead us to the unexpected and highly crafted forms the artist of the word and the artist of the wood may produce.

And they remind us of the last ethnologic principle that rules our *Word Carving:* To perceive life like a stranger, with a renewed sense of wonder for all that surrounds us.

A-A Farman-Farmaian

Hiding Places

SOMETIME IN OCTOBER 1978, A COUPLE OF MONTHS before the Shah of Iran was finally overthrown, my mother called me and my brother to her room to tell us we were going on vacation to Europe. She told us to pack two suitcases and get our homework assignments from school. Then she warned us that, if things got worse, we might end up staying a little longer than planned. She asked us how we felt about that. She was very good at this, anticipating and cushioning a potential trauma without creating an unnecessary one. I was twelve, my brother was ten, and we didn't know what to make of it, so we packed our bags.

By then, a few movie theatres had been set on fire and a curfew had been imposed. At night, we could hear shots fired somewhere in the distance. But the Islamic revolution of Iran broke out in full force only a few weeks after we left. And so, this time in a hotel in Geneva, my mother called us into her room once again. She told us things were not looking good and we would not be returning home any time soon. Before she could ask how we felt about this, my brother and I jumped up with joy. Quick to grasp the essential implications of the Islamic revolution, we realized we no longer had to complete our homework assignments.

Portentous events have always been transmitted to us in my mother's rooms, and in one of those rooms we got the news about our home back home — in her first or second room in Geneva, with its verdant motif, floral curtains, green bamboo bed, paisley throw, almost like a greenhouse, a shelter for uprooted life. Other parts of the apartment were not like it at all. She wanted it that way, so vastly different in style and in spirit, to completely mark off her realm from the rest of the world. It was a private corner in which she took refuge whenever life came harassing her with bad news. One of the anecdotes she repeated often back then was about Voltaire jumping across the border into Geneva every time he saw French officials creeping up to arrest him. I think she saw that room as her Geneva within Geneva, a personal haven in her country of refuge.

But then her rooms have always been a realm apart. In our palatial house in Iran — which had become my mother's dominion after my father's early death in 1973 in a skiing accident — her room was tucked into a far corner of the second floor, yet it was the centre of everything, an inner sanctum of enigma and authority, a place we needed permission to enter and a place in which we sought permission. We would wait for her to wake up, and her waking would be announced by an electric bell connected to a box in the pantry where Fatemeh Khanoum, the bright-eyed, over-efficient maid with a white headscarf, sat ready next to a tray of fresh orange juice, tea, and toast. She'd scramble up and whisk the tray off the table, and we'd dash excitedly, beating her to my mother's room, knocking impatiently, then rushing inside while the curtains were still drawn and the room dark to ask permission for something we needed desperately to do. "Can we go in the pool?" "Can we go see our friends?" Fatemeh Khanoum would enter, arrange the breakfast tray on my mother's bed, and slide open the curtains. Daylight would pour in, suddenly illuminating a woman's sacred world of mirrors, jewels, and silk-soft sheets.

10

I remember her room mostly in the dark, though, with the curtains drawn, because we were usually in there early in the morning or at night. Not long before we left Iran, she had gotten into the habit of reading us stories and poetry. We would lie in our pyjamas on her paisley quilt, passed down from her mother and a mother before that, and she would read to us from an abridged version of *Merchant of Venice* or a few verses from Saadi. We'd also be there whenever she was getting ready for her dinner parties. Her pearls, her boudoir, her glamorous wardrobe evoked an enchanting feminine world out of our reach, a place reserved for certain special people who drank whisky and were allowed to stay up late and play in the world of adult games. They had their own Barbie and GI Joe world, just as we, thanks to a few American-style stores, had ours.

The wonder, the sense of awe in that room, was partly in the young eyes, but even later, when we had grown up, my mother's rooms transmitted the same sensations. Once in Geneva, we moved several times, and in each apartment she reconstructed her room as though she were fashioning a new universe, giving it its own laws and its own aesthetics. She was, perhaps, trying to capture the specialness of that first home, not its size or grandiosity, but some of its meanings, some of its light and some of its shadows. Those first years in Geneva, our deadly quiet little place of exile, were difficult for her, suddenly adrift alone with two children. She tried to shield us, but the trauma would seep out, as trauma often does. She would explode into irrational rage, usually in the kitchen, where our negligence in allowing the pot of rice to burn would somehow transmute into a major cause of the revolution, with possible links to the Iran-Iraq war and the destruction of the environment, and with that kind of irresponsible behaviour, it was no wonder that the world was in the state it was in. Then she would retire to her room and shut the door.

When we walked into that room, that same night, to comfort her and ourselves, or for that matter at any other time, we walked in gingerly. In our now older eyes, her room may have appeared less magical, but it still felt like a sanctified realm and a locus of authority.

We would gather in her room to hear bits of news about people "back home" or the fate of the belongings we had left behind. We could tell when my mother was talking on the phone to Iran because her voice would resound with a sad authority and be louder than usual, perhaps to help it cross the gulf of loss more than the physical distance. The other telling feature was the strange language. In the early days after the revolution — actually, even today — everyone was convinced that the lines were tapped; that an army of young bearded students was sitting with headsets in some basement, hoping to intercept a crucial bit of information about the debauched elite or foreign spies. So people devised a sort of adolescent code, a substitution of the names of valuables with the names of ordinary goods, peaches for carpets and letters for money. When she was done talking, my mother would call us into her room and from her bed, propped up on pillows, she would transmit news of a life that once seemed irrevocably ours, but with each phone call was fading and fraying, from the fringes all the way up.

We heard that the caretaker, a seventies romancer type with a Bee Gees beard and blow-dried hair named Mr. Ali, had hidden some of the art and the carpets in a vault to the left of the main staircase and plastered over the entrance. Then we were relayed these bits of news in quick succession: that the bank accounts had been frozen, then repossessed; that my father, though dead for seven years, had nevertheless been placed on a wanted list and everything belonging to his children and spouse no longer belonged to them. That included our house, which was now officially owned by others. So Mr. Ali removed some of the silver and carpets from the sealed vault inside our now ex-house to a safer refuge in his own house. Still later, we heard that some paintings and carpets (yes, carpets were always part of it), along with photo albums and old letters, were smuggled inside a watermelon truck and would reach Europe at some unknown time. Some of it was lost or stolen or hijacked along the way, and some of it reached us, stained with watermelon juice.

The only truly sad moment came when my mother told us that our seventy-five-year-old Romanian nurse, Madame Irene, who raised us, had fallen down the stairs in the children's quarters — dark stairs we had taken thousands of times, descending from our bedrooms to the cavelike playroom below and the garden outside, stairs connecting two happy, exclusive realms via a small landing halfway down, on which stood a wrought-iron radiator. Madame Irene split her head open on that radiator. It was later rumoured that it wasn't a simple fall. She and her cantankerous drunk of a husband, whom we called simply Monsieur ("Moossyo"), had been arguing at the top of the stairs.

Of all the news that came out of Iran — uncles jailed, death sentences on family members, friends in hiding — Madame Irene's was the only story that made me cry. A tragic end made more painful by its location, in a children's playroom, among bits of Lego strewn about the floor, under a wall pockmarked with the patterns and stitches of a football we used to bounce against it despite Madame Irene's pleas. My tears, I think, were of love and guilt, of regret for all the times we kids tortured her. I imagined her mottled, corpulent flesh and her melliferous scent, confusing it probably with the smell of sweets she brought us whenever she went home on holiday, which she did not do often on account of her husband's unbearable moods and occasional violence. I remember Moossyo's cane and his droopy eyes, lambskin cap, gravelly voice, and vodka breath. Every time my mother suggested that it was time for

Madame Irene to take a break, rest at home with her husband, Madame Irene would respond in her heavy and slow Farsi, "No, Madame, I am too tired for a holiday."

Madame Irene had lived on with us long after we needed care. At first she was angry at her sudden purposelessness, but in the final years she reconciled herself with just being around and often said she never wanted to leave. She never did. She lived there longer than we did and died there too, without us, and I cannot remember or imagine that house without her.

That house was a home in the fullest sense of the word, not a shelter but a place speckled with meaning and discovery, where we first found food, love, fear, art, death, solitude, and pain. It was where we found out what being was made of, among the brick and mortar of our metaphysics: The great big columns on the veranda and the hot white stone we lay on in the summer after a day in the pool, baking our bellies. The round lawn at the geometrical centre of which I at the age of three would sit and wail when chastised or rejected. The balustrade through which we spied down on the huge living room and its hairy, grown-up inhabitants. The smoky, mirrored wall in which I used to stare at myself, trying to see how that face I saw matched me, until one day my mother noticed and told me it is not good to look at myself in the mirror. And there was my father's study presided over by a Picasso watercolour of a musketeer, with tragic, dissimilar eyes, my father's wedding gift to my mother, accidentally lost in the aftermath of the revolution to a paper shredder.

In its less communal spaces, there were far-off rooms with the smell of wet laundry and an unending river of soap bubbles flowing out from under the door, dark vaults like the one under the staircase in which Mr. Ali hid the carpets, musty nooks and crannies containing iron safes, pistols, and my father's fencing gear from his Oxford days, with the smell of metal and leather blended with the smell of his sweat. Surrounding all this, enveloping it in a semi-man-icured embrace, was a giant garden, along the farthest edges of which were untrod pathways and unused sheds that would yield their silent mysteries only to children.

In those corners, where nothing unwanted could touch us, we shaped our secrets and found our private selves. They were our hid-ing places. My brother liked to hide things, I liked to hide myself, and sometimes all the kids would hide together from the adults. Behind sofas, mattresses, antique tables, and stacks of rugs piled up in storage, we carved out The Invisible City, with tunnels connect-ing one "room" to the next. While sitting quietly inside, we often heard adult voices shouting from out in the world, "I know you're in there, come out or I'll lock you in" — we never came out and they never locked us in. Another favourite hideout was a tree house at the very end of the garden on a "King-berry" tree, where only the boys and a handful of honorary tomboys were allowed in. I had two of my own exclusive hiding places, which like most children's hiding places were dark corners that had to be crawled into: inside the doghouse, mostly in the company of a mute Dalmatian, and in a ditch in a remote corner of the garden, sometimes filled with leaves waiting to be burned.

And one day, in her greenhouse room in Geneva, about two years after we left, my mother gently told us of the fate of that home in Iran.

"I have some bad news," she started. "It's the house." We had done this before, sitting in my mother's room in Geneva talking about other rooms in Iran. Living one life and keeping another, keeping it less and less, partly because there was less and less of it to keep.

"They destroyed the house," she said, the angle of her head and her deliberately softened voice showing not her own pain but con-cern about how we'd take the news. And we, my brother and I, sat there for a few seconds trying to understand its implications. She continued, "Apparently, the neighbours across the street said they came in the night with bulldozers and tore down the house."

Finally, my brother sighed, "Oh, no, all our secret hiding places are gone." We laughed, and it seemed that nothing else needed to be said. In fact, that was all that was ever said. Every conversation about the house from that point on referred not to the building or the garden but to my brother's innocent wisdom.

Of course, we had pictures of it. Not long after we determined that we would stay on in Geneva, my mother began obsessing about our belongings. How to get them out? What to get out? How much would it cost? Her most immediate concern was to recover my dad's letters and the pictures from her family albums. She quickly arranged for those to be carried out, by a Belgian diplomat I believe, but not far behind on the list was obtaining photographs of the house and the garden. I'm not sure who came up with the idea, but I know that at some point we noticed we had no pictures of the place — at least not without a smiling relative taking up most of the frame — and felt we needed them, we needed some representation of the original home, some fetish to stand in for its meanings. We asked Mr. Ali to take pictures with his black Instamatic and send them to us. We got on the phone one by one to make sure he wouldn't miss the one corner or feature that seemed most impor-tant to us. When they finally arrived, the pictures were a disap-pointment, and not because they were too cyan (developed in Tehran in the middle of revolution). We angled them this way and that, trying to slip beyond the borders of the picture behind the great pine tree with its crunching bed of dry needles. But we couldn't; the borders of the Kodak paper were absolute. The pictures seemed like lifeless snapshots taped to the windows of a realtor's office. They captured the columns and the steps and the lane of cypress trees, but not the hiding places, not the cosmos inside the home. After the house was razed, the pictures turned even more poignantly inadequate, making the lifestyle rather than the meaning of the place jump out.

I'm not sure what we felt that night, when we got the news, but I think my mother cooked some veal strips with lemon and sage, and we went to my brother's room to watch a video.

By then, it was clear that we would not be going back in the foreseeable future. The mullahs, firmly in power, had a visceral dislike for anything that smacked of the old regime, and their roaming militias of armed youth went around practising the familiar alchemy of history: taking old wealth and making it new by making it their own. It left us little to go back to. Of the extended family, only a few uncles or aunts had stayed on, some of them under house arrest or in jail, as well as my maternal grandmother who refused to leave. There was certainly a sense of longing in the first years abroad, in our first two apartments. But if I longed for anything, it cannot have been Iran, even if I said so because it was something to be said, something everyone said, and consequently something to be felt. The fact is I had very little idea of what Iran was.

We were spoiled and overprotected and too young to have developed the teenage thrill and lust that drives a discovery of the wider and wilder world. Until the last few months, we had very little exposure to the world beyond our walls. We heard about it from the sons and daughters of those who worked for us, with whom we played cowboys and Indians in the garden. They occasionally brought us tokens from there, such as fresh yogourt and switchblades. We caught other glimpses of it through the car window, literally like moving pictures, as we were shuttled to school or to an uncle's or friend's house; and there were the accompanied outings to the cinema or the Ice Palace skating rink. But what exactly was that world and why was it there? Did some mischievous deity prop all this up to mock us and entertain himself? Was it real or was it a show, like the one at the Ice Palace?

I remember having these primitive and paranoid Cartesian thoughts as I watched the shop signs flit by and hundreds of unknown faces stream past outside the car. What can a child believe about a world outside his or her own, a world that seems to be in independent motion? There was little sense of continuity between my skin and the world's. Little sense that we were on the same timeline, held down by the same forces.

Home on the other hand felt like an organic part of me, an extension of my insides, with corners for my thoughts and sheds for my moods. Even as I began to see more of the outside world, in the final year in Iran, and then later as I grew into my early teens and adapted to a life elsewhere, that sense of home as a physical place seemed to stick. Forever concerned with aesthetics, my mother regularly bought *Architectural Digest* (as well as *Vogue* and *Elle Décor*). There was always a stack of them, under a square glass table, in our Geneva apartments. Periodically, I would leaf through them with my brother and a cousin, the three of us building our dream house out of a collage of color photographs and adolescent fantasy. We knew those homes were unattainable, but they managed somehow to feel concrete, something we could grasp, like the home we once had. To this day, my mother speaks of a home she plans to build in Spain or Morocco or Turkey.

I view all that now as a confusion, a case of the outer shell posing as the inner self. For if it was not Iran I missed, it wasn't exactly the house either. It was the hiding places I missed. In the most obvious sense, the hiding was a form of psychological refuge, a shelter from such common things as a mother's occasional rage or a public humiliation by some diabolical cousin. To think of it in those terms alone, however, would be to diminish it. The hiding places were much more than that, much grander than the space they occupied, extending beyond their perimeters and opening up beyond their volume, beyond the dimensions of Euclidean geometry or

Freudian shelter, beyond these and into an infinite recess where possibilities seemed different, where the self and the world could be prodded, probed, questioned, and built differently. To the leaves and to my Dalmatian, Igor, I posed my why and what-if questions: Why had my father died? What if I were someone else's child? I told them the silliest joke of the day and practised absurd kung fu chops copied from Bruce Lee movies. And sometimes I'd cry and sometimes I made beautiful designs peeing and sometimes I thought about how much I loved my brother and sometimes about how I wanted to smash his head against the brick wall. But always I was whole, existing without judgment or contradiction, a big mix of beast and angel in the unfragmented silence and solitude of hiding. Could I have asked for a better home than that, than what was given me by a doghouse and a mute dog, or a ditch with dry leaves waiting to be burned?

We like to bind the most ephemeral parts of our being to physical things, to make the unknown known, the unseen seen, and the untouchable touched — statues for liberty, gravestones for the dead, beads for our prayers. Without them we might drift away into a vacuum. We need a terra firma, some solid territory, on which to map out the more vaporous territories of the mind. That is why we take refuge in an attic or basement or a bathtub: it's a home for the primal subconscious, a shell to fit the soul. But what's the use of a soul if it's stuck in one corner? What, to paraphrase Gertrude Stein, is the use of a home if you can't take it with you?

As long as the house existed physically, even if officially it was not ours anymore, my memories lodged themselves between the bricks, waiting. They could bind to something in the world I hoped to lay eyes on or touch again, if only I walked long enough on that carpet rolling out into the past. Then the house crumbled. It took a few years for the dust to settle, so to speak, but when it did, I looked up and the memories had been dislodged from the masonry, and I felt as though some mirthful spirit had descended with the delight of a kid stomping all over a sand castle, shouting: Look around, you are milling about in the rubble of an old house and a garden reduced to dirt and that place you called home is nothing more than a square patch of earth. There are plenty of places to hide. This is your world. Take your self and go and remember to praise the bulldozers.

Camilla Gibb

Foreigners

ADIQO USED TO CALL ME THE FARENJI, "THE FOREIGNER," even though it was she who had come to Canada as a refugee and I had spent most of my life here. She was 5'2", a tiny woman weighing less than a hundred pounds, wearing jeans and a T-shirt large enough to clothe two of her. She had long, paper-thin hair, dark skin, and even darker circles around her eyes, and she smelled like the warm butter she rubbed into her hair to make it shine.

I was the white giant standing beside her — 5'10" with shockingly red hair and a pierced nose, wearing a miniskirt and steel-toed boots. Still, if you cocked your head at a particular angle and squinted your eyes, you might have seen a similarity. Both of us looked a bit like bruised fruit drop kicked off the back of a passing transport truck.

When we met, I was a student in my early twenties, studying social anthropology, a discipline that had greeted me with open arms: a refuge for people like me who wanted to escape the conventions of the world they were born to. This passport to other worlds had taken me to Kenya and then Cairo, where for a year I navigated streets that reeked of urine, exhaust, and overripe mangos, studied Arabic, fell in and out of love, and omitted a lot of significant detail in my letters home. Back in Toronto, I was wandering around like a dazed adolescent dreaming of other worlds when I first caught sight of Adiqo. I didn't notice her because she was black, but because she was African. She was closer to Kenya and Egypt — the places where my heart was lingering and my head was lost — than anyone around me. She was the embodiment of elsewhere: a living connection to my dreams.

Adiqo had arrived at Pearson Airport that August carrying a small suitcase and a canvas bag she had been given by her sponsors, World University Services Canada. She had won WUSC's prestigious scholarship for refugees and was headed for the University of Toronto. The university gave Adiqo a room in residence, a meal plan, and a part-time job — anything else she might have needed, she was left to find on her own.

When I met her I wanted to wrap my arms around her, protect her, know her secrets, be her best friend. Adiqo told me I was "different" from the other white Canadians she had met: I was interested in the world beyond. We talked about Egypt and Kenya, places we both knew. We peppered our phrases with Arabic expressions like "thanks to God" and "if God is willing," and we linked arms and sang *Hakuna Matata,* Swahili for "no problem." We became friends for a reason: We were both, in our own ways, *farenjis.*

Adiqo couldn't have known that I was *only* interested in the world beyond, not in the world she was entering. I didn't realize that she wished to embrace this new world and eventually call it her own. My feet weren't planted on this ground. My head was in the clouds, dreaming of other places as I had since childhood — since the day I fell in love with a foreigner who moved into my mother's house.

When I was a young girl, the world was white and English. My father believed in a strict British upbringing. If children had to be seen at all, they certainly shouldn't be heard. He was a rule-bound, rigid, public-school–educated, ex-British Army officer who had been thrown out of the military for his racist comments about a black superior. Long after the British Empire had collapsed, my father was still preaching the gospel of colonialism — standing at the pulpit of his private church, with his family his captive congregation.

My father's opinion of women was no more enlightened, and my parents' marriage broke up in part as a result. I was ten — just five years after our arrival in Canada. Our tightly knotted world began to unravel, and a new man appeared in my father's place. This new man was nothing like my father. He was dark, swarthy, and very, very hairy. He had scars on his face, spoke with an accent, read newspapers in Arabic, and had a name we couldn't pronounce. He spoke in a loud voice and was openly affectionate with my mother. I thought he didn't have a "proper" job because he didn't wear a suit and go to an office. He was an actor who wore hip-hugging Levis and loose white shirts without collars, and he grew tomatoes and marijuana in the backyard.

As soon as he moved in, the foreigner threw out the single beds my parents had always slept in and built a double bed for my mother and himself in the basement. I was horrified. I was sure that public displays of affection were not only rude, but possibly unhealthy, and that sharing a bed was a moral transgression. I was convinced that the dark, swarthy foreigner was corrupting my mother, and I was furious that she could so easily stray from the path of righteousness my father had laid down.

My father collaborated with me on our alternate weekends together — criticizing my mother for having taken up with a "Paki." My brother, who had been terrified of my father, fell head over heels in love with Ara, as did everybody who met him. I stood apart, scowling at a firm distance. My only recourse was to stop speaking, and stop speaking I did for the better part of the next year.

I kept vigilant, bitter watch until we visited the farm of a friend of my mother's. I had spent the day swimming solitary laps across the pond while the foreigner, my brother, and a host of other children ran around naked and rolled down the muddy bank. That night there was a wrestling match where the foreigner was taken on by the combined forces of four children. From my vantage point on the stairs, I found myself overtaken by envy and possessiveness as the other children shrieked in delight and pinned him down.

When he was seated again, I walked across the room and slid onto his lap. I glared at the other children and stated defiantly: "He's mine." Silence overtook the room then, and quiet tears started tumbling down all the grown-ups' faces. I wrapped my arms around Ara's neck and thought: "Gross, I wish all these other touchy-feely grown-ups would go away."

After that, Ara was mine, and I was his. I adored him. He was intense, passionate, and dramatic. I clung to him like a barnacle: followed him from bed to kitchen to market. I even defended him. "Don't call him a Paki," I pleaded with my father. "He's Armenian, and he's from Lebanon."

Over the next year I cultivated a taste for kibbeh and baba ghanouj and accumulated a vast arsenal of Arabic words for naughty bodily bits and what one could do with them. Many of these dishes and bad words are still part of my family's diet and vernacular, even though the man himself is no longer part of our family. When he left it broke my heart. He squatted on my bedroom floor one night and said some things that were probably profound, each of them beginning "Life is …" Crying, he handed me a cheap Avon ring obviously designed for someone with grown-up hands. The next day he was gone. His Ravi Shankar and Leonard Cohen albums remained while he travelled west to start a new life.

Things became quieter and much blander at home after that. My mother worked hard and felt unhappy, and I was a moody and aloof teenager, slamming my door, writing bad poetry, and day-dreaming my way to Beirut. Because of Ara, I started to dream of places, necessarily foreign, where people's lives were different: meaningful and even happy. I remember how I used to watch him as he sat in the sun on the back porch and read a newspaper from right to left. I imagined him entering a secret and magical world. I was prepared to spend the rest of my life searching for the door.

I used to think knowing Ara had taught me how to overcome prejudice. What was at work was far more complex: the fear and disgust my father had instilled were replaced by romantic idealization. I was brushing up against the soft underbelly of racism, where "love" can be as loaded and limiting as hate.

It wasn't until I started studying anthropology at university that I found a framework for my dreams of other worlds. I found answers — *scientific validation* that life could be different. *Concrete evidence* of radically different alternatives to the confines of a repressive British upbringing. If I had had a religious upbringing, I may well have had no need for anthropology. I might have found refuge in spiritual notions — heaven, the afterlife, or reincarnation. But my parents had always insisted we were atheists. Religion, in my father's estimation, was for people who lacked the strength to face the unknown on their own, so I was left to stare at the bleak and the vast without a prophet to guide me. Luckily, I found relief in anthropology rather than drugs. A homeless non-believer, I found refuge and faith through immersing myself in other people's worlds. Naively, I thought I could make those worlds mine, or make myself a part of them.

Shortly after meeting Adiqo, I asked her whether I could write an article about her for our college magazine. I suggested the Queen of Sheba, the only Ethiopian restaurant I knew. I asked Adiqo to order. "Do you like meat?" she asked. "*Kitfo,*" she told the waiter. He asked her a question and she shook her head.

"What did he ask you?"

"He asked whether we wanted the meat cooked or not cooked."

"You mean raw?"

"Yes."

"Do *you* eat it raw?"

"Yes."

"So, let's eat it raw," I shrugged.

"Are you sure?" She looked at me curiously. "You are not like any other *farenji* I have ever met."

She didn't see me eat more than two mouthfuls of raw meat that day. The platter of injera, pancake-like bread the size of the table, with its mounds of blood-red *kitfo,* cottage-cheese-like *iab,* and dangerous amounts of *berbere,* Ethiopian hot pepper, sat untouched between us. I was too taken with her and her story; she was too upset to eat. She spoke in harsh whispers about the oppression of her people, the Oromo, the largest ethnic group in Ethiopia — a ferocious anger muted by a current of fear rippling just under her skin.

Adiqo apologized repeatedly for being so emotional. I was equally emotional: my eyes welling up with tears, I reached out to squeeze her hand. "I have heard people celebrate Ethiopia because they think it is the only country that was never colonized," she finally said. 'Who are these strong Africans?' they wonder. They have no idea that these strong Africans, especially the Amharas, persecute and oppress other Ethiopians. We Oromo know the worst kind of colonialism."

"Is this restaurant run by Amharas?" I asked her.

"Yes," she nodded.

I felt mortified. My choice of restaurant meant "dining with the enemy." Ethiopia has long been ruled by Christian Semitic-speaking populations from the northern highlands — the Amhara, and most recently, the Tigrayans. The Oromo are different: originally animists from the south, they speak a completely unrelated language. They have been marginalized by the country's successive rulers, treated like third-class citizens, and officially called the *Galla,* or "uncivilized." According to explicitly racist agendas, Ethiopian governments have denied the Oromo land, rights to speak their language, and freedom of cultural expression. Their "Ethiopianness" is also rejected by those who consider them migrants from black Africa.

"It's OK," she said, forgiving me for my mistake. "I have some Amhara friends. I don't have to only be associated with Oromos. It's about personality, not ethnicity."

Persecution of the Oromo had reached its zenith under the *Dergue,* the military dictatorship that overthrew Haile Selassie's long-lived imperial regime in 1974. During its reign of terror, the *Dergue* implemented radical socialist reforms through force, conscripting children as young as twelve into its army, and kidnapping, torturing, and killing hundreds of thousands of citizens perceived to be dissidents or objectors.

The Oromo, who established an independence movement at the end of the Haile Selassie era, were seen as the *Dergue's* biggest enemy. "Simply speaking my own language made me an enemy of the state," Adiqo told me. "I could not speak in Afaan Oromo to my family on the phone. We were even forced to change our names to Amhara names. Can you imagine? This is the extent to which they wanted to erase our identity."

Adiqo saw her neighbours massacred in the street, and her brothers seized from their home, beaten, blindfolded, and thrown into the back of a truck. Taken to faraway jails, they were only let out of solitary confinement to crawl across fields of broken glass on their knees. On her walk home from school, Adiqo often saw bodies riddled with bullet holes and rolled over onto their stomachs with the words "Red Terror" across their backs.

School, although frequently shut down for political reasons, offered some respite. "Studying was an escape for me. When I was in a classroom I could fully concentrate — and I loved it. It was the only place where I had a mental break from the chaos." Adiqo did so well that she became one of the first Oromo women to go on to higher education. After graduating from Addis Ababa University, she worked in a government office — in a country where everything is nationalized, government jobs are the only ones to be had. "From day one I knew I couldn't get any other job," she told me. "My choice was doing this, or going to prison. And I thought it would be stupid to just rot in prison."

As the only Oromo in the office, she was considered suspect, and she was ridiculed and harassed because of her ethnicity. "It was hell," she said. "It was as if I was a corpse — only my dead body was there." Adiqo remained resolute, refusing to change her name. She was placed under surveillance and isolated from other Oromo. "Every time I walked toward that building I was terrified. As if I was being led to a house full of snakes — that's the way I felt. They were constantly watching over me. I was so scared I didn't know what to do. You know that book by Orwell?" she asked me. "*1984?*"

I did indeed. Orwell's description of totalitarian nightmare was assigned reading in my Grade 11 English class, shelved under science fiction in our school library. For Adiqo and her contemporaries, though, the book was a window on the world they knew, passed clandestinely between friends in a brown paper cover. "That book was banned," she told me, "because it captured the feeling of growing up in the communist state *perfectly*. Big Brother was watching. From day one, I thought, 'I have to leave.' "

Adiqo embarked on several life-threatening attempts to flee the country. In 1988 she made it. One day after finishing work, she took a circuitous route to a friend's house, cut her hair, changed into servants' clothing, and walked away. She took nothing more than a change of clothes and some money she'd sewn into the waistband of her skirt. She spent two months travelling the more than five hundred kilometres to the Kenyan border and arrived emaciated at a refugee camp.

Today she is widely celebrated by members of the Oromo diaspora as the first Oromo woman who escaped from Ethiopia alone. Yet she was always determined to do more than escape. She wanted out of the refugee camp, a place she found demoralizing and oppressive, and soon found a job working as a radio announcer for an Oromo-language program based in Nairobi — a service created by Swedish missionaries to broadcast news back into Ethiopia. Bright, articulate, and determined, she reached out even further, applying for and winning the highly coveted and competitive scholarship that brought her to Canada in 1991.

Minutes into our first conversation, I was certain that I had met someone who would leave an indelible impression on my life. Over the next year we became close friends. We went to Kensington Market and bought the ten spices she needed to make *berbere,* without which food was not *food.* We shopped at Goodwill for cheap winter clothes: an olive-green parka and boots for her, and a motley assortment of moth-eaten sweaters in various shades of black for me. We drank endless cups of coffee — mine black, hers with enough sugar to keep a spoon standing — and spent hours and hours talking about politics, racism, religion, family, and friendship.

"They are so rude and so ignorant!" she said of many of her fellow students in residence. "They think I was some poor, starving African who ran around naked before I came here. They ask me whether I've ever worn jeans before. They ask me why my English is so good. They ask me if I am a famine victim or a Rastafarian.

They don't know anything about anything except the names of different kinds of beer."

We closed the door to the other students, and she taught me to cook one of Ethiopia's national dishes, *doro wot,* over a single element in her room.

By the end of her first year in Toronto, Adiqo had two Canadian friends. I felt awful because both of us were leaving the country to go to graduate school. In some way, though, I was taking Adiqo with me. I left for England in 1992 to start my doctoral work at Oxford with the determination — partly inspired by my friend — to conduct my thesis research in Ethiopia. Just before I left, Adiqo gave me a letter to deliver to her brother, Guracha, whom she had not seen in several years.

Guracha — the only other member of their family who had left Ethiopia — was an outspoken Oromo nationalist living in exile in London, where he was completing his doctoral thesis on Oromo social and political organization. I arranged to meet him in the student bar of the School of Oriental and African Studies. It was a dark, wet, and depressing autumn night, and we drank pints of bitter and tried to make out each other's faces through thick cigarette smoke, mostly of our own making.

I sensed that I failed to impress him (a fact he later affirmed), and I found him tough and unapproachable. He didn't understand my relationship to Adiqo, refused to make eye contact, and looked right past me as he ranted on about the fact that his thesis had just been rejected because of its perceived political bias. He was in the stages of formally protesting this decision and demanding re-examination.

When he talked about Adiqo, though, his countenance completely altered. He softened and became animated. He praised her courage and said people grossly misjudged her. "They assume she's a meek and submissive African woman. But she is so hotheaded! She has had to fight *so* hard," he declared. "Someone like you could never imagine what she's been through," he then added dismissively. "Do you know she was sent to Czechoslovakia to be trained by the Soviets? Yes, yes. They wanted her to spy against her own people. That is why she was forced to leave the country."

I was shocked. There were obviously large parts of her history Adiqo hadn't felt safe to tell me. There were other things I would never understand unless I witnessed them first-hand. In 1994, after a year of archival research in England, I took two planes and a three-day drive over bumpy terrain to reach the walled Muslim city of Harar in eastern Ethiopia. I had been drawn to the city because of its history and cultural complexity. Although the city's indigenous inhabitants form a single ethnic group known as the Harari, their origins are diverse. The community developed through the inter-marriage of Oromos, Somalis, Arabs, and former slaves from south-western Ethiopia. Harari religion, language, and culture consequently draw upon very different sources, creating the unique forms of expression that were the subject of my research.

For a year and a half, I struggled to speak the obscure, unwritten language of the Harari, wore a veil, abstained from alcohol, and lived with a local family of ten. The mother, daughter, visiting female relatives, and I slept on adjacent raised red-earth platforms in one room, and we passed a water jug between us to bathe. We ate all our meals together, sharing one bowl of watery, fenugreek-laden stew twice a day, fishing for tiny morsels of carrot and potato with our hands. We lived in two rooms, battled rats, cockroaches, and various intestinal parasites, and, like any other family, we shared triumphs, tribulations, news, gossip, and the mundane details of daily life.

Often, those details were dramatic. The *Dergue* had been overthrown in 1991, and the country was in a period of great uncertainty. The eastern frontier where I lived in 1994 and 1995 was under threat of civil war. Despite illness and frustration, a curfew after dark, and bombs routinely exploding in the streets, I felt happy: my mind was on fire and my heart was full.

When I returned to England I felt utterly disoriented. I felt caught between distant and partial worlds; uncertain about where and whether I belonged. I was doped up with a foreign language I had nowhere to speak, and otherwise felt I had nothing to say. I was also overwhelmed by the daunting obligation before me: to produce a seamless text using jargon that would be meaningless to anyone outside the tiny world of the initiated. Sadly and perversely, this language would exclude the very people about whom I was writing.

Crushed by the weight of Oxford's relentlessly grey skies and the formality of the world around me, I found myself crying in all the wrong places. Anthropologists have a term for the post-field-work propensity to burst into tears in supermarkets. We call it "reverse culture shock." My doctor, however, had another word for it and promptly sent me off to Boots with a prescription for Prozac and sleeping pills. I spent the next few weeks staring at the henna on my palms — needing this tangible reminder of where I'd been as assurance that I wasn't losing my mind.

The henna began to fade and I had to begin writing my thesis. This work required navigating the distance between lived experience in all its colour and chaos, and a text that demanded citations and footnotes rather than poetry. The register sounded fraudulent and empty. It felt counterintuitive and dishonest to have to freeze and frame my observations and experiences in academic language. I did not want to lose the sensation of what I felt when I writhed with stomach ache, argued with my neighbours, suffered under the Evil Eye, danced among the possessed, and slept crammed between bodies strewn across a red-earth floor. I did not want to lose the passionate memory of my friendships by turning people into subjects and mining and interpreting their experiences for some intellectual purpose. But if I wanted my degree, this is precisely what I would have to do.

A year and a half later, it was time to defend my thesis. At the appointed hour, I climbed the three flights of stairs to the attic library where my examination was to take place. Across the table sat two anthropologists of considerable repute — all three of us dressed in subfusc, Oxford's requisite sartorial dress designed to lend austerity to every possible occasion. The initial silence was interrupted when my internal examiner scraped back his chair, stood up, and dropped my bound thesis onto the table with a thud. He then resumed his seat and shoved the tome across the table at me. "I don't know," he said, shaking his head. "Why don't *you* tell me what it's about?" I wouldn't be exaggerating if I described him as looking disgusted.

My first instinct was to burst into tears. I knew my job was to "contextualize this work in terms of its theoretical contribution to the advancement of the discipline." The emotional value of my experiences would be irrelevant to the examiners, as would the care and compassion I applied in making my observations. With these points in mind, I began speaking about the thesis as an analysis of gender relations within a locally defined framework of Islamic orthodoxy. After three hours of interrogation, they extended their hands and congratulated me on my successful "acquittal." *Clearly,* this had been a trial.

Technically speaking, I was now a proper, grown-up anthropologist with a doctorate from a very prestigious institution and a promising academic future ahead of me. Emotionally speaking, I was a wreck. The intellectual process had forced me to abandon all the reasons I had been drawn into anthropology in the first place. It wasn't until well after graduating from Oxford, though, that I began to understand why I became an anthropologist. It wasn't because I held strong convictions about the discipline's importance. In fact, I felt ambivalent about its theoretical underpinnings and usefulness. As a dreamer, I was full of other worlds and words to describe them, but as an anthropologist I was at best an apologist; at worst, mute.

In all this, one of the key things that had been disrupted was my friendship with Adiqo. Although I had made many friends in Ethiopia, Adiqo had been the first to inspire my interest in the country and was a crucial bridge between these worlds. Just before I left England for Ethiopia, Adiqo had married, and shortly there-after, moved to California. An invitation to her wedding had sat at my mother's house for over a year. I had no forwarding address and my efforts to find her proved unsuccessful. My last hope was her brother, but by the time I returned to England, he had defended his thesis again and left London.

In 1997, I was one of more than three hundred "Ethiopianists" who gathered in Kyoto, Japan, for the Thirteenth International Conference of Ethiopian Studies. This was the first conference of its kind since the overthrow of the *Dergue* in 1991, and it brought together many influential intellectuals who had well-grounded sus-picions about the alleged democracy of the new government. Freedom of the press had been short-lived, opponents of the regime had started mysteriously disappearing, and the army had begun encroaching on the newly separate state of Eritrea. The government was concerned that this particular gathering would foster political opposition, and sent its (not inconspicuous) delegates to monitor the proceedings.

At the end of one of the last panels, an Oromo intellectual from Addis Ababa University delivered just what the government dele-gates were waiting for — a passionate, aggressive polemic about the continued denial of Oromo claims to nationhood. In a matter of minutes, he had successfully enraged almost everyone in the room and there was yelling from all sides. The government officials were the only ones who remained silent, and I knew — we all knew — he had taken a monumental risk.

I approached him after the panel to commend him for his courage. A tall, heavy, brooding man, he gave me a patronizing nod, and then abruptly asked if I would come and have a drink with him. I knew it was probably unwise to agree, but he seemed dangerous and that was too compelling to resist. We wandered out into a wet Japanese night, and I asked him whether he felt his position at the university would be compromised by the paper he had just delivered. He gave a fatalistic shrug and said that short of killing him, there was little any Ethiopian government could do to him that had not been done to him before.

"But I don't understand why a British girl like you would have any interest in Ethiopia," he then said.

"Actually, I grew up in Canada, and there are a lot of Ethiopians there. I had an amazing friend who came to Toronto as a refugee and she taught me a lot about Ethiopia."

He grabbed me by the shoulders and turned me around to face him. "Who are you?" he barked, nearly causing my heart to stop. I was scared and perplexed. He repeated the question. "Don't you remember coming to a bar in London one night and meeting a man ..."

"Oh my God," was all I could say. It was Guracha — Professor Guracha Legesse now. I couldn't believe it. We burst out laughing and threw our arms around each other, overwhelmed by this unusual connection between lives and worlds. We literally skipped down the sidewalk, our conversation much less formal now, me asking question after question about Adiqo, and him telling me that he had been suspicious of me when we first met. "Who is this woman?" he had asked himself. "And why is she so interested in my sister?"

After several beers, we stumbled back to the hotel intent on calling Adiqo in California. She had married a man to whom she had once lent a brown paper–wrapped copy of *1984* on the Addis Ababa University campus, and they had two babies now. "Adi?" Guracha shouted. "I've found an old friend of yours in Japan!"

When he finally passed the phone to me, I spluttered "Adi? Ngaya. Faya?" greeting her in Orominyya and bursting into tears.

"Camilla!" Adiqo gasped. "Don't be silly, stop crying!" I had to laugh. The confidence in her voice was amazing. "I didn't know what to think when you didn't come to my wedding!" she shouted. "I thought Guracha must have offended you when you went to see him in London. I felt terrible for sending you — I should have warned you that he's a notorious womanizer!" I assured her that on that occasion he had been perfectly decent. What I didn't tell her was that he was doing his best to grope me while I was on the phone with her from his room in Kyoto.

I am flying to San Francisco, having exchanged numerous letters and phone calls with Adiqo over the past year. The purpose of my visit is twofold. In addition to wrapping my arms around someone I have not seen in years, I am going to record her story, something I have been wanting to do since we first met. What I knew already amounted to an incredibly painful and beautiful story that might have political and emotional significance not just for Adiqo and her children, but for a wider audience. But as Guracha had intimated, there were secrets still to be revealed.

At the airport, a voluptuous and elegant African woman stands before me with her arms outstretched. She has short auburn hair and wears large gold earrings, false red nails, and fitted jeans. I don't recognize her. She is the only black woman standing at the exit, but I look over her shoulder, searching for the tiny woman I know Adiqo to be. "This is me!" the black woman shouts, seeing my confusion. "This is what I am *supposed* to look like!" I search for Adiqo in this woman's face; for that faraway look of Africa; the dark circles of worry and sadness. I seek the bitter butter scent I have come to associate with Ethiopia and inhale a cloud of Opium instead.

We drive down Highway 5 to Palo Alto, passing a giant bill-board poster of John Lennon and Yoko Ono preaching love not war from their rumpled post-coital sheets. "Do you know who they are?" I ask Adiqo.

"No."

"Have you ever heard of a band called the Beatles?"

"Like insects?"

Adiqo may look now like the embodiment of America, but she lacks a western history. John Lennon was the first person I "knew" who had died during my lifetime. Where was Adiqo when John Lennon died? It was the end of the Red Terror. She was hiding in a bunker as her classmates were being gunned down in the school-yard above her, while I was crying in my living room and listening to a warped forty-five of "Strawberry Fields Forever."

Adiqo opens the door of her apartment. Her daughters, Milto and Albu, are glued to the image of Barney the purple dinosaur. Her husband, Solomon, is glued to another screen, scrolling through the day's e-mail postings from the Oromia Support Network. "Hi, hi," he waves, reluctantly tearing himself away from his computer. "So this is the man who waited eleven years for Adiqo," I think to myself.

"Milto! Albu!" Adiqo exclaims. "Come and greet Camilla! Turn the television off!" The younger girl, Albu, jumps up and throws her arms around her mother's legs, giggles at the sight of me, and hides her face behind her mother's knees. Milto gives a bored glance over her shoulder and turns back toward the television. The floor is littered with Barbies with butchered hair in various states of undress.

In the morning the kids eat large bowls of Froot Loops. Adiqo and I drive them to the Kiddie Academy where they spend their days fighting and playing with little blond girls and boys with names like Tiffany and Travis. On the weekends there are sleepovers and birthday parties and swimming lessons. Adiqo looks exhausted. She is trying to juggle the demands of a job, part-time studies at university, and two cute but extremely spoiled children. For all Solomon's "Americanness," he leaves Adiqo to single-handedly do all the cooking and cleaning and the vast majority of the child care. "He's a typical African man," she says, rolling her eyes.

For two weeks Adiqo and I sit together for hours as she recounts her entire history. We tape her story by day and I transcribe those tapes at night. The conversation between us is punctuated with frequent laughter, lots of tears, and occasionally, phone calls from my lover at home. "My best friend," I tell Adiqo, ashamed of my own secrets. Unsure how to tell her my most significant relationship is with another woman, because not only are same-sex relations considered unnatural in Ethiopia, they are stigmatized everywhere else as well. Unsure because Solomon has made a couple of homophobic jokes. Unsure because here, in the suburbs of Palo Alto, a haven for young, upwardly mobile families, Adiqo's friends are good Christian women, happily married mothers of toddlers — *like* Adiqo, except for the fact that they are white, and *unlike* me, except for the fact that they are white.

Adiqo was right, I am unlike most other *farenjis* she has known: I am a *farenji* among *farenjis*. My dreams have never been about being married with children and having a comfortable life in the suburbs. No matter how much I might flirt with the idea of normal I've never really thought I could cut it — or be happy there. I became an anthropologist because something in the same landscape Adiqo has aspired to inhabit seemed meaningless to me. I couldn't see a home for myself within it. I went far away to find some sense of belonging — which I found, provided I remained veiled.

Adiqo roams more freely, shedding skin, acquiring more. She is part of this suburban landscape — a comfortable place free of nightmares. In retrospect, Adiqo says she spent much of her first year in Canada in a daze. She was plagued by nightmares, terrified of the police, startled by loud noises, and thoroughly depressed by the Canadian winter. Ten years later, she has a name for what she was experiencing then: "I was suffering from post-traumatic stress disorder." I had not appreciated the magnitude of her suffering at the time. What she did reveal then, I had romanticized, considering it enviably heroic.

"Really, now I have everything I have ever dreamed of," she says, though she seems to say it without conviction. In two hundred pages of transcribed text, she has revealed her secrets — her motivation, catharsis. Another new word in her vocabulary — one she learned in a communications class at San José State University. We discuss her circumcision, her feelings about sex and orgasm, her childhood, her parents' divorce, and her experiences in Czechoslovakia; things she tells me she would have felt ashamed to speak of ten years ago. She has a North American language now, one that allows her to speak of the atrocities she has endured. "English allows you to talk about suffering. It is shameful to do so in my language. But still, I can't really speak my heart in this language," she says sadly. I wish I could tell her that I have trouble speaking my heart in any language.

Nine years ago when Adiqo came to my apartment for the first time, she commented that my roommate and I must be very good friends. There was only one bedroom in the apartment — and only one bed. I knew she wasn't making any more of it; in fact, she remarked that it was just like Ethiopia, where any number of people shared a bed without any inference of sexual connection. "We are very good friends," I agreed.

No matter how close I might feel the friendship between Adiqo and me, I have cultivated a certain image of myself, and have kept the complexities of my life a secret from the beginning. Despite myself, I am, apparently, an anthropologist — as veiled as I was in the faraway field. When Adiqo was alien too, I identified with her much more strongly. But that small woman I met in 1991 was not Adiqo, but a traumatized sliver of the woman Adiqo is. "This is me!" she had shouted in the San Francisco airport, standing large and voluptuous before me. I had looked past her, in search of something familiar.

I imagine Ara would probably also be unrecognizable to me today. Last year I wrote to him for the first time in twenty years. I sent him a copy of my first novel, directing him to the chapter where the protagonist's parochial world is shaken up when she meets a Sikh man. I wanted him to know that twenty years ago, he had changed a young girl's world. I inscribed the book with bold words of love and thanks, and several months later got a short note in return. It was signed: "Sincerely, David Hovan." In the years since I knew him, Ara Hovanessian has become David Hovan, married a white American woman, and become a chartered accountant.

I wonder if he still has his scar, and I hope that he has kept this one reminder of the past.

He used to run his finger across his cheek in disgust and say he was going to have to have plastic surgery if he continued to be type-cast as a thug, terrorist, or Mafia hit man. But I liked the scar, the evidence of his endurance: bullied and beaten up and dodging car bombs in Beirut. It proved that life was worth fighting for and marked him as a hero. As a child I needed a hero; I needed to know life was worth fighting for. The romance of such beliefs obviously continued well into adulthood — preventing me from appreciating that there is as much heroism in mastering a new set of cultural expectations as there is in dodging bullets. The suburbs are full of heroes.

ALYSE FRAMPTON

My American Father

THOUGH I WAS ONLY SIX, I SENSED THAT, EVEN BEFORE HE spoke out, my father cut an unusual figure among the casually dressed parents lined up for the Saturday afternoon matinee in White Plains, New York. His bearing was military (the legacy of prep school), his face handsome, with a cleft chin and thick, dark hair that met his high forehead in a widow's peak. He wore a crisply laundered shirt, pressed pants, and black leather shoes that gleamed with polish.

Until we had joined the shuffling line of families waiting to buy tickets, he had not realized that the movie was a western. He took in the lurid playbills depicting the American cavalry firing on tomahawk-wielding redskins, stepped out of line, and in his clear, carrying voice denounced the film to me, and to the world at large. The West was not won, but stolen, he declaimed. The true story was a shameful one, full of lies and racism directed at the American Indian. He urged his fellow parents to reject this film, just take their children and go, as he was about to do.

A burly man in line near us objected. Then several adults in the crowd chimed in; the words "pinko" and "un-American" were shouted. (The year was 1956.) I tried to ignore the smirks and stares of the other kids. Finally, the burly man shoved my father, hard

41

enough to make him stumble, and abruptly the shouting stopped. My father surveyed the crowd as if daring people to meet his eyes. Then he took my hand and led me off at a slow, deliberate pace.

I understood. Those people did not chase us away; we had turned our backs on them. The confrontation did not surprise me. My middle name is Harriet, my parents' way of honouring a black woman who risked her life as a conductor on the Underground Railroad. At home, Harriet Tubman's stern, sad face gazed out from the portrait hung on my bedroom wall. Taking my responsibilities as her namesake seriously, I had set some of my all-white Grade 1 class straight about a playground rhyme that included the lines "Catch a nigger by the toe. If he hollers let him go." Say *tiger* instead, I corrected the other kids. At a drugstore lunch counter where my mother and I were having milkshakes one day, I decided to personally apologize to the black man who sat on the stool next to mine. Leaning over to get his attention, I whispered, "I'm sorry that white people are mean to Negro people." After a long moment during which he and my mother made impenetrable eye contact over my head, he replied, "I'm sorry, too, honey. I'm sorry, too." But the scene with my father at the theatre was different. I was a little frightened by the people ganging up on him. It was also news to me that the Indians, like the Negro people, were downtrodden and needed our help. And I still wanted to see that movie.

In bed that night, I lay open-eyed in the dark, feeling proud of my father and protective of him. I was also troubled by a disturbing undertow of mingled embarrassment, confusion, frustration, and guilt. It is my first clear memory of the strong emotions that he rarely failed to provoke in me.

I was not quite seven years old when my parents divorced. A year later my mother left the United States and took my younger brother and me back to her hometown, Montreal, where we moved in with my maternal grandparents. After that I seldom saw my father, Albert Frampton, a man who wanted to change the world, and was in the end crushed by it, and by himself. We were not close. I calculate we shared roughly seventeen visits, exchanged some three hundred phone calls, spread over forty years. He died in 1994. His life has increasingly seemed an enigma to me. Yet an enduring attachment tugs on me, ever more insistently. That is partly why, early one May morning eight years after his death, I found myself standing on the oldest Quaker burying ground in Philadelphia.

A section of the cemetery is built over by the handsome red brick meeting house that dominates the property. What remains is a neglected lawn, with weedy clumps and bare spots. There are no grave markers, because the colonial Quakers who interred their dead here scorned such worldly vanity. They were avid chroniclers and bookkeepers, however, and the surviving records pointed me to this place. I discovered that somewhere underfoot lay my great-great-great-great-great-great-great grandfather, one William Frampton, buried on September 11, 1686.

I first learned about old William from a small, leather-bound book that I found when sifting through the dusty piles of my father's papers after his death. A history of William Frampton and his descendants, the book was apparently published at the behest of a distant relation around 1914. Before that, my only inkling of this paternal family history came first not from my own father, Albert Frampton, but from my mother, Sylvia.

It seems that not long after my birth in 1950, a piece of mail arrived from the Daughters of the American Revolution, at that time an organization well known for its political arch-conservatism and genteel but steely racism. It was a letter congratulating my parents on producing a female infant, who, by dint of "lineal, blood line descent from an ancestor who aided in achieving American independence," would one day be eligible to join their star-spangled society. This honour could be mine because a descendent of William Frampton had fought as a militiaman in the Revolutionary War. (That man, also called William, was my great-great-great grandfather.)

To my mother, a left-wing, working-class Jew from Montreal, the letter was hilarious. She was sure that, had the Daughters known about the true origins of Mrs. Albert Frampton, the invitation would have been instantly rescinded. I was fourteen when I heard this story, and politically sophisticated enough to enjoy the irony on my own terms. What if the Daughters had found out that my father's greatest hero was not Thomas Jefferson or another laurelled member of the American patriotic pantheon, but the crusading union leader, Eugene Victor Debs? EVD was my brother Gene's acronym for his namesake, about whose noble deeds as co-founder of the American Socialist party we'd heard plenty from my father. (Though my mother admired Debs, she thought the full "Eugene" too prim a name to inflict on her infant son.)

My father's hometown was St. Louis, Missouri, where he grew up and returned to live the last third of his life. Born to wealth in 1918, he was the youngest child and only son of Anna Goodchild Frampton, a resolute Episcopalian and Women's Christian Temperance Union advocate, and Albert Stuart Frampton Sr., a self-made, staunchly Republican businessman who grew rich selling steel, then cars. My paternal grandfather's firm, the Hudson-Frampton Motor Car Company, held the distribution rights for Hudson and Nash throughout the Midwest. In 1933, Albert Sr. returned to St. Louis from Switzerland with a case of undulant fever, contracted from drinking unpasteurized milk on a mountain-climbing excursion. At risk for dizzy spells, he was forbidden to rise from bed unaided, but he nevertheless tried to go to the bathroom without ringing for the nurse. He fell, hit his head, and died two days later.

Although his company was hard hit by the Depression, he left a sizable estate to be divided among his widow, son, and two daughters. I don't know the total value of my father's inheritance, but I do know that from the age of eighteen he received income from a trust fund. On turning twenty-one in 1939, he took possession of the capital of a portfolio of blue-chip stocks worth at least three hundred thousand dollars — equivalent to over two million dollars, at a conservative estimate, in today's money.

When he died in St. Louis in 1994, my father was penniless. Soup kitchens fed him. A tiny veterans disability pension had kept him off the street, in a cramped, dingy rented room with shared bathroom at the Mark Twain Hotel in the city's gritty core. He chose the place because he relished its name. He was convinced to the end that his stubborn dream of what he called the third American Revolution — the triumph of democratic socialism — a dream that had consumed his entire adult life and his inherited money — would someday come to pass.

My father had more schemes and causes than I will ever know about, but he did tell me about some of them. After he was demobilized in 1946, he moved to New York City with the idea of establishing himself as a freelance publishers' representative specializing in antiquarian publications and books on labour history. He also tried, unsuccessfully, to find his way as a writer, a poet. Of this ambition remains an unpublished collection of war poems and essays, mainly tributes to Debs. He planned an even more extensive tribute in the form of an anthology of famous authors' writings about the man. Fumbling for his own writerly voice, he sought vicarious satisfaction, I believe, by establishing the small, short-lived but grandly named Arts and Science Press, which he ran out of his apartment in Manhattan.

The World Fellowship Center, a country haven for left-wingers in the White Mountains of New Hampshire, was one beneficiary of his largesse. The Maryknoll Sisters, an American Catholic activist order with a strong presence in Latin America, was another. My father's more quixotic ventures were long on vision but disastrously lacking in common sense. The last of his money went on a doomed, Thoreauesque scheme to establish a sort of halfway house for ex-convicts by a peaceful, unspoiled lake in the Ozark Mountains.

In my growing-up years, I looked up to my father. In my twenties, bothered by what seemed to me his paternal shortcomings, I took to calling him "Al" rather than "Dad." There were other strains on the connection. I began to find his political views outdated and simplistic. I started to develop a career and gain a toehold in the "booboisie" (to use the contemptuous term that he borrowed from Mencken) just as my father's slide into poverty began. And increasingly, his obstinate grip on his ideological convictions, and his use of his life as a kind of self-destructive, anti-capitalist demonstration project, seemed to me less and less explicable, and ultimately an existential puzzlement. Part heroic ideologue and intemperate dreamer, part grandiose dilettante, and part angry rogue male, my father ignored the pressures and accepted none of the answers that steadily eroded the American Left in his lifetime. I still find myself asking why he ran his life into the ground; if, in the end, the consuming flame was worth the candle.

On a research excursion to Swarthmore College — one of the main repositories of American Quaker archival material — I had located the burial place of the original William Frampton. He was a prominent merchant, religious leader, and politician in the new colony founded in 1682 by his associate, William Penn, as a haven from persecution for the Religious Society of Friends and other groups. Frampton had just been named register general of Pennsylvania when he died suddenly at age thirty-six, leaving a widow and three young children. Following William's trail, I located the site of his plantation on the Delaware River, and in the old quarter of Philadelphia I walked by the lots on Second Street where his "great brew house" and bakery had stood. These moments delighted me, and I imagined that Al, with his deep interest in history, might have felt the same.

Yet his failure to mention the Frampton family history does not surprise me. As I eventually discovered, the book was the work of a professional researcher hired by a distant female relation who had aspired to join the Daughters and needed proof of the requisite lineage to support her application. The research library at the society's headquarters in Washington has a copy. My father had no use for this brand of genealogical genuflection, with its implied claims to social superiority. To him, the book was probably tainted as an exercise in ancestor worship.

My father's line of the Frampton family left the Quaker fold during the War of Independence. Pacifism was and is a central tenet of Friends' faith. Based on the family history, I surmise that my great-great-great grandfather William decided to bear arms and fight if called on to do so by the patriot forces. During his lifetime, the family became Baptist and stayed so for successive generations until my paternal grandfather, Albert Sr., joined his bride, Anna, in the Episcopal church.

Early in life, my father rejected organized religion in any form but especially the one in which he had been baptized and confirmed. Episcopalianism, he said once, was church for the country club set. Yet he was, in his own way, a spiritual man. As I stood on the old burying ground, I saw affinities between him and his Quaker forebears, dissident Christians with a resolute belief in the primacy of individual conscience and unmediated communion with God.

It was my cousin, Ernest — the son of my father's adored older sister, Ciel — who opened Al's world to me in a wholly unexpected way. Because he bears another surname, Ernest decided to send me the Frampton memorabilia that belonged to my late aunt and paternal grandmother. About two years after my father's death, two large cartons arrived in the mail from California. Stuffed among the heavy, dank-smelling portrait albums of long-dead relatives in Victorian dress, I found bundles of letters that Al wrote to his mother and sister in the thirties and forties, as well as dozens of loose family snapshots that I'd never seen.

One of these, taken in St. Louis in 1934, records his departure for military prep school. Albert Sr. had died the previous winter, and my widowed grandmother decided that her son needed the masculine influence and discipline the school would provide.

Albert Jr. and his sister Ciel stand in bright sunshine on the broad stone steps of the family house, behind which looms a massive portico. Aged sixteen, my father faces the camera with a boy's eyes, guileless and unguarded, a hint of childlike roundness softening his jaw. He looks half-proud, half-embarrassed in his absurd uniform, a costume out of an operetta or a tin-pot dictator's closet, replete with brass buttons, epaulets, and frog closings. He carries his hat, a kepi, tucked under his arm. His sister turns toward him, arms flung upward, in a pose of beaming admiration.

Absent from this scene was my father's oldest sister, Ruth. She was away at university and, in any event, not close to her young brother. But why wasn't my grandmother, Anna, part of this stagy send-off? Perhaps because, like most women of her social class and time, she left the care of her offspring to servants; throughout his childhood Al was tended by a succession of black nannies.

Still, my grandmother's absence seems pointedly characteristic of the old lady I remember from my childhood, who had a severe, chilly manner to match her snowy, pinned-up hair. When she arrived for a visit, she would turn away my hug until her coat and hat were neatly stowed in the closet and she had washed her hands.

Once, when I was around five, she took me to an amusement park. She did not allow me to ride the merry-go-round on the grounds that I would have nothing to look forward to. Another time, when I was left in her care overnight, we had a showdown at breakfast. I refused to eat the loathsome, decapitated soft-boiled egg placed in front of me. Didn't she know I ate only perfectly blended, evenly yellow scrambled egg, the membrane sieved out? When my father came to pick me up hours later, I was still confined to my seat at the kitchen table, staring at the cold mess of mucousy white and congealed gummy yolk. "Alyse really oughtn't be allowed to behave like this," my grandmother told him. He mumbled some lame reply. The bossy, rigid, old bat, I saw, spooked him as much as she did me.

And who held the camera? Probably the family chauffeur, a black man named John. As I knew from other photographs, John had a sleek Packard sedan waiting in the driveway to drive my father to his destination. Looking at the snapshot, I felt sorry for Al Jr. His mother was sending him, surely still mourning the loss of his father, to live among strangers far from home. It struck me that Ciel was dressed for an excursion in her smart outfit and laced pumps. I hoped, an anachronistic impulse, that she kept her young brother company on the ride to the train station, staving off the inevitable moment when he must have felt unpleasantly alone.

"I had it easy back then," my father used to say of his cosseted youth, his tone mixing wonderment and dismay. Appearances to the contrary, I think that the pampered white boy who rode off to his expensive boarding school in a chauffeured car already harboured radical ideas. Born in 1918, my father came of age during the dozen or so years leading up to America's 1941 entry into World War II — a time when the Left held a tenable minority position in American politics. In the 1912 presidential election, Eugene Victor Debs won almost six per cent of the vote. Jailed for sedition, Debs ran his presidential campaign as Socialist Party leader from a prison cell in the

1920 election and captured 3.5 per cent of the vote. The Depression inflicted mass suffering that made socialism attractive to many more Americans. Elected president in 1932 on his New Deal ticket to revive the economy, Franklin Delano Roosevelt undoubtedly drew some left-wing support to the Democrats. Even so, nearly a million Americans voted Socialist or Communist that year. One of them was my Aunt Ciel.

Seven years older than my father, Ciel was a charismatic, vivacious redhead. As a teenager, she had rejected her detested given name, Clara Louise, in favour of her initials. Eventually, she learned that "C. L." made a homonym of sorts for the French word for sky — *ciel* — and adopted that spelling instead. Loyal to her upper-middle-class roots until she went to college, Ciel was a debutante in St. Louis in the late twenties. Among her beaus was a young lawyer, Clark Clifford, later a powerful Washington insider and an adviser to three presidents. At Sarah Lawrence College, she was voted runner-up "Best Dressed Girl" in clothes she designed. But before she graduated with a fine arts degree in 1932, she had started to move in bohemian, politically progressive circles.

Ciel once told me a story about the domestic fallout of the 1932 American election at the Frampton household in St. Louis. Albert Sr. by all accounts held liberal social views for his time. He forced his neighbours in the affluent community of Webster Groves to abandon their tacit agreement to exclude Jewish families, and he spoke out for civil rights for Negroes. He was, however, an economic conservative and a fierce opponent of the Democrats. He and many like-minded Americans feared that FDR's murky, undefined New Deal strategies would ruin the country. In November 1932, Albert Sr. sat down to a post-election family dinner expecting his four womenfolk to share his outrage at the results. One by one, his wife, mother-in-law, and older daughter declared that they had voted for FDR. Then Ciel dealt the *coup de grâce*. Her vote had gone to the Socialist Party candidate, Norman Thomas. (Eugene Victor Debs had died in 1926.) Aghast at this betrayal, my grandfather is said to have flung down his napkin, stalked out of the house, and given the culprits the silent treatment for several weeks.

I picture my fourteen-year-old father taking in this scene, mesmerized by Ciel's daring, impressed by her bold gesture of independence. After their father died and Al Jr. was dispatched to boarding school, the siblings exchanged letters often. He was intrigued and inspired by Ciel's increasing activism. Newly married, she and her sculptor husband had gone to teach art at Hull House in Chicago, an institution famous for its pioneering delivery of educational and social services to the neighbourhood poor. They were also busy helping to raise money for the Abraham Lincoln Brigade, one of the volunteer international units that joined the Soviet-supported Republican forces in the Spanish Civil War. Fatherless, I think Al. Jr. sought a father-hero and, with Ciel's encouragement, found Eugene Victor Debs. Like Martin Luther King in the civil rights movement decades later, Debs was widely revered as a martyr to his beliefs. He remained an iconic figure to the Left long after his death.

Throughout the thirties, leftists like my aunt and her husband saw themselves as the political vanguard. Democratic socialism, they thought, had a real future in American life. By the time Al went to study history at the University of St. Louis, he was a convert to the cause. He was drafted early in 1942 after three years there. A pacifist inspired by Gandhi, but wanting to help fight fascism, he elected to serve as an unarmed medic and was shipped out to the South Pacific.

A letter, written from Dutch New Guinea in 1944, after Al learned that the family house in St. Louis had been sold, may have been intended to disconcert its recipient as well as the army censor:

Dear mother,

Invest your capital from the sale of 433 West Baker in farm property not too far from the city. Open your gates wide to all! Take care of the poor and the weak. Let it be bread and wine on your table for all. Have plenty of dogs — sometimes I think I could live the rest of my life with them they are so self-contained and contented. Am planning on visiting an Aboriginal settlement next weekend. Still like ice cream, good beer, and crazy people. Have talked to many workers and soldiers who know of and remember Eugene Victor Debs.

    I love you, Al

While the Depression diminished my paternal grandfather's fortune, it forced my maternal grandfather, Abraham Papiernik, a Polish-born Jewish immigrant to Canada, to wield a pick and shovel in the aluminum mines of Arvida, Quebec. He was a cabinet maker by trade, but no such work was available. His wife and daughter didn't see him for months at time in the thirties. My mother, Sylvia, born in Montreal in 1923, recalls this period of her childhood with a stoical shrug. "He had to put bread on the table. That's the way it was." While retaining a strong attachment to Jewish culture, my grandfather had long since rejected his religion in favour of workers' solidarity. Short but stocky with a barrel chest and powerful arms, he worked as a construction foreman in the 1940s and 1950s. His dictatorial manner apparently earned him the sobriquet "little Napoleon" from his mostly Italian immigrant crews. My mother spoke Yiddish as her first language and was raised a socialist of the combative school.

In 1946, her visit to a girlfriend living in Manhattan turned into a protracted stay. Clerical jobs proved easy to come by. New York, exploding with post-war energy, was an exciting place. Greenwich Village had a short, sweet renaissance as an epicentre of art, free-thinking, and, according to my mother, great parties. Pete Seeger presided at come-one-come-all hootenannies at his apartment. At one such event, my mother met the friend who later introduced her to my father, himself a recent arrival to the city.

My parents were, I think, exotics to each other. When at the age of fifteen I came across some early photographs of my mother as a young woman, I was amazed that she looked like Elizabeth Taylor, whose cinematic portrayal of Cleopatra as voluptuous femme fatale I had recently cut classes to watch. Though my mother barely scraped through high school, she has always had a sharp mind and an ingrained respect for scholarship and artistic endeavour. Seen through her eyes at that long-ago meeting, my father was rail thin (the legacy of malaria contracted in New Guinea), a romantic intellectual, appealingly intense yet shy, with the kind of insouciance conferred by lots of money in the bank (though that was a secret he kept from Sylvia while courting).

My father invited the Jewish, socialist beauty to accompany him to a political rally. Six months later, in 1947, they were married, first by a minister at Ciel's home in Croton, New York, to satisfy my paternal grandmother, then by a Reform rabbi in Montreal to convince the Jewish relatives that Al was not an anti-Semite. My mother says that her new husband didn't mention until some time afterward that he had any income apart from what he earned selling books on commission. Since he lived modestly, there was no reason to think otherwise. Years later, my mother would say, "I'd never met anyone before who didn't have to work for a living." She was stunned to discover she had married money.

My father expected to see the values of democratic socialism flourish after the war — lighting a moral beacon for American life, attacking the inequities of capitalism and racism, influencing public policy for the better. This was not purblind optimism. The Left had enjoyed brief mainstream respectability from 1942 to 1945 when the United States and the Soviet Union were wartime allies; during this period, waves of government propaganda told Americans that the Russians were their friends. Leftists like my parents had high hopes for the post-war Progressive Party led by Henry Wallace, a prominent New Dealer who had been FDR's vice-president and then his commerce secretary. They campaigned to get Wallace on the New York State ballot for the 1948 federal election, believing that the Progressive Party could make a good showing and establish itself as a real contender in American politics. But Wallace won a humiliating three per cent of the popular vote. The Progressive Party disintegrated.

As the Cold War accelerated, the political climate quickly turned hostile to my father's views. The Republicans, led by, among others, California representative Richard Nixon, hammered Harry Truman's Democratic administration as favourable to socialism. In 1950, my parents, by then living in California, campaigned unsuccessfully for Nixon's opponent, a progressive democrat, Helen Gahagan Douglas. (His forces put out "pink sheets" detailing Douglas's votes in Congress.) In the Senate after 1950, Joe McCarthy made himself the poster boy for anti-communism, organizing red-baiting inquisitions that ruined reputations and lives. The 1952 election was a landslide victory for Dwight D. Eisenhower's Republicans.

My father had returned from the war with a small, ridged scar above his right ear — the souvenir of a sentry's bullet fired when, lurching to the latrine with the malarial runs, he forgot to give the password. The experience made him a fatalist. "When your number's up, it's up," he told me as a teenager. He was not willing to betray what he saw as the true values of American democratic socialism, the cause for which he had fought and risked his life. As he would explain to me much later in Montreal, when we marched together in a protest against the Vietnam War, the defeat of Helen

Gahagan Douglas demonstrated the folly of leftists who sought a haven in the Democratic Party. Those who continued to do so were, he believed, witless sellouts and gutless compromisers who helped perpetuate a status quo in which the abiding evils of capitalism, racism, and militarism would be largely ignored.

Disenchanted with California, my parents moved back to New York City in 1952. By this time, my father's book-selling activities had brought him into association with dozens of progressive publications and groups across the United States. These contacts did not pass unnoticed. My mother says I was asleep in my crib when, on a winter afternoon that year, two self-described "representatives of the U.S. government" knocked at the door of our West 98th Street apartment. Against her wishes, my father invited them in. Although the living room was overheated, she recalls, the men kept their coats on and sat on the sofa, side by side. Out of their briefcases came lists of names and dates for every contact my father had made during the previous five years. My mother was petrified. But my father, she says, enjoyed the encounter, especially the climactic question: "Are you now or have you ever been a member of the Communist Party?" "What is a Communist according to you?" my father parried. His interlocutor shot off the sofa, clasped his hands behind his back and recited, "A Communist is one who is dedicated to the violent overthrow of this United States government." "We couldn't help laughing," my mother told me years later. After a few days, the agents returned with a transcript of the interview for my parents to sign. My mother sent them away. The next week, they tried again. "What, one goodbye isn't enough for you?" she said as she shut the door in their faces. "Here's another one."

Like other avowed socialists, my father found himself swept to the eccentric fringes of American political life. But he took things a step further and withdrew from mainstream life altogether. He was unable, it seems, to envisage finding in the American capitalist economy meaningful work that would not require him to compromise or dilute his beliefs on one level or another. He refused, as he put it, to "play the game." The "game" had, I suspect, even less appeal because Albert Sr. — a driven, striving businessman, a model of entrepreneurial success — had played it so well.

I think my father's idealism, while genuine, masked his fear, conscious or not, that he would fail to make his independent way in the world. According to my Aunt Ciel, my grandmother had been a distant, domineering woman who instilled a deep sense of inadequacy in all her children. Both my aunts led troubled lives marred by alcoholism and divorce. My father's grandiosity was perhaps psychic infill for an aching hollowness, the lack of a sense of self-worth at his core. He may also have had a hereditary tendency toward depression.

These are all commonplace problems. The sheer necessity of earning a living forces most people to confront and, in one way or another, move beyond them. Temperamentally a loner, and possessing independent means, my father was able to hold himself aloof from conventional concerns. I doubt he realized his decision not to work at a paid job could have disastrous personal consequences. He would fight the good fight, as he saw it. Above all, he dedicated himself to preserving and defending the legacy of his boyhood hero, Eugene Victor Debs.

Another snapshot plucked from my cousin's trove shows my father holding me, a squirming infant, on one knee while he peered at a heavy, open book balanced precariously on the other — an apt image of our nascent relationship. My strongest early memories of him revolve around the years I was five and six. In 1955, my parents had rented an apartment in White Plains, New York, a bedroom community of Manhattan. It was the last place we lived together as a family.

As it seemed to me then, Daddy's main activities were reading (page after page of tiny black print, a baffling code, no pictures), thinking (which looked deceptively like doing nothing but required absolute "peace and quiet"), taking long walks all by himself, and shaving.

I liked to watch him shave, looking up at him from my perch on the toilet seat, my short legs dangling. Half-dressed in unbelted trousers and a sleeveless white undershirt, he used a stubby brush to spread creamy lather over his face, like icing a cake. Sometimes he dabbed a sudsy moustache under my nose. Though I wheedled, he wouldn't let me shave it off or do it for me, because the razor was dangerously sharp. Angling his face to the mirror and twisting his mouth to draw taut the skin, he stroked the blade over his cheek-bone until every speck of whisker was gone. I liked his low-pitched voice, the way he snapped words out with the hint of a twang. Acutely conscious of the way grown-ups smelled, I inhaled his odour, mingling soap, spicy aftershave, and a musky whiff of peppery sweat.

Around this time it dawned on me that my dad's habit of shaving around noon was not standard practice. Why didn't he go to that place called "work" with the other fathers in our apartment building? I'd seen them, briefcases swinging, rushing for the elevator even before the milkman came. Since piping down was the price of my presence in the bathroom, I went on wondering. Was "work" a place, something to do, or both? My father had his own work. It was very important and somehow connected to the small, bodiless metal man's head displayed prominently on a shelf in our living room. Sometimes he took the train into the city to a place he called his "office," but that was surely different from "work," because it never seemed to matter when he arrived, or if he went there at all.

Even then I must have been dimly aware that my father was a solitary, inward man. But he was not merely a bookworm, without any physical presence. One day, swinging on the jungle gym in the playground beside our apartment building, I turned to see my three-year-old brother, Gene, with blood streaming down his head, bawling. Told not to throw rocks at the chain-link fence enclosing the area, he had hurled one up in the air instead, thus acquainting himself with the law of gravity the hard way. I grabbed him and headed for home. The two of us emerged from the elevator just as a neighbour lady stood waiting to board it. Catching sight of my blood-drenched brother, she let out a screech. Gene wailed louder, and my mother, poking her head out the front door, came bellowing down the hall. Afraid of being blamed for Gene's injury, I started crying, too. Into this chaos my father calmly inserted himself. Scooping up my brother, he carried him into the kitchen, set him on the counter, and probed his matted hair. As he swabbed and dressed the wound, he told my mother it was just a scalp nick, a real bleeder but nothing serious. Though it was disappointing to learn that my brother's life was not in danger after all, I was impressed by my father's mastery of the crisis.

And yet he did seem to live mostly in his books and papers, away from my material world. I sensed, for example, that he was too gentle to smack me, unlike some luckless playmates' fathers who administered ritualized spankings with a hairbrush or belt. I had never been so much as swatted by either of my parents. But just to be sure, one day I decided to test my father with a campaign of provocation that culminated with my lying on the floor, gnawing on his ankle, while he tried to read the newspaper. "Cut that out!" in a raised voice was the most he managed.

My mother ran the domestic show. My father seemed not quite an adult, more like one of us kids, a moody, introverted older brother. This had distinct advantages. Getting his attention was hard, but time spent in my father's care was like being let off a leash, a bit scary but oh so thrilling. Sunday afternoons, he sometimes took me to my favourite place in New York City, the Museum of Natural History. He retired to the restaurant with his paper, leaving me to roam the museum as the spirit moved me. I was the only young child unattended by an adult. Public spaces were safer then, but the museum guards always stopped me to ask where my parents could be found. At an appointed hour, I was supposed to meet him under the huge wall clock in the rotunda. Since I couldn't tell time, he showed me what to look for by moving the hands on his wrist-watch. Every so often, I interrupted my wide-eyed charge through the galleries with a detour to check the clock. When the time came for our rendezvous, I stayed put on a pre-selected bench. He was always late. It was my private game to spot him just as he emerged from the corridor leading to the cafeteria, folding his newspaper, striding toward me with his fast, jerky walk.

When my parents started to fight in front of us, my father was plainly on the defensive. My mother seemed to grow larger, louder, more threatening, while he appeared to physically contract. I under-stood the divorce to mean that she would not allow him to live with us anymore. I worried about him, wondering why he had been ban-ished. After the divorce, my mother briefly rented a house in Mamaroneck, New York. Sunday afternoons, my father visited Gene and me there. His misery was obvious in his closed face and long silences as he feigned interest in a game of Snakes and Ladders or whatever contrived activity we were trying to share.

A year later, my mother decided to move us back to Montreal to live with her parents. Certain that my father could not survive without us, I wrote him letters intended to reassure him that he was not forgotten, and even forged some in large unsteady print on behalf of my six-year-old brother. My mother had promised my father would come to visit as soon as we were settled in Canada, but two birthdays passed before I saw him again. (I found out years later that my fears for him were justified. He suffered a breakdown. Ciel checked him into the Institute for Living, a psychiatric facility in New Haven, Connecticut, where he spent eighteen months.)

In the fall of 1959, he arrived in Montreal and was expected at my grandparents' house around two in the afternoon. I stationed myself on the front porch. Finally, a man rounded the corner at the far end of the block. I knew his walk before I could make out his face. I nearly ran him down in my eagerness to embrace him. Once in his arms, I recognized his smell. "So, sweetheart," he asked as we walked back to the house together hand in hand, "are you still on your old man's side?" On future visits, I came to expect this question. Yes, Daddy. Sure, Daddy. But already it felt a bit odd, calling him that, because despite myself, I felt closer to Grandpa, present every day.

I also had a guilty secret. Rummaging in my mother's jewellery box one day, I had found a blackened dog tag. It was retrieved, she explained, from the plane piloted by her first fiancé, shot down over Belgium during the war. Her first fiancé! The divorce had broken my world of family into unmendable pieces. Feeling disloyal, I constructed a rich fantasy in which this other man starred, unthwarted by destiny, as my true father in our picture-book family, a family that would never disintegrate, with a father who would always be there. It was a short-lived daydream. I reluctantly accepted that my own unalterable destiny was to be Al's daughter, and none other.

Montreal, 1960

"I am Ozymandias, king of kings. Look upon my works, ye mighty, and despair." Ten years old, wearing my mother's blue chiffon party dress, my mouth red with her lipstick, I declaim this poem on the wobbly stage of my grandparents' comforter-heaped bed. No one attends the performance. My audience is myself, reflected in the dresser mirror. After months of warring with Grandpa, my mother moved out a few months ago, leaving Gene and me to stay with our grandparents. Mummy has

a new job, helping performers get on TV and into nightclubs. Her apartment is a few blocks away. On visits to her place, I've seen some of her "acts," including a folk-singing trio and Vladimir the Great, a giant, moustachioed burning-coal walker, fire eater, and snake charmer, who, between performances, stashes his cobra in my mother's bathtub. These people seem okay to me, and I saw Vladimir on TV once, but Grandpa was furious. Once I overheard him tell Granny that Sylvia has gone crazy. Two weeks ago he died after a freak car accident. My mother collapsed at his funeral and was taken to hospital. No one has said exactly what is wrong with her, including my dad, who came up from New York a few days ago. But she's never even phoned, so maybe she'll die too. In the kitchen down the hall, Daddy and Granny are talking in low voices, impossible to decipher, hard as I try. After a while, he comes in and perches awkwardly on Granny's side of the bed as I recite the poem again, for his benefit. "I'm very proud of you," he tells me. Wishing that he'd take Gene and me back with him to New York, I somehow know that he'll be gone tomorrow, without us.

A week later, my brother and I are called out of class, down to the principal's office, where a large woman with a horsey smile sits waiting for us. Miss Powell is her name. Her job, she explains, is to look after children whose families can't take care of them. That means us, because our mother is very sick and Granny is too old. Sitting in the back seat of Miss Powell's car, I look out the window as she drives, out of the city, over bridges and past snowy fields, until I have lost all notion of where we are.

She says we're going to stay at a special school called Allancroft. It turns out to be a holding tank for children awaiting placement in foster care. No learning takes place in its single, all-grades classroom, a chamber of intimidation run by a pointer-slamming, chalk-hurling banshee named Mrs. North. I spend the school day staring her down and trying to protect my brother and the weaker kids from her inexplicable, volcanic wrath. We sleep in sex-segregated dorms, supervised in shifts by a *squad of tired-looking, middle-aged women with work-reddened hands, two of whom, Thelma and Ivy, show with little pats and kind words that they actually like children. Every night at bedtime, Thelma reads aloud a few pages from* The Secret Garden; *the thought of this quarter-hour sustains me all day long.*

After three months, on March 17, 1961, a foster home is ready for me. Waiting for Miss Powell to take me there, I sit on my dorm bed thinking, "I don't care if they send me to Siberia and I never see anybody I know again." Despite myself, I do miss Thelma and my brother during the first few weeks with my foster parents, a lower-middle-class couple with Scots–Irish Protestant roots. My foster mother has sewed a frilly pink bedspread and matching curtains especially for my room. Their house has no books. For dinner they eat sausages with gluey mashed potatoes or pork chops with creamed corn. They are dull as doorknobs and kind enough. All things considered, I decide I'd be better off staying with them until I am grown up. This choice is not mine to make. About fifteen months later, the day after school ends in June, Miss Powell takes me back to my grandparents' house. My mother, a pale, puffy stranger, thankfully keeps her distance as I lie on my old bed, face turned to the wall, for an endless afternoon.

None of this was my father's doing. But a time came when I blamed him for it, and other things besides.

A year after my sojourn in foster care ended, I spent ten days in July on vacation with my father and Aunt Ciel. We met Ciel in Croton, the town on the Hudson River where she lived. It was a long, hot drive from there up to the World Fellowship Center in Conway, New Hampshire. Lying across the back seat of the car, I listened to the adults praise the bravery and worry about the frail health of the Center's director, Willard Uphaus, who had recently spent a year in prison. My parents, separately, had already told me about Senator

Joe McCarthy and his evil ways. So I understood when my father looked over his shoulder to explain that Willard had been tried because he had refused to give the attorney general of New Hampshire a list of the centre's visitors. (The government pursued Uphaus through the courts for six years. In 1960, he was finally sentenced to a year in jail for contempt of court.) I no longer knew where I stood on all this. The foster parents in whose care I had spent fifteen months, a period that included the Berlin Wall crisis, were terrified of Communism. They had fashioned a fallout shelter in the basement and considered Nikita Khrushchev the devil incarnate.

After we settled into our rooms at the World Fellowship lodge, I wandered down to the lake. Two older girls in their early teens were getting ready to take out a canoe and invited me aboard. Once we were well out on the water, they stopped paddling. They had an important question for me, apparently some kind of initiation test for new kids. Would I rather be Red or dead? Perversely, I chose the latter. The result was more than I bargained for. They tipped the canoe and swam away with it in tow, leaving me to make it back to shore alone. I was outraged. Those girls could call themselves communists or socialists or progressives or whatever name they went by, but in my book they were bullying creeps. Meaning to take this up with my father, the next day I met Fiona, a proud young leftist with enviable, corn-silk yellow hair who became a real friend. I decided that my place was on the rosy end of the political spectrum after all.

In the ensuing years of my adolescence, which coincided with the sixties, my father's politics made him almost a trophy dad to show off to my friends. Although old, here was a cool guy who felt as strongly as we did about the evils of capitalism, the dead hand of imperialism, racial oppression, environmental degradation, corporate hegemony, and the military-industrial complex. And unlike my mother, he did not try to chaperone my sexual behaviour according to the traditional double standard.

The summer I turned fifteen, my first boyfriend and I took the bus to Manhattan on a lark. I was supposed to stay with my father, my boyfriend with an aunt. When we arrived, my father took us out for dinner, then flipped me the keys to his apartment, and went off to spend the night at his girlfriend's place.

My father's building was a well-kept brownstone on East 83rd Street, cater-corner to the Metropolitan Museum of Art. My seventeen-year-old boyfriend was a smart, sweet boy from a Jewish household of comfort, cleanliness, and order. Though I had tried to drop hints, he blanched at the sight of my father's "foxhole," as he called his semi-basement studio. Heavy red curtains filtered dim light that fell on wall-to-wall shelves crammed with books. Like stalagmites, dusty volumes rose from every available surface, including the floor, in tall, unsteady formations that you had to negotiate carefully when making even the smallest journey in any direction. In this book cave, a pulled-out sofa bed with tangled greyish sheets almost bumped against the huge wooden desk. On top of the desk, propped against the wall, loomed a huge framed reproduction of Goya's *Satan Devouring His Children*. Except for a quart of milk, the fridge was empty, the cupboard bare save for three half-size tins of spaghetti neatly stored in a row. My unnerved boyfriend and I did less that night than we would have with my mother lurking within earshot, loudly munching an apple, as she was wont to do.

Much as my father's flouting of convention delighted me as a teenager, his more abrasive peculiarities began to try my patience. These, I see in retrospect, grew steadily more pronounced as my father himself grew older in the self-built bubble he either couldn't or wouldn't break out of. When it suited him, he had a fine disdain for social graces. Self-absorbed, he more likely than not let the door he had just preceded you through swing shut in your face. At a restaurant meal convened to introduce my brother's girlfriend, Al removed his dental bridge and laid it on the white tablecloth so that he could eat his steak more comfortably. "Fine" was almost never the answer if you asked about his health. Either prone to hypochondria or afflicted with a delicate constitution (perhaps weakened by recurrent bouts of malaria), he always had a headache, sore back, or some other pain. He popped Aspirin the way some people use breath mints or Lifesavers. This habit, I think, gradually damaged his hearing, a common consequence of ASA overuse. He talked too loudly, which made conversation wearing. On his perennial subjects — the shameful neglect of Debs's legacy, the countless outrages and deficiencies of American capitalist society and two-party politics, the nefarious conspiracies of the CIA — he could be a ranter. Avoiding these topics won the listener no reprieve. Offer him a breakfast glass of orange juice, and you'd soon be talking about the plight of migrant fruit pickers and the poisonous practices of agribusiness.

By the time I entered college, an outing in my father's company sometimes made me squirm with embarrassment. And although I continued to admire his idealism, I grew newly skeptical of Al's sputtering, inconclusive Debsian literary projects. My own coursework in history and political science made me realize that he approached his subject not with a tough, scholarly eye but with near-hagiographic reverence. He was ruled by emotion, not intellect, I thought with more than a trace of condescension. Certain things affected him viscerally. When we discussed the rape and murder of four Maryknoll churchwomen in El Salvador, his hands shook and he was near tears. A conversation about Richard Nixon and Henry Kissinger, whom he regarded as war criminals, once made his temple vein swell so alarmingly I feared he'd have a stroke.

In 1970, my father had his first brush with destitution. I was nineteen at the time, registered at McGill University but living in Brighton, England, doing one year of my undergraduate history degree at the University of Sussex — a sojourn largely funded by my father, I later realized, out of a bank balance fast dwindling to zero.

In January of that year he scrawled this note to Ciel:

Dearest sister,
Am broke and desperate. My back injury is acting up again — can't look for a job. Can you send and loan me $75 to keep the landlord at bay?
    I love you, Al

My seventeen-year-old brother went down to Manhattan to help him move out of his apartment. They put his things in storage, Gene told me, taking only clothes, some books — a poetry anthology, a history of the Spanish-American War — and a small bust of Debs to our father's new digs in a rooming house on a rough Soho street years away from gentrification. Within a week, he was sporting a shiner, the result of a tiff with a fellow resident who took offence when my father asked him not to shine his shoes on the communal kitchen table.

Where did my father's inheritance go?

As I've said, he had his projects, his causes. With help from him and others, the Eugene Victor Debs house at Terre Haute, Indiana, was saved from demolition and converted to a museum. He travelled a good deal, usually on purposeful group tours to promote world peace or some other worthy cause. I remember him proudly showing me the letterhead and business card of the Arts and Science Press. His intention was to provide an outlet for socially progressive work. This may have remained a pipe dream; I'm not sure what he published, if anything at all. In the mid-sixties, he undertook a one-man mission to Moscow to encourage détente by persuading the Soviets to issue a postage stamp depicting Debs and Lenin side by side. (A great admirer of Lenin, Debs called the Russian Revolution "a luminous achievement ... the beginning of the self-government of the people throughout the world.") The stamp project was not successful, but judging by the letters to my father that I found among his papers, he did leave a trail of bemused and bewildered Russian officials and academics in his wake.

Although he helped me pay for my university education, he'd been unreliable about child support, often skipping payments — perhaps vengefully. Maybe he feared that my mother would use any funds he sent for her own purposes. My father did show my brother and me a good time on our visits to Manhattan. He put us up in the Stanhope Hotel, around the corner from his apartment, in quarters that seemed palatial compared to the bedroom I shared with my mother at my grandmother's cramped house in Montreal. He took us to the 1962 New York World's Fair, introduced us to Broadway musicals, and taught us to order the perfect steakhouse dinner (shrimp cocktail, a T-bone cooked medium rare with a baked potato dripping butter, topped off with a hot fudge sundae).

There were women, including one in New York and another in Finland, with whom he had long-standing liaisons at different times. I sometimes heard about but never met them. Probably he showed them a good time, too. While he had money, he always wore good clothes, favouring a well-cut topcoat, conservative suits, mildly splashy ties, and leather dress shoes. No doubt his prolonged treatment in residence at the Institute for Living had depleted his fortune too. And given his disdain for inherited wealth and wilful ignorance of his own investment portfolio, he may have been fleeced by unscrupulous brokers.

Then there were his books. "Your old man's a bibliomaniac," he used to say half-apologetically as he pulled me into yet another stop on his trapline of second-hand and antiquarian bookstores. He was also an amateur philatelist. His library and stamp collection were valuable. I know he hung on to these treasures as long as possible, though eventually he had to sell them.

My father's financial predicament did not surprise my mother. She said he had always been wildly impractical about money, unable to grasp the simple fact that no fortune would withstand steady erosion of its capital. This, I think, is only half the truth. He was acutely aware that his life of principle, as he saw it, was supported by inherited funds amassed in the economic system he professed to despise. My grandmother and aunts had managed differently, and their share of Albert Sr.'s estate sustained them in comfort all their lives. My aunts did sometimes work (Ciel taught art for a few years and Ruth had a job as a social worker) but not because they had to. My father, with prudent stewardship of his resources, could have stayed prosperous. He must have been at least partly glad to shed the money, if only to see what it felt like. It's also possible that he expected to receive a second inheritance, sooner rather than later, from his then eighty-eight-year-old mother.

A year later, that is what happened. My grandmother died, and her will restored my father to solvency. He moved back to St. Louis, ostensibly because it was cheaper to live there than in Manhattan, but also, I think, because it felt something like home.

In 1974 I was living in Toronto and working on a graduate degree in history when my father sent me a train ticket to visit him in St. Louis. To my relief, he had a decent apartment — not quite a book cave yet, but he was clearly working on it — and seemed to have constructed a life for himself. Touring around, he showed me the table at the university library where he did his work. He was particularly pleased to find that one of the librarians knew a lot about Debs and was very helpful. He had made a few friends. I met Larry, a clerk in a second-hand bookstore, and Charlie, a Vietnam vet who lived in a van with his dog. There was a girlfriend around somewhere — on the young side judging by the voice I heard when I answered the phone in his living room, but he kept mum about that.

I hoped my father had learned his lesson. I had no idea how much my grandmother had left him, but at twenty-four I knew that earning money was tough. Apart from his desultory stab at book-selling decades ago, Al had never held a job or even tried to find one. Whatever he had received from his mother's estate, he would have to make it last. So I was infuriated when he unveiled his latest project. Through the Debs Society, he had endowed a $500 prize for poetry, to be called the Edwin Markham Award. It was, to me, a huge sum — almost enough to cover the annual tuition at McGill, where Gene — his son! — was holding down two part-time jobs to pay his way through social-work school. Any spare money should rightly go to help Gene, I protested. My father's face fell. Things should not come to a boy too easily, he argued. In retrospect, I think this was sincere, if misguided and self-serving — my father's tacit admission that inheriting money too early had deformed his life. At the time, it made me that much angrier. My last shot was to call Edwin Markham a bad poet. Who read that hoary old chestnut "The Man with the Hoe" anymore? You might be right, my father said mildly. You might very well be right.

"Sweetheart, your father was never all there." This remark, from an old friend of my mother, made me bridle in my early twenties. A decade later, a girlfriend of my own blurted, "I've never met any-one like your father. He's absolutely awful." Though I disliked her for saying it, by that time I more than half agreed. I'd tried to dis-suade him from his last, in my view, crackpot venture, the lakeside halfway house for ex-convicts, pointing out problems of insurance, security, the neighbours' reaction, not to mention his trusting disre-gard for personal danger. He assumed any guest of his establishment would be a good man at heart. The next thing I heard, the proper-ty was bought and he was shopping for canoes. The project went bust for reasons never made clear to me.

By 1983 my father was broke again, this time permanently. The next year he showed up on my doorstep in Toronto, clothes reeking from a straight twenty-four-hour bus trip up from St. Louis. He had a can opener in one trouser pocket, a spoon in the other, utensils for eating the tinned baked beans and pineapple he'd carried to eat on the way. (A bank teller who had known Al at this juncture wrote me a long letter after he died. This woman whom I had never met still felt guilty for refusing my father's request to sleep in her garage.) He stayed with me a week in Toronto, then, provisioned with more tinned food, bussed back to St. Louis. There he again landed on his feet, sort of. Having managed to secure a veterans disability pension, he took a rented room at the Mark Twain Hotel. Sharing this news by phone, he sounded chipper.

Unfortunately for both of us, the last, most difficult decade of my father's life coincided with a period when I was consumed by problems of my own — the aftermath of a failed marriage, a job that went sour. Fearful of slipping under myself, my view of him hardened. As a father, he'd failed me, even betrayed me, I decided. He was selfish, lazy, self-indulgent. Born with every advantage, he had inherited more money than most people earn in a lifetime, and having spent it all, he evinced no compunction about accepting a state-funded pension largely paid for by working taxpayers. Worse than a hypocrite, he was a parasite. For several years, I virtually ignored him.

In 1989, my father developed cancer of the esophagus, with a life expectancy, his doctor told me, of six months. That fall, I went to St. Louis to see him, expecting this visit might be our last. His grungy rented room in the Mark Twain Hotel appalled me. If it bothered him, he never let on, nor did he appear to regret his self-imposed one-way ride on the "downalator" (a word he used). His veterans pension, he told me, was the first income he felt he had ever earned. My elderly father's situation, suffering in poverty and alone, tormented me. I was angry, with him and with myself. Why had he let his life come to such a pass? And what could or should I do about it? I lacked the means to help him pay for better living quarters. My three days in St. Louis had cost twelve hundred dollars, including airfare and hotel, not a trip I could afford to make often. Because he had cancer, I could not buy travel health insurance to cover the cost of any treatment he might need if he came to Toronto. Even so, I sent him a plane ticket. He did not use it.

Determined to beat his disease and ignoring nearly all medical recommendations, my father outlasted his initial prognosis by five years. During his illness, I talked frequently to the staff in charge of his care at the Veterans Administration Hospital. He was variously and affectionately pronounced "an amazing guy," "a real piece of work," and "stubborn as a mule" by a resident physician, a radiation technician, and a social worker. Only the oncologist was at a loss for words. "Your father is … is … is …" he'd sputtered. "Eccentric," I supplied. "Eccentric! That's it," he seized the word gratefully. I suspect the phrase on the tip of his tongue was "a royal pain in the ass." Every Sunday afternoon at 5 P.M., I placed a call to the pay phone in the Mark Twain's lobby, the desk clerk having agreed to answer it and fetch my father from his room. Every so often, I asked if he would like a visit. "Not right now, dear. Next spring, maybe." I never did see him again, both of us pretending there was more time than there was.

The Jefferson Barracks National Cemetery in St. Louis looks like a study in perspective, its vast, rolling expanse overlaid with precise rows of identical white headstones that diminish steadily in size as they approach the horizon. There, on a frigid February afternoon in 1994, with me, my brother, my partner, and my father's few friends from the Debs Society and the Democratic Socialists of America looking on, an urn containing his ashes was placed in Section 1-F, grave 2319.

He left no will or instructions of any kind. On the trip down, in my haze of confused grief, I fretted about the death notice that had appeared in the *St. Louis Post-Dispatch,* courtesy of the Veterans Affairs department, complete with a tiny picture of a half-mast American flag. A pacifist, deeply American but a patriot strictly on his own terms, Al probably would have nixed the flag. I also regretted having withheld consent for an autopsy. The medical director at the hospital was crestfallen. Since my father lived so much longer than expected, his corpse had special value. Probably he would have wanted science to learn from his body. Unable to contemplate its dissection in the aftershock of his death, I was not ready to make that time-limited decision.

The Veterans Administration covered the costs of my father's cremation, funeral, and interment. I accepted this final entitlement. Probably he had not cared about such matters one way or another. Encouraged by the unctuous funeral director, I did pay for a "wooden urn upgrade" to replace the no-frills metal model, not wanting to watch my father's remains vanish from the cold, radiant world in a glorified tin can. In the event, the upgrade — a pale pine canister — looked like something from the kitchenware pages of an Ikea catalogue. My father would have told me to save my money, or better yet, donate it to the Maryknoll Sisters. His bank statements showed that, out of his $685 disability pension, he regularly contributed $25 to the Maryknolls, the last debit processed two days after he died.

Maybe he would have laughed at the prospect of spending all eternity in the care of the U.S. Armed Forces. The war had "made a man of him," he once told me, but he had hated military service — far worse than the regimentation was the near-constant din and clatter. Maybe he would have joked that the cemetery was the one quiet place army life had to offer, or been amused by the orientation package for mourners, which contained a detailed map of the property, a schedule of hours of operation, and a policy sheet on flowers.

I did what I could for my father. For years I agonized over having abandoned him to his solitude and having let professionals ease his end. But guilt, that heavy, watery emotion that assumes any shape and fills any space you give it, has seeped away, leaving a fine, adhesive silt of love on the membrane of my heart, and also a shard of shame, durable and piercing.

In 1995, a year after his death, a letter came from one of my father's Debs Society friends, a labour lawyer whom I'd met at the funeral:

> Your father Al was a delightful person. We stood in awe of his knowledge of Eugene Victor Debs, and smile remembering his fury at a historian whose book called Debs "an uncultured man." He had an idea for a drop-in coffee house for lesbian and gay teenagers, which we are now in the process of setting up in a community center in his honor. Do you have a picture of Al that we could frame and display on the premises?

The cache of Frampton memorabilia had yet to arrive. All I had to offer was a single, zany colour snapshot of my father that was taken in 1973 in Toronto. The photographer was a sculptor friend. The high-ceilinged studio that he semi-legally occupied in a rundown old warehouse was furnished with a greasy-looking Louis XVI–style brocade upholstered sofa and an armchair from the Salvation Army thrift shop. The floor was strewn with detritus, a source of spare parts for my friend's art — the rusted corpses of bicycles, a decrepit shopping cart missing one wheel, a faux-marble replica of Michelangelo's *David,* badly chipped with its internal wire framework exposed along one arm. In the snapshot, my father sits in the armchair to one side and just in front of the statue, wearing a white shirt and tie. His longish, salt-and-pepper hair, combed back, curls over his collar. He gazes past the camera; unsmiling, the right corner of his mouth pulled into a small, sardonic twist. He looks like the last curator in a bombed-out museum. I sent an enlarged copy of the snapshot to St. Louis.

I did not hear from the lawyer again, and I have not tried to find out if Al's Rainbow Café — its proposed name — came into being. A chip off the old block, I prefer to hold fast to this comforting notion and tell myself it did.

PHILIP MARCHAND

Lea and Me

IN THE FALL OF 1964, AS A SEVENTEEN-YEAR-OLD, I
left my home in Niskayuna, a suburb of Schenectady, New York, and
came to Canada to study at the University of Toronto. I loved it. A
provincial youth going to Paris in a Balzac novel couldn't have felt
more of a sense of release, of adventure, of expanded horizons, than
I had in that city and that university. For the first time in my life, I
was happy in my unhappiness.

Although I had been raised Catholic and was in residence at
St. Michael's College in the university, I also stopped going to mass,
immediately. No spiritual crisis, no troubled conscience, I just
stopped going. Curiously enough, in that first year or two in
Toronto, I did become intrigued with an intellectual side of
Catholicism that I had never encountered before, the Jacques
Maritain and Etienne Gilson school of neo-Scholasticism, and all
those terribly intense, terribly spiritual Catholic novelists such as
Bloy and Bernanos. That these intellectuals were all French had an
almost symbolic importance — they stood in dramatic opposition
to the defiantly philistine Irish American priests I had known as a
child. These French intellectual Catholics had a kind of austere
glamour, compounded of the light from the Rose Window of
Chartres and bottles of good, honest peasant burgundy, served in the
cafés where they argued with Jean-Paul Sartre.

So I cheered them on from a distance, as it were, as if they were my team in the major leagues of philosophy. But even their glamour began to fade in the next few years, as various revolutions appeared on the horizon. Timothy Leary, with his promise of hundreds of orgasms per incident of sexual intercourse on LSD, not to mention cosmic enlightenment, Abbie Hoffman, with his vision of politicized hippies — all this was infinitely more exciting than the church had ever been.

All the while, unbeknownst to me, the nuns and priests at St. Michael's College — or many of them, anyway — were quietly embarking on their own revolution. In the very year I came to that college, in 1964, these doctoral students in theology, experts in the philosophy of St. Bonaventure and the phenomenology of Edmund Husserl, were sitting in a comfortable, cedar-panelled room with a woman named Mrs. Lea Hindley-Smith and weeping over their negligent fathers or their angry mothers.

Mrs. Hindley-Smith was not a psychiatrist or a psychologist or a psychoanalyst. She had no credentials, even as a psychotherapist. She sold real estate, and she occasionally read palms and tea leaves. She was not alluring. She was corpulent, beady-eyed, with a bouffant hairdo slightly smaller than a papal tiara and two outfits she wore alternately — a gold satin smock and a purple satin smock. She had no social or academic status — born in Cardiff, Wales, in 1916, she had witnessed, as an eight-year-old, her father being carted off to a lunatic asylum, which he never left. Despising her mother as a weakling, she faced the grim task of making a living with no resources but her own ingenuity and determination.

Fortunately, these were considerable. She worked as an artists' model and a nurse, while studying at a psychoanalytic institute from which she emerged a confirmed Freudian, with a sideline in the art of hypnosis. She married a man in the textile business and with their three children moved to Canada in 1948. Her husband developed a heart condition and was unable to hold a job; once again, Lea was thrown on her own resources. She worked hard, reading tea leaves at parties, running a boarding house, dealing in antiques, buying her own house — elegant, but dilapidated — restoring it, buying others. Her first love, however, was emotional healing, and slowly she built up a clientele, in the teeth of opposition from her husband, a cranky, disappointed man who was bitterly jealous of her therapeutic work. He could hardly stop it, however, since she was now the breadwinner. And in fact it was a very slight move from reading palms and tea leaves and tarot cards — the arts, in reality, of gauging the feelings and reactions of people — to psychotherapizing.

By 1964 she had an extensive practice. Then the priests and nuns came and were enchanted. For the first time in their lives, they encountered someone who listened to them, who understood them, who wanted to help them.

Were they deluded? Hardly. That she was a canny judge of human beings there was no doubt. And when she spoke, people listened. Her voice was the kind that instantly alerted the nervous system of the auditor, vibrant with feeling, slightly high pitched, but unwavering and sympathetic. It was not a voice made for small talk. Whatever she said, she believed absolutely. She knew how wretched her clients felt, and she was determined to do battle with that wretchedness, to salvage their lives. There was almost a desperation in her resolve, as if — and this was something she herself pondered — she were somehow reaching out to the father in her unconscious, trying to save him from his fate.

She was also, without being fully aware of it, a true revolutionary. She was a figure whose time had come. It was partly by accident that she conducted the first experiment in group therapy with Roman Catholic priests and nuns in history, but history was leading up to this moment. Something in the atmosphere of the early 1960s favoured enterprises like unorthodox psychotherapy. If happiness can be defined as a temporary cessation of anxiety, then perhaps this period represented a cessation from Doom. It was as if, in the collective psyche of the West, people looked around and realized that their world was going to survive after all. After the slaughter of World War I, the catastrophe of World War II and the Holocaust, the dropping of the atom bomb — manifestations of destructiveness unprecedented in scale — the rubble had cleared, at least in western Europe and North America. The threat of nuclear annihilation remained, of course, but western Europe was prosperous, democratic, and stable, and North America was experiencing remarkable economic growth — no, the Great Depression was not going to return; no, the Communists were not going to overrun all of Europe; no, the Apocalypse was not staring us in the face. It was as if a man living a nightmare had awakened one morning and felt — happy. Perhaps life could be different.

A pope in Rome called the Second Vatican Council in 1962, to reconcile the church with the modern world, as if he had heard the first tremors of what Tom Wolfe would later call the "happiness explosion," the search for individual fulfillment unparalleled in history. The priests and nuns at St. Michael's College heard those tremors. And their response — to seek therapy — would also set a precedent for the years to come. Of course, people had resorted to Freud long before this, but Lea Hindley-Smith offered something more than classic psychoanalysis — that austere, rigorous practice involving a lonely analysand and an equally lonely analyst, scrupulous in his detachment from the outpourings of his patient. Hindley-Smith would use any technique that came into her head. Above all, she refused to be detached, to stand aloof from the treacherous undertow of a patient's "transference." Positive transference, negative transference — good mother, bad mother — Hindley-Smith treated the whole package like a loving but firm schoolmistress. Every thought and feeling was allowed, every thought and feeling was accepted — and then put in its place.

In theory, negative transference was just as welcome as positive. After all, both were basically irrational psychic mechanisms — they clouded reality — that could be put to good use by a therapist. But as time went on, positive transference — the longing for the benign giantess of the nursery, as it were, redirected to the person of Mrs. Hindley-Smith — began to seem natural and fitting. The role suited her. She was the good mother. In fact, she was more than that: she was a life force. The priests and nuns asked her to initiate them into the mysteries of Freud and Wilhelm Reich. Just two or three years ago, they had been ministers of a church that remained, in its essentials, a medieval institution. Now they had moved beyond that, moved beyond even the model of a "relevant" post–Vatican II Church, into a new evangelism, the emotional liberation of the repressed human being.

Houses were purchased in which people could live together, counsel each other, explore their conflicts — and the concealed emotional dynamics underlying these conflicts — in weekly groups led by a therapist. A hundred-acre farm was acquired in the rolling countryside north of Toronto. At its height, in the 1970s, the Therafields complex included eighteen houses, an eight-suite apartment building, four rural houses with extensive land, two vacation properties in Florida, and two office buildings in Toronto. Eight hundred people were fee-paying members of the organization.

Lea Hindley-Smith had long since thrown out her smocks. Now her outfits were elegant and tasteful, with only a few accessories — silver shoes, massive floral-patterned silk scarves — to testify to a certain impulse to the gaudy. (As well, she no longer weighed two hundred pounds, though her weight fluctuated, and she remained stout.) Her surroundings were equally well appointed. There was something disconcerting, however, in her tendency to acquire and then to discard palatial accommodations. A home in Rosedale had been bought, lived in, and then sold. The Willow, an immense country home, designed according to the principles of Frank Lloyd Wright, by an architect named Visvaldis Upenieks, Lea's lover, had been built by Therafields members — I worked on the plumbing — as a suitable residence for Mrs. Hindley-Smith. She saw it, pronounced it good, lived in it for a while, and then bought a suite at The Palace Pier.

In later years, after Therafields had disappeared into history, we who were not intimates of Lea Hindley-Smith found out something of the truth. At the time we had no idea what was behind this restlessness. We had no idea that she was even then hearing a knock on the door from her worst fear. It was a familiar presence, it was her father's nemesis, it was the shock that had never gone away, it was madness — coming for her now. Changing residences did not help. It knew her address.

In 1968, I married a fellow student at the University of Toronto in her hometown of Pittsburgh. Thereafter, we returned to Toronto and rented an apartment while I worked on an MA in English literature at the same university. One day, in early 1969, I received a visit in our apartment from a friend, another former student at St. Michael's College, and the conversation got around to some problem I was having in my marriage. My friend suggested the problem was much deeper and the answer might be found with a group called Therafields. He was involved with this community devoted to "communications therapy." He gave me a telephone number.

My wife and I had heard of this group. One day in the neighbourhood we passed a man on the sidewalk, a former student at St. Michael's College, one of those serious religious types who read Teutonic theologians, attended guitar masses in the college chapel, and was now a known member of Therafields. He looked lost in space. "What is it with this organization?" my wife and I asked ourselves. We did not use the word "cult." At the time, cults were not the news item they have since become. In our minds, however, Therafields had acquired something of the aura of what we would later call a cult, a tightly knit group sealed off from the rest of the world, engaged in mysterious quasi-religious practices. It was not appealing.

Nevertheless — perhaps because I trusted my friend, a man of discernment — I phoned the number and made an appointment with a man who had been a controversial priest when I had been at St. Michael's College, condemning the church's stand on birth control as evidence of a "celibate psychosis." The man himself looked like a born celibate, with his severe brush cut and rather distant manner. At the time he interviewed me, however, he had cast aside his own celibate psychosis by leaving the priesthood and marrying a former nun. The couple produced two children and then separated. A few years ago, I saw him at a Gay Pride Parade in Toronto, with two or three buddies.

All that was in the future, however. During the interview, he was far from the stereotype of a cult recruiter as a smiling, unctuous individual who is anxious to be your friend. He asked me, in the spirit of Mr. Rorschach I assume, to do a drawing. I did, complete with stick figures, and somebody peering out from behind a tree in a surreptitious manner, which I thought would give whoever looked at the picture some pretty good psychological material to work with, right off the bat. I told him, at the close of the interview, that I didn't want some old lady as a therapist. I don't know what I was thinking. I suppose I was afraid I would get stuck with somebody like my eleventh-grade history teacher, Mrs. Gogarty. (Not her real name.) He informed me that Therafields did not have any old lady therapists.

In fact, I started out with two therapists, Larissa and Andre, who both looked in their thirties. In return for one-hour sessions once a week, I paid a monthly fee. I forget how much I paid — it wasn't a lot. On the other hand, I think Larissa and Andre were "learning therapists," so seeing them was like getting your hair cut at barber college. They were nice enough, though a little clean-cut for my taste, since I was in my shaggy hippie stage. Andre was, in fact, an accountant with Ralston Purina; Larissa looked like the insurance saleswoman she later became after her therapist career. We sat, one evening, in a house in the Annex, in what would have made a nice sitting room for a bed and breakfast, with comfortable armchairs, subdued light from a floor lamp, a thick rug over a well-urethaned oak floor, and the ubiquitous cedar panelling of the era.

Andre, who had a vaguely continental accent, was the more relaxed of the two, leaning forward in his sleeveless V-neck sweater and thick rimmed glasses, looking at me with not unfriendly curiosity. Larissa, with her equine face and carefully coiffed blond hair, did have, to my mind, an unfortunate air of a schoolteacher or well-trained real estate agent. For a long time, I told them, I believed that I was on a kind of automatic maturation escalator. At eighteen, I was more clued in than when I was fifteen, at twenty, more evolved as a human being than I was at eighteen. But now, at the age of twenty-two, I had lost faith in this process. I was who I was, and age alone would bring no more improvements. They nodded in agreement.

So began my introduction to a twentieth-century method of remaking the soul; of achieving the secular equivalent of sanctity — what people now refer to as "taking control" of their lives. The human being, it was believed in Therafields, had to wrest this control from repressed emotions. And the struggle lasted a lifetime — just like the pursuit of sainthood.

I started talking about my feelings. In 1969 this still seemed like a brave and revolutionary undertaking — our culture had not yet become obsessed with therapy. Oprah Winfrey and "grief counsellors" were as yet unknown. It was an unsettling experience. "What do you think would happen if you did say something to him?" Larissa would ask when I mentioned my reluctance to confront my landlord on some issue. That was a good question. There was a rational answer to it, based on reasonable probability, and there was an answer that seemed to emerge from the bubbling, half-conscious swampland of the imagination, where fearful creatures lived under the water. That answer was: Something Terrible. Was it worth it to trace that phantasmal something down the pathways of the nervous system to some buried memory, some childhood trauma perhaps?

And did one have to be totally honest all the time? How useful was that? In one session, I felt impelled to tell Larissa I thought she was less than physically attractive. She sat there with a determined smile on her face as I slowly forced the words out of my mouth. The smile said: See, I don't mind a bit. That was nice of her, but now I cringe at the memory.

Gingerly, Larissa and Andre would hint at some of the mysteries of repressed emotions and unconscious desires. We didn't go far in that direction, but not because of any skepticism on my part. The notion of "family dramas" and how parents and siblings forced you into certain roles made sense to me. The mysteries of the Higher Freudianism were more daunting — oddly enough I never read a single work by Freud in all the years I spent in Therafields — but these, too, I was prepared to accept.

My wife entered Therafields at the same time as I did, and she saw a different therapist. After a year and a half, we entered different house groups, effectively ending our marriage. That the marriage was over saddened me — but I never said much about it, and the subject was not raised in my therapeutic sessions. Whatever regret I felt was brushed aside in the adventure of living in this new, extraordinary situation, a house full of people dedicated to expressing their true feelings at whatever cost. The theory was that living together would inevitably bring out the family dramas of each individual — Susie would find herself playing out her martyr complex, Bill his isolated child-in-hiding role. Only now those roles would be challenged by other house group members, and Bill and Susie would be forced into clear consciousness of what they were doing — clearing the way for expression of even deeper, murkier emotions.

Each of us still had our individual therapists — Andre and Larissa bowed out, in my case, for reasons that were never made clear to me, and I began seeing Ian, a quiet-spoken, thirtyish, former Scot. This was a step-up for me. Ian was a member of the inner circle of therapists, the group called "Hypno One." This group, adepts in hypnotherapy, consisted largely of the nuns and priests who first saw Lea Hindley-Smith in the early sixties.

One lesson that Therafields did teach me, in retrospect, is that explicit hierarchies, as exemplified by the Catholic church, are far less dangerous than implicit hierarchies, exemplified by Therafields. In explicit hierarchies, you obey the bishop because he's the bishop, or the colonel because he's the colonel; in private, you are perfectly free to express your conviction that the man is an idiot. In implicit hierarchies, you obey your superior because he really is superior. Hypno One was superior. Below this group was a more recent group of therapists, called by its acronym CAG (character analysis group). They were less superior. Below them was a group called the Brunswick Learners Group, named after Brunswick Avenue where several Therafields houses were located, and below them was the Gemini Group, consisting largely of people who entered Therafields at the same time I did, or later. Very few people in this latter group were ever anointed as working therapists — to become a therapist was tantamount to being declared cured of your "drama" — before the whole structure collapsed around 1980.

Looming above everyone was Lea, the ur-therapist, who had become invested with the quality of infallibility by the time I entered Therafields. She had no official position in Therafields, but her word was final. Moreover, control of Therafields was vested, after 1971, in a corporate structure known as Therafields Environmental Centre (York) Ltd., whose president was Rob Hindley-Smith, Lea's son. Its vice-president was bp Nichol, winner of the Governor General's award for poetry, whose devotion to Lea was unquestioned. Barrie, as his friends called him, was also Therafields's greatest walking advertisement. His reserves of warmth, confidence, energy, humour, and genuine regard for others seemed to have no limits. People felt good around him. He had friends not just in Therafields but in the literary and artistic world — countless writers, artists, and musicians were devoted to him. Esteem for his work, at least among the avant-garde literati, in Canada and internationally, was and remains high. And there he was, helping to run this strange corporation, which even the therapists began to question. When some of the Hypno One therapists wanted to exert a little more direction over the often-capricious handling of Therafields affairs, their concern was dismissed as a "power drive" by the Hindley-Smithites. (For anyone to question the financial affairs of Therafields was also dismissed as "paranoia" — and Lea made it clear that she had had enough of that in her lifetime.) In 1980, when Therafields was undergoing a financial crisis due to overextension of properties, the corporation paid Lea $900,000 for one of her residences, while the therapists were not getting paid at all. The situation could not last.

None of that was on the horizon when, in the fall of 1970, fresh out of graduate school, and recently employed by McClelland and Stewart as the "manuscript editor" — I read and reported on the submissions on the slush pile — I moved into my first house group.

Now, in addition to my sessions with Ian, I met with my fellow residents once a week with the house group therapist — he lived elsewhere — who was a former priest and a member in good standing of Hypno One. We paid rent cheques to Therafields in addition to our monthly fees.

The house was a two-storey duplex in the Annex, a red brick house built in the twenties, with plain walls and ceilings and oak tongue-and-groove flooring. Twenty-four people — twelve men and twelve women — lived in it. Four of the larger rooms were shared by two occupants, which left sixteen smaller rooms, one of which I occupied. The basement was converted into a kitchen and a large common area used as a dining room and a place where the "groups" took place one evening a week, with the therapist present.

Off to the side of this room was a smaller unfinished room. Since part of our obligations as house group members — assumed, rather than specifically assigned — was to maintain the house and undertake needed renovations, it was determined that we would finish this room. What for, I can't recall. It could have been a nice television room, except none of us watched television. The point was that it needed work. And work — physical work, at any rate — binds us to reality, as Freud pointed out. "Work therapy," therefore, was a major part of the Therafields agenda, for at least two reasons. One, it was therapeutic. Two, it resulted in houses and buildings owned by Therafields being constructed and renovated in handsome style.

This room, about ten feet square, defeated us, however. The big problem was the cement floor. To install flooring on top of that, we had to lay down two by fours and then make sure they were uniformly level. It's the kind of job that can drive an experienced carpenter mad. Since none of us knew what we were doing, it took forever. That wretched floor was a standing rebuke to everyone in the house group for the entire year the group lasted, especially the men, because the men were responsible for physical repairs and construction. (The women did more womanly things. If we decided to devote a day to working on the house, for example, the women would prepare lunch and dinner, and clean.) We were defeated by our "passivity," by our "transference" to the house (bad mother), perhaps even by our hidden homosexual feelings. (More on that later.) The women did not get off scot-free, either. They weren't "supportive." Who knew what secret jollies they were getting from our failure? The truth was this entire house group was a failure, a maelstrom of emotions nobody could get a handle on.

The first night I stayed in the house set the tone. While I was unpacking my books and putting them in carefully arranged order on my little brick bookcase, I heard shouting from downstairs. Later, Neal knocked on my door and expressed concern that I might have been freaked out. What happened was that Neal had been shouting at George — not for anything that George did but because of the impact on Neal's nervous system of George's very presence. It might have been a conflict of body types. Neal was tall, narrow boned, with a pronounced jaw, and an open homosexual. George, a real estate salesman who had been born and raised in Greece, was built, on the other hand, like a football player. He had a habit of stroking his trim moustache with his index finger and his thumb whenever he volunteered his pithy comments. While almost always genial, he did seem tough. He once showed me photographs of himself in his younger days as a member of some quasi-military outfit in his native Greece, in a dangerously fascistic-looking uniform — his headgear had a tassel on it, I think. He supported the Greek junta then in power, and when somebody in the house group came back from watching the movie Z, he explained Costa-Gravas's mistake to him. Neal might have been afraid that George would metamorphose into a storm trooper and commit unspeakable acts on his body.

Neal was trying to be true to his feelings. Neal was on the edge quite a bit. One might almost say that he was on the verge of hysteria most of the time. When things got too much for him — when repressed feelings were getting too close to the surface, is the way we understood it — he would do something naughty like cruise the gay bars. At one point, he took some drugs and ended up in a room at the Clarke Institute of Psychiatry. Therapy was a true drama where Neal was concerned. (On the other hand, if you were upset about something, he was often the person you wanted to hear your troubles.)

If Neal's response to George, in particular, was exaggerated, that was par for the course in those early years of house groups. You would walk into the house after coming home from work, and in the dining room or in a bedroom, there would be an impromptu group. Somebody would have had a fit about something, and other house group members would be dutifully trying to sort it out. The idea was that one person in the gathering, at least, would be "objective." Sometimes these impromptu groups helped. Sometimes they made things worse, despite the therapeutic insights proffered on all sides. When this happened, it was said to have created a "heavy" atmosphere, and that was not good.

As time went on, extreme displays of emotion in the course of daily house group living were discouraged by therapists. The notion was that exchanges of feelings should be "crisp," to the point. Let's say house group member X noticed that house group member Y left dirty dishes in the sink. X, without further ado, would then "confront" Y on his or her negligence. Perhaps Y was subconsciously expressing anger toward the house group. No matter. If there was smouldering resentment in the aftermath of this confrontation, the idea was to "save it for the group," that is, the weekly group with a therapist in attendance. The therapist, as an ultimately objective person, would help prevent the swirl of emotion from becoming "heavy." Besides, if you were going to bare your very soul — why waste that revelation on a smaller, unofficial audience?

A lot of my feelings were directed toward Martin. Although Martin has remained a friend of mine for thirty years, I didn't much like him when I first met him. In the subtle competition among Therafields members over whose family was worse, Martin won easily. Both his parents, by then deceased, had been hopeless drunks. His brother was an ex-con. His sister was a welfare case.

Martin and I, for some reason, aroused each other's competitiveness in many ways. The astute reader will have inferred from this that a big part of our drama in this house group was sibling rivalry. A rather amusing example occurred one night when I walked into an impromptu group in that room we were trying to finish. I don't know how it started — perhaps some flare-up had occurred among the men working there — but I'll never forget the urgency in Neal's voice as he confronted Martin: "Do you want to be pre-Oedipal all your life?"

This was no joke. Freud postulated that boys, about the age of three, begin to experience desire for the mother and rivalry with the father. Upon the successful outcome of this dynamic much of the son's future sexual and emotional life depends. If it goes funny, the lad's personality will be seriously warped. If he "wins" the Oedipal, for example, he may become a great success with women in his later life, but he will be unable to trust in the strength or reliability of other men.

Much worse is the problem of boys who, for some reason or other — usually horrid parents — never reach the Oedipal phase at all. This is the case, pre-eminently, with homosexuals. Freud himself was rather sympathetic to homosexuals, but some of his disciples, notably the late psychoanalyst Edmund Bergler, whose books were widely read in Therafields, were not. According to Bergler, homosexuals, being pre-Oedipal, were stuck in the earliest phase of sexuality, the oral phase. They were swamped with psychic masochism, prone to injustice collecting and pseudo-aggressive behaviour with others, and possessed a raft of other unpleasant characteristics.

At Therafields, this was taken seriously. Poor Neal was in no very comfortable position as a gay man. Yet, in an odd way, his overt homosexuality gave him a kind of authority. At least his pre-Oedipal dilemma was not hidden. What was really deadly was the suppressed homosexuality of ostensibly heterosexual men. Martin, for example, was not homosexual. But Neal's question implied that his hetero-sexuality was thin, as if Martin's Oedipal phase had been a sham, a formality, a going through the motions. Underneath, he was a screaming oral infant, with megalomaniacal delusions, psychic masochism, and all the rest of it.

There was nothing like a bunch of men on a work site to bring out covert "homosexual feelings." I must admit that I spent ten years on Therafields work sites and in groups discussing what happened on those work sites, where "homosexual feelings" — always attrib-uted to heterosexual men, by the way — were often cited as the cause of whatever screw-ups occurred, and to this day I do not understand what people meant by it. The term seemed to have no connection with actual desire of any sort.

Neal doggedly attempted to graduate from his pre-Oedipal phase for twelve years. Since work and sexuality were closely linked — both requiring a flow of energy, an ability to deal with reality rather than fantasy — he became a champion joint cementer. Wherever gyproc walls were going up, you could count on Neal being there with his spatula and his bucket of joint cement. At one point, when he finally made the painfully slow transition from pre-Oedipal to Oedipal, and left homosexuality behind him, he acquired a "relationship," that is, a girlfriend. That did not last, how-ever. One night in bed, after Neal had been thrusting away for what seemed forever without much result, he jokingly told his girlfriend that he finally understood the relation between sex and work. As I write this, he has been living with another man for the better part of two decades, and he seems content with the arrangement. He would now strangle you if you presented him with a bucket of joint cement.

That evening, however, there was nothing but passionate sincerity in his rhetorical question to Martin. And I remember clearly that Martin, spotting me enter the room, turned to me. I do not remember what he said. But his look clearly stated, hey, what about you? That annoyed me. It was pure sibling rivalry. He just didn't want to be the only sham heterosexual in the room. But being pre-Oedipal, I will state for the record, is not my problem. Technically speaking, I suffer from having had a negative Oedipal. The reader interested in the full implications of this may consult the works of Dr. Bergler. I'll only say that it's much better than being pre-Oedipal, because it is an Oedipal, but it remains an affliction, which I bear as I may.

And the women in the house? Perhaps because they tended to be more stable than the men, they did not leave such vivid traces. Except for Anita, an attractive brunette with intense blue eyes and sharp features, who was an actress. I never saw her onstage, so I cannot judge her talent, but in the house group she showed true histrionic ability. Well do I recall one day in that gloomy basement living room, an impromptu group in the corner, where sat Anita, a rather handsome young man named Stuart, who had a semi-skilled job with Ontario Hydro, and a few other house group members, desperately trying to be "objective."

Anita was upset with Stuart. Again, I am not sure why. Who knows what triggered these sudden influxes of emotion, these tempestuous convictions that the hand of the emotional plague was upon us? At that moment, Anita was deeply agitated, and nothing could have stopped her from expressing it. "You sit there in your room, and I can feel it," she nearly shrieked. "I can feel you in your room, you're just sitting there and stewing, and your fucking anger's spreading all over the house." Stuart sat there silently. He did look a bit pissed off. "One of these days you're going to act out all that … that murderous feeling," Anita continued. "I feel like I'm living with a murderer."

If this was over the top, it was not obvious. Anita felt the truth of her words. There was conviction in them. She really was, as she uttered them, a young woman sleeping one night while Stuart — this is her vision — full of silent rage, grabs a carving knife from the kitchen, tiptoes into her room, and slits her throat. The other people in the group were nonplussed. Stuart had no response either. No one thought to say quietly, "Anita, Stuart is not a murderer."

Jane, an Australian, was self-possessed, by contrast. In appearance and style, she was not unlike Lois Maxwell in the role of Miss Moneypenny in the James Bond movies — lanky, with heavily framed eyeglasses, short hair, and a meticulous air. She was also great fun, born to trade witticisms with Noel Coward and other highly presentable men of dubious sexual orientation. As it happened, she became a memorable participant in our first house group marathon.

A marathon was an intense weekend of psychotherapy, usually held at the Therafields farm — known to members simply as "The Farm." Located in the rolling Caledon Hills of Ontario, an hour's drive northwest of Toronto, The Farm was an old farmhouse and barn converted into offices, dormitories, a dining room, and a huge kitchen. Off to the side was a small building consisting of one large room with a fireplace. In this room, couches and chairs lined the four walls, with armchairs reserved for the therapists (usually two).

I don't know how many times I sat in that room. Members of a house group would file in, sit in a chair or couch or a cushion on the carpeted floor, and wait for five or ten minutes for the therapists to arrive. During that wait, the room was full of tense silence.

Sometimes a person would say, before the therapists arrived, "I'd like to talk," and then another person would say, "I'd like to talk, too," and then a third person, and so on. But it wasn't a dance card. The flow of the group could be unpredictable. And if in the middle of a group you were dying to talk, to be the centre of attention, as it were, you had to have a good sense of timing, to know when a "piece of work" had finished with so-and-so, and the therapists had said the last word on the subject, and you could speak up and say, "I'd like to talk." And if it were indeed your turn, you never knew what would ensue. It could be scalding tears, or pounding a cushion on the floor to liberate raw, suppressed anger. Or it could be a confrontation of the first order, with the therapist and fellow house group members forcefully telling you of the destructive and dishonest things you were doing. That could leave you dry-eyed but badly shaken.

Aside from the groups, there was always work during a marathon. The men would do construction; the women would head for the fields of carrots and potatoes or to the kitchen. The division of labour never altered. No one felt it was "sexist." To raise the issue would have been like talking about bourgeois false consciousness at a meeting of Pentecostals — it would have been the introduction of an alien vocabulary into the seamless Therafields discourse. The language would swiftly have changed to talk of repressed feelings about one's mother or father or even of latent paranoia.

Politics aside, if you want to stir up feelings easily, having men work with men only, and women work with women only, is still a potent formula. Lea Hindley-Smith's instincts in this regard were sound. Ironically, she herself was the quintessential "strong" woman, with pronounced Queen Bee tendencies. Queen Bees do not tolerate other Queen Bees.

Occasionally, she would make an appearance at The Farm, moving in unhurried procession from room to room. Her lover Visvaldis encouraged her matriarchal role, with himself as princely consort. Sometimes the two, during an evening, would walk into a group in that little building, she with her bouffant and flowing gowns, he with a caftan and gold medallion, as if for all the world they were rulers of a fantasy kingdom. This always brought whatever therapeutic work was in progress to a screeching halt. When they had seated themselves, the work might resume, but haltingly, because everyone was poised to hear what Lea might say. Very often what she said had an oracular quality only tenuously connected to the emotional disturbance at hand. "You know, people sneer at Norman Vincent Peale, but he has something very important and useful to say," she might state. "He has helped very many people." Or she might refer something to her own experience. "I cannot believe it when people tell me they have trouble maintaining something because it's not theirs," she would remark, apropos members who were lax in keeping up their house. "I remember when I had an apartment in London, I painted my telephone silver."

In later years, in my experience, whenever the subject of Visvaldis came up among Therafields veterans, no one had a good word for him, but I confess I found him an impressive figure. He was not tall, but well built with a handsome, squarish head, robust enough to make the bangs he wore not ridiculous, and a deep voice. He seemed to know what he was talking about, without being pompous. One summer, early in my Therafields career, when my confidence was still non-existent — perhaps I should say here, lest I give the impression that everything about Therafields was ludicrous, that I felt very much better about myself when I left Therafields after a decade or so than when I first joined — I was walking with some other people down a gravel road from The Farm to another part of the property, when Visvaldis came roaring toward us in a convertible. When he reached us, he brought the car to a halt in a cloud of dust, greeted us with genuine warmth, it seemed to me, with his smile and his gold medallion, asked what we were doing, exchanged a few more pleasantries, and then roared off. I felt like a peasant who had been graced with a visit from his lord.

When I've mentioned this story to other Therafieldians, they more or less shrug, as if they couldn't conceive of such a feeling. Visvaldis, we later learned, was an alcoholic, a deeply insecure man who would become furious if he lost a tennis match, an architect who had no practice except for Therafields. But he was always gracious when I saw him, and I must say — no one would have dared even think this in the heyday of Therafields — he was a lot sexier than Lea was.

It was during an evening session of the marathon that we "worked with" Jane. I remember the dimly lit room — there may have been a floor lamp in the corner — and Jane leaning forward in her chair, with a quizzical stare, as people talked to her. As usual, it is impossible to recall with what grievances or feelings she began this session. She, like the rest of us, had moved into the house with the vague notion that she would be paid attention to. Although it was never put this way, she, like the rest of us, had a hope that she would be loved. But everyone was far too preoccupied with his or her emotional states to offer love. The premise of the house group experience was that we would find not love, but truth, a bitter medicine.

So Jane was unhappy and irritated for a dozen different reasons, and probably resentful. As the group went on, that resentment assumed darker and darker proportions. She was even admonished against committing suicide. Maureen, a young woman with long, straight red hair and a soft Irish voice that could convey immense disapproval, sat with her legs tucked under her, in a chair in the corner, and said, "People who kill themselves don't really believe they're going to die. They really believe they're going to live on in their anger."

Better suicide than murder, as Stuart might have said. Jane continued to lean forward, as if braced for the worst. And it came. The therapist, Kevin, was burly, balding, with the face of an Irish pug and a rumbly baritone that never wavered in conviction — a born homilist's voice. He meant well. But he was on the track of something, a deep, buried and dangerous emotion within Jane's psyche. With the fervour of a recent convert to depth psychology, he decided that Jane was ripe for the emergence of this emotion.

To penetrate quickly to deeper layers of the psyche, a number of techniques were usually employed in Therafields. There was "hypnotherapy," in which the therapist put the subject into a light trance by saying, "Your feet are getting heavy, your ankles … You will hear noises outside the window, but they will not bother you …" There was "psychodrama," in which two or three people would enact roles in the life of the subject — say, insulting and harassing the subject, like his or her brothers and sisters used to do. (That could be fun, if you were one of the role players.) There was "bioenergetics," borrowed from Reich — the old slam-the-mattress-with-a-tennis-racket technique to activate emotion. Later in the Therafields experience, "abreaction" became popular — as far as I can recall, it involved just lying on the floor and wailing like an infant.

This evening, none of these techniques were used. A tension had gathered in the room, around Jane, and it seemed like something might burst. "What are you feeling?" Kevin asked. Jane frowned. It was so hard to say. Her stare intensified. "I feel agitated, like I want to …" Her voice trailed off. "What do you feel like doing?" Jane shrugged. "I don't know, I feel like getting up, and just walking." "Get up and walk." Another frown from Jane. "Get up and walk?" Kevin nodded vigorously. "Get up. Walk around." She stood up hesitantly, paused, and then slowly started pacing back and forth. "That's right. Walk back and forth." Her tempo increased slightly.

"What are you feeling?" Jane continued to walk silently. If pacing would produce this searing emotion, she would pace. It was there, obviously, but tantalizingly out of reach.

"Jane, there's something you want to do," Kevin said, ominously, in his deepest baritone. Jane kept walking back and forth. "You're holding on to it, Jane. Let it come out." Sitting on a couch, wedged between a couple of other house group members, I marvelled that Kevin knew what Jane was holding on to. "I don't know," Jane said, with a plea in her voice. All of us watched, waiting for Jane's grip on this feeling to let go. What sinister thing did Jane want to do? It had something to do with eating, Kevin had suggested earlier, with an infant's visceral and enraged fantasy of devouring the other. "You're furious. There's something you want to do." Jane paused in her pacing, as if to think about what she wanted to do. "Keep walking," Kevin barked. She resumed pacing. She did not look at any of us as she did so, but fixed her gaze on a spot on the floor a few feet ahead of her. "What is it you want to do? What do you want to do to Mommy? What do you want to do to her? Don't stop to think about it. Don't stop! You can let yourself feel this; you're safe here. You can do it here. It's all right to let it come out."

I'm not sure how long this went on. It seemed like a long time. And then something happened in the room. Not an outburst of furious keening from Jane, but the opposite, a realization on everybody's part that it would never be forthcoming, no matter how much Kevin exhorted her. The realization was almost shocking. Her pacing slowed down, her determined look became woeful, and Kevin turned grim. He shook his head. "There's something in you that wants, I mean literally wants, to devour the mother, Jane. I'm talking about the whole basis of paranoia and what it can do to you and people around you, unless you let go of it."

As the group filed out of the building, Jane was alone. Her failure to locate her emotions seemed a moral failure, as if she deliberately wanted to hold on to a deeply destructive impulse. If we were Amish, we would have shunned her. If we were a Bronze Age tribe, we would have been tempted to pick up stones. An unclean one was in our midst. That feeling faded afterward, particularly when Jane's therapist disagreed with the house group therapist's diagnosis, but I think Jane lost her appetite for therapy after this episode. When the house group disbanded after a year — house groups were supposed to be temporary, and they rarely lasted more than a couple years — I never saw her again.

Years after its demise, Martin and I would discuss Therafields and never come to an agreement. (We worked out our sibling rivalry and became lifelong friends.) Martin at the age of eighteen had suffered a nervous breakdown — though "suffered" is probably not the right word, because in later years he viewed his breakdown as the best experience of his life. In the course of it, he felt uplifted; he felt powerful. He experienced what prophets and visionaries undergo. He received insights and shed inhibitions. He talked to homeless people on the street. He dreamt of becoming an architect and designing the perfect building that would bring everyone together. He took his alcoholic mother to the ballet and, transcending embarrassment, was sublimely unruffled by her obvious drunkenness.

One day, after a sleepless night, he was seized with the notion that his father should go to confession and receive the sacrament of penance. He virtually dragged the man to a nearby church. This was his undoing. Shortly afterward, Martin was hospitalized. In 1965, few options were available to people experiencing emotional turbulence, a crucial point to remember about Therafields. And the psychiatric ward certainly was not always the best of those options. It didn't take Martin long to realize he wasn't getting out of there until he did what they told him to do. He underwent electroshock treatments, though he had never felt depressed. The treatments humiliated him, devastated his memory, and removed forever the possibility of his feeling uplifted and powerful again.

A few years later, when he discovered Therafields and told this story to Lea, she said, "Ah, that was you." She already knew about him. When he was imprisoned in hospital, one of his high-school teachers had come to her in the hope that she might be able to do something. "We can't help him now, but he will come to us," she told the teacher. Martin will never forget the magic of that moment, the beauty of it. In her prime, Lea had a knack for arousing such feeling because of the burning sincerity of her pronouncements. Irony was foreign to her.

There was an ideal of sanity or freedom or truthfulness in the house groups, the gatherings at the farm, and the individual sessions with therapists. It was as if everyone was always being challenged to rise to greater heights. Unfortunately, these challenges were linked to Freudian concepts, to beliefs in such things as orgone energy (Wilhelm Reich's notion of a "creative force" from which all nature evolved), which seem dubious now, to say the least.

I can't say I have a high opinion of the kind of therapy we received in Therafields. Still, the effects of it were not entirely illusory. A couple of years after I began therapy, I ran into an old university professor, who remarked on how I appeared much more relaxed. Evidently, as an undergraduate I had a hunted look, despite the liberation of being in Toronto. In fact, it does relax a body to express emotions, air obsessions, tell the person standing next to you (calmly but firmly) to get off your toes. Therafields offered that opportunity—which was still, I repeat, something of a novelty. And although I am now an agnostic on the question of the existence of the unconscious and body memories and so on, I do recall a moment or two, during my time in Therafields, of hitting a vein of buried childhood anguish. Those feelings had never gone away, and it was good for me to relive them. At the very least, the experience inoculated me against the men's movement, so that years later, when I reached middle age, I felt no temptation to join Robert Bly and other middle-aged men beating a drum in the woods.

At Therafields, I learned how to install a toilet, hang drywall, deal with a leaky tap. This certainly boosted my self-esteem, because I had a profound uneasiness, on the scale of Woody Allen's, around handyman tasks. But the deepest appeal of Therafields was the promise of friendship. Martin to me is like an old army buddy. We went through the psychological wars together. Like young men in the army, we had experienced a world of intense emotion apart from the normal one of finding mates, building careers, having children. Throughout the decade I spent at Therafields, I can't remember one word being uttered about investing for retirement. The concept would have seemed odd. The twenty-first century was a long, long way away, and when it came it would be different anyway. Maybe the whole of Canada would be a gigantic farm modelled on our Caledon venture and devoted to work therapy and bioenergetics. In the meantime, comradeship was possible. I felt a degree of it then (that I have never experienced since) with a couple of men, including Martin, who had a sense of humour attuned to my own.

Back then, we would have denied we were part of a cult. We had nothing but contempt for Scientologists and believers in est and T-group junkies. We were serious; they were fools. In hindsight, however, it is obvious that something cultlike was happening in those Annex houses. Until the end, Lea's word was not to be disputed. Few popes were ever as revered by pious Catholics as she was revered by these former priests and nuns. (If some in the group were less than worshipful, they were discreet about their misgivings.) This devotion had its inevitable effect. When you're constantly told you can do no wrong, you tend to believe it.

A number of things did go wrong. The most serious involved Lea's elder son, Malcolm, a highly intelligent man, gifted in math and music, who lived in Therafields houses but had never had any overt role in the organization. What he did for a living was a mystery. Crusty, bordering on the surly, he stayed clear of Therafields activities. Then, in the late seventies, he was visited with an inspiration, which received his mother's enthusiastic imprimatur. He started an alternative school for the children of Therafields members, called Ka School, after an Egyptian word meaning "life force," with himself as virtually the only faculty. Nearly all Therafields parents sent their children to this school, later renamed Heliopolis.

Soon the school became a cult within a cult. An inner circle of older students — most of them in their early teens — with strong attachments to Malcolm began to fire off manifestos with a decidedly anti-parent tone. Ka School, in their eyes, was a beacon of light that threatened the uncomprehending outside world, including Therafields — though the school would never have been founded, and could not continue, without the support of the organization it condemned. Their mentor decreed that some parents were bad influences on their children. In 1985, by which time the school was defunct, Malcolm was arrested for sexually abusing two former students. Despite his defence — that he had tried to protect his students from the mind-control cult of Therafields — he was convicted of two counts of sexual misconduct and sentenced to three years in prison.

By this time, Therafields itself was a memory. For all its property, it had so little equity that when the credit crunch came in the early eighties, most of the real estate had to be sold off at a substantial loss.

Meanwhile, Lea's health had worsened, and her mental powers began to fail. Her force of personality — her great good sense about people — which had inspired and encouraged and uplifted so many, could not save her. There was a tragic irony in the way she foresaw her fate when she told associates that it was almost impossible to work with manic-depressives, who didn't think they needed help in their manic phase and didn't think anybody could help them in their depressive phase.

Something very like manic depression took hold of her in her later years, a condition aggravated by diabetes and her attempts to treat the disease holistically. She and the therapists in general were enthusiasts of alternative medicine, and the regimens undergone by people in Therafields were numerous and varied: there were distilled water fasts, carrot juice fasts, diets requiring a person to eat five different vegetables at each meal, macrobiotic diets, the works. Unfortunately, some of these were contrary to the diets prescribed diabetics, and her health continued to deteriorate. She died in 1987 at the age of seventy-one.

Therafields Environmental Centre disbanded, and Rob Hindley-Smith and bp Nichol, for the most part, went their separate ways. Bp died while undergoing back surgery in 1988. Rob busied himself with an Amway dealership, spreading the fad among many people who were still attached, one way or another, to Therafields, but that faded, too. He and his family moved to King City in the mid-eighties. He seems to have no connection whatsoever with the people he once presided over as the official head of Therafields. Visvaldis Upenieks, after suffering months of severe depression, committed suicide by jumping from an apartment window.

My first therapist, Andre, continues to work as an accountant. His partner, Larissa, died of cancer in the mid-eighties. The former priest who first interviewed me separated from his wife a few years after our interview. He left Therafields in the early seventies to teach at a Catholic high school. His former wife has been married for many years to Kevin, my first house group therapist. Kevin taught at York University throughout his career at Therafields and continued after he left. He and his wife are now retired in a town outside Toronto.

My friend Martin wound up a teacher with the separate school board and is now retired. Neal, after a decade of working in different capacities for Therafields — as a receptionist and a therapist — also became a teacher, but in the public school system. My first wife, who sought counsel at Therafields at the same time as me, eventually remarried and now lives in Toronto with her husband and two sons.

I also remarried a couple of years after I left Therafields. I have returned to the Catholic church and have not seen a therapist in more than twenty years, though I don't dismiss psychotherapy. As with religious faith, I believe in its potential for both good and evil.

Our memories of Therafields may be murky at times, but for those of us who shared a year of our lives in the red brick house on Walmer, some moments remain razor sharp. Like the night a cop showed up at the door on a routine errand. As he gazed inside, his curiosity was piqued. He asked how many people lived here and whether we all lived in common. When told we did, he mentioned a television documentary he had just seen on communes. According to this documentary, he said, communal living was the way of the future. Everybody would be living like this. Far from being appalled, he seemed taken with the prospect.

In a way, we were the future. Thirty-odd years later, we find ourselves living in a culture saturated by therapy. The language of repressed feelings and family dramas and emotional honesty has become part of our vernacular. But the revolutionary, communal aspects of Therafields did not survive the 1970s. The days of dreaming of a new community, a society run not unlike The Farm, came to an end. Members went on to buy houses, marry, have children, and, in the ultimate backlash against the 1960s, save for their retirement.

TED BISHOP

The Motorcycle and the Archive

I HAD JUST BOUGHT THE NEW DUCATI, "IL MOSTRO" —
the Monster — but it was nothing monstrous. A lithe sport bike,
the arc from its front forks up through the trellis frame and down
to the rear swingarm. It has the line of a panther in mid-leap. Always
in motion, even parked at the curb. Ducati makes the most stylish
and best-handling bikes in the world, and I'd bought this bike to
ride, not just to pose in front of the local cafés (OK, not *only*), or to
blast down a winding road for an hour on a Sunday morning and
then put it back in the garage.

Then the grant money came. Expenses and travel money to go
to the Harry Ransom Center in Austin, Texas, the improbable location of the best archive of modernist writers in the world. I was
heading to Austin to track the first readers of *Ulysses,* not the
reviewers for the big newspapers and the literary quarterlies, but the
buyers whose responses never made it into print. The grant agreement did not contain the usual threatening clauses about how
"receipts, boarding passes, and original air tickets must be submitted
before reimbursement can be approved." It said, "Your cheque will
be waiting for you."

Most noble scholars. I decided to ride.

My friends looked at the short wheelbase and hard, sloping seat of the Monster, and said, "You're riding to Texas on *that?*" Why not? I'd take it one short stretch at a time, the way I read one file at a time in the archives. If you thought about the whole project, you'd never start. I bundled up my research notes and bubble wrapped my laptop, and shipped them by UPS. I'd be travelling light. I looked forward to escaping my academic persona, trading tweed for leather, transforming myself into a lone rider heading down the highway. I didn't want my literary work to taint that image. The biker slogan is "Ride to Live. Live to Ride." "Ride to Read! Read to Ride!" wouldn't sell a lot of black T-shirts.

And yet the riding and the reading, the bike journey and the print journey, strangely meshed with one another. The motorcycle and the archive both proved to be vehicles of discovery and visceral thrill.

Rhythm

It was good to be on the road. In the first few days, I began discovering my rhythm for the ride: in the first half-hour or so, I tend to drive around the speed limit. Then when the bike is warmed up and I'm through fiddling with gear, I start to blast — a steady 140 with occasional bursts up to 160 to clear the carbs and get the adrenaline going. I usually have the road to myself and rocket along, focused on the road, ignoring the scenery.

I eat a monster truck-stop breakfast around eleven (bacon and eggs and toast and hash browns, with a few sips of appalling coffee to cut the grease), and from then until mid-afternoon, I get progressively slower and more dozy. I just cruise. I obey the speed limits, I look at the view, I stop at Sites of Historic Interest, and if I can find a secluded picnic site and it's warm enough, I take a seventeen-minute power snooze to chase the drowse away. In the late afternoon, I pick up the pace again. That's often my best riding. After being on the bike all day, I have that good tiredness that makes you relaxed and more efficient, yet not sloppy. I find a motel before dinnertime, and I tighten the chain every evening after checking in, taking care of the bike before taking a shower, like the old cowboys — you make sure your horse is looked to before you go feed yourself.

When I tighten the chain, I feel like a real mechanic. I mean, I'm using *two* wrenches. Clearly, *Ted and the Art of Motorcycle Maintenance* would be a short book. I don't tune the carburetors. For a Ducati, you need a two-year training course and proficiency in Italian even to find the carburetors. And to set the valves, you need special tools and special shims that come handcrafted from Bologna and cost twice as much as those for any other motorcycle. (Shims are the bits of metal that go under the valve stems to change how far they open and close; I've never seen one, but I'm assured they exist and when they appear on my work order, they are extravagantly expensive.) I'm told that for old BMWs, you can, in a pinch, make them out of beer cans.

My biker friends wonder why I, the least Mr. Fix-It of mortals, would buy such a complex bike. They miss the logic of it: even if the bike were simple to work on, I would still have to take it to a mechanic. With the Ducati, no one can be expected to work on it, and you can complain about those perverse Italians who make it impossible to do your own maintenance, suggesting, without saying so, that you'd otherwise be stripping and rebuilding the engine every morning before breakfast for the fun of it.

Woolf Library

My first stop was Washington State University, on the Idaho–Washington border. I wanted to look at the Leonard and Virginia Woolf library, which had somehow wound up not in New

York, not in London, but in the little college town of Pullman, Washington. When WSU (the students call themselves Wazoos) acquired the Leonard and Virginia Woolf library, it was housed intact. But special collections libraries are on the border between a library and an archive, and archivists and librarians order things differently. When a new curator — a librarian — took over, he dispersed the collection, shelving all the books by their call number, refusing to see that the Woolf library constituted a text in itself.

"Archive" derives from *arkheion:* a house, a domicile, an address, the residence of the superior magistrates; that is, the *archons,* those who command. The documents or laws were filed in their house, and they have the power to interpret the documents. It is in this "domiciliation," this "house arrest," that archives take place. The concept of the archive as the repository of law, watched over by those invested with the power of the law, is disavowed but inescapable. When I worked in the New York Public Library, in the Berg collection under the infamous curator Lola Szladitz, a junior librarian staffing the desk at lunchtime asked me on my way out, "Have you felt the lash yet?" I had not, but I was there because a friend had been ejected from the archive when Lola discovered he was a mere graduate student.

"She shouted at me, 'I won't have *my* material used for *cheap theses!*' And that was that. I left the next day. You might as well do the edition," he said. "She'll never let me back in."

I had always suspected that the most fulsome thanks in a book's acknowledgements were directed to the most difficult archivists. In any case, what I wanted in Pullman no longer existed.

"Just tell us which books you want," they said.

"I want all of them," I said, and left.

Off the Map

For my money, the best motorcycle road in the universe is Highway 31 from Fairview to Huntington, southwest of Price, Utah. It's so small it doesn't appear on my western states map. This is what you want — no truckers, no tourists in their Winnahoggos. It was three in the afternoon, and I was grumpy, stabbing at stale pie delivered by a surly waitress who took so long she must have been putting apples and raisins in one by one. I'd never make Moab tonight. I slurped some of my lukewarm coffee with nondairy-petrochemi-cal-byproduct-whitener. I paid the bill and walked out.

Five minutes later, none of it mattered. My memory of the country is a blur — bright creek, slender pines. I grabbed it in laser-glimpses between corners. I tried to ride fast and stay off the brake, fast and smooth, keeping the bike in third gear, exploring the Duc's linear power. It pulls hard all the way from 50 to 140, and when you back off, it's like throwing out an anchor. So this is why people love big twin-cylinder bikes, I thought. I found myself going faster, a little faster, a little faster ... Then I blew by a slow camper, snapped down my visor, and dived into a bend at 125 — and found every-thingoingintoslowmo. Instead of feeling fast, I felt like I could get up, do a tap dance on the tank, smoke a Havana cigar, get back down, and finish the corner with time for a snack. Glorious.

Then I saw the roof lights on the jeep in front — a County Sheriff. Damn. I throttled back and shut down. But I waited, found the groove again, and stayed with it until the winding gorge dumped me, like a swimmer off a water slide, into the flat grey desert of Castle Valley. The best rides take you off the map.

The Archival Jolt

Archives also have surprising curves and can produce moments as intense as any highway. Sometimes it feels more like a crash than a ride. Fifteen years ago, I had been working in the British Library's Manuscript Room, looking for material related to Virginia Woolf's first experimental novel, *Jacob's Room*. The hoary clerks, with tufts of hair coming out of their ears and noses, had with bad grace been bringing me what I needed. The windows were open, and we could hear traffic noise from across the parking lot: an unobtrusive drone that glided in on the warm June air and drew you gently toward sleep. You weren't even aware at what point you stopped reading, when critical reflection turned to daydreaming, when your eyes slipped out of focus and let the print blur, and your measured breathing took on that hoarse quality just shy of a snore.

My eyes fell shut. They just dropped down like the metal shutters on a Paris shop at the end of the day. Bam. I forced them open. I felt like I was doing bicep curls with my eyelids. I got them up, licked my middle finger, and swabbed saliva on my eyelids, the old cross-country driver's trick. It gives you about ten seconds, better than nothing, and helps break the rhythm of heaviness. I slumped forward, elbows on the table, thumb and forefinger on either side of my face, my thumbs at my cheekbones pushing down, my forefingers at the edge of my eyebrows pushing up, stretching the skin, using the pain to keep my eyes open. "Is this really reading?" I wondered.

I opened up the next manila envelope and slid out a single sheet. It was handwritten and my eyes winced after the sojourn in typescript. Still, it was only a single page and it was well spaced. I'd be out of here soon. I found myself reading a letter I'd read in print dozens of times before. Anybody who works on Woolf practically knows it by heart; it's reprinted so often. It begins "Dearest, I want to tell you that you have give me complete happiness. No one could have done more than you have done. Please believe that. But I know that I shall never get over this: and I am wasting your life. It is this madness …"

I felt a physical shock. I was holding Virginia Woolf's suicide note. I lost any bodily sense, or rather I felt like I was spinning into a vortex, a connection that collapsed the intervening decades. This note wasn't a record of an event — this was the event itself. This writing. And it was not for me. I'd walked in on something unbearably personal. It probably took less than thirty seconds to read the letter, and in that interval I'd been blasted back to March 1941 and staggered up to the present, time roaring in my ears, and no one had noticed. The other readers in the room were still nodding away.

I placed it on the reading stand, wiped my fingers, which turned out to be cold and dry, and turned the sheet over. There Leonard had written in green ink the date: 11/5/41. This detail set off an unexpected aftershock. I realized I seldom thought of him, of how he'd had to wait twenty-one days before the body was found. Three long weeks, answering questions from the *Times,* taking calls from friends. Then a group of teenagers, throwing rocks at a log in the river, found it was not a log at all and dragged what was once Virginia Woolf ashore.

The coroner misquoted the suicide note, and so did the newspapers. Leonard had to issue corrections, and at the cremation, which he went to alone, they played the wrong music. He went home that night and played the "Cavatina" from Beethoven's String Quartet Op. 130 to himself on the gramophone. A few days later, he carefully dated the note I had in front of me. I remembered none of the scholarly discussion about the dating. I only saw the pain, and the attempt to order, by dating and noting the circumstances of the letter.

I decided to call it a day. I put the letter back in the manila envelope, wound the string around the roundel at the top, and took everything back to the desk. I retrieved my bookbag and umbrella from the coat-check kiosk and walked out into the brilliant sunshine. I was far too sophisticated for biographical readings of Woolf, so the note was of no use to me. What I didn't know was that I'd just become an archive junkie.

Later, I read the work of anthropologist Paul Stoller, who, in *The Taste of Ethnographic Things* and later in *Sensuous Scholarship*, argues that we must include the tactile, the auditory, the gustatory, and not just the visual, in our scholarship. He quotes Walter Benjamin on "corporeal knowing," a useful concept; I now see that the suicide note added nothing to my "textual knowledge," but it added enormously to my "corporeal knowledge," a knowledge difficult to quantify or describe, but not for that reason to be dismissed or ignored. It did make me aware of Leonard's place in all of this. I had become the recipient of the note. Part of the reason we work in archives is, I'm convinced, for the archival jolt. But that jolt is the portal to important knowledges.

Woolf on Wheels

The first motorcycle was invented in 1885, when James Joyce and Virginia Woolf were both three years old. In the 1920s, when their work came of age, the motorcycle too discovered a form that would define it for the century. Often emerging from the factories that had produced armaments, motorcycles became part of the motoring mainstream.

In 1927, with the profits from *To the Lighthouse,* the Woolfs acquired a car. Virginia's lover, Vita Sackville-West, recorded Virginia's driving attempts in Richmond Park:

Leonard [Woolf] and I watched her start. The motor made little pounces and stopped dead. At one moment it ran backwards. At last she sailed off, and Leonard and I and Pinker went for a walk at five miles an hour. Every five minutes Leonard would say, "I suppose Virginia will be all right ..."

Virginia herself wrote to her friend Ethel Sands, "I have driven from the Embankment to Marble Arch and only knocked one boy very gently off his bicycle."

She never did manage to learn to drive a car, but she apparently considered becoming a biker. After meeting Virginia, Frances Marshall wrote "I was bowled over by her irresistible cracked charm ... She is going to be the newest motor-bicycle addict, for she says Leonard won't let her drive the car and a motor bike is just what she wants."

Travelling over the high passes in Colorado, I tried to picture Woolf thundering across the Sussex downs or roaring up Oxford Street on a motorcycle. *Mrs. Dalloway* would certainly be different if the character had gone to get flowers on her Royal Enfield. I couldn't imagine it. I doubted Woolf would have lived as long as she did had she taken up motorcycling, and we never would have had those last great novels.

Buzzards and Dillos

Motorcycling always involves risk. I skidded and swerved up ten miles of gravel road to visit D. H. Lawrence's ranch high above Taos, New Mexico, and then zoomed through west Texas on the straight, empty back roads, singing in my helmet, "Life is a Hiiiiighway, And I want to riiiiide it. All. Night. Long. Boom chuka boom-chukchchch." Luckily, I never hit anything. The biggest dangers in west Texas are the buzzards — they flap slowwwwwly off the road-kill like a fully loaded 747.

"If you hit 'em in your truck, they can take out a windshield," a Texan told me. Hit one on a motorcycle at a hundred, and it would probably take your head off.

The other things to watch out for are the armadillos —

"When they're scared they don't run. They jump straight up, and their shell is so hard it'd flip a bike jest like that."

And the tarantulas —

"Wahl, they won't hurt you, but in migratin' season they stretch for miles. In a truck ya jest go over 'em, and you can hear the crunchcrunchcrunch as ya squish 'em. Trouble is, the road gets real slimy. On a bike you'd slide out for sure."

I only ever saw one tarantula on the road and avoided it easily.

"Then thar's the killer bees …"

Right. So much for folk wisdom. My source was Jim Haule, a Woolf scholar who lived down on the Rio Grande, but who hailed from Detroit and liked to josh the newcomers to the lone star state.

Non-riders did ask me, "Don't you think motorcycling's dangerous?" in the tone of a foregone conclusion. It could be, I agreed, but I was a conservative rider, and I knew I would be one of those people who rides for thirty years and never drops a bike. Besides, I said, motorcycling is only one of a million ways you can die. You can just as easily go in your La-Z-Boy recliner. In the spring, or when I haven't been riding in a long time, I have a moment of fear thinking about what I'm going to do, but as soon as I'm up and riding, I'm fine. I give the answer my father gave when people asked him, "Isn't mountain climbing dangerous?" "Sure," he said, "but at least you go doing something you like."

When I ride I always carry a book, and I choose the book in part by what will fit in a jacket pocket. You don't want anything too thick. For airline reading, I want something with action, like Martin Cruz Smith, but on a motorcycle I seem to need something quieter, like Carol Shields. Sometimes while travelling you begin to feel you're some kind of gigantic open nerve on the verge of overload, and that if you see/smell/touch/taste/hear one more thing, you'll explode and splatter your sensory data all over the wall. The right book creates a space and orders things for you. When you look up from it, you are ready again to take in your own impressions, whether it's of pink sandstone arches soaring up from the desert floor, or a clubhouse sandwich with too much mayo and a side of limp fries. I'd bought *The Stone Diaries* before I left and though it was a bit lumpy for the jacket, it carried me well into Nevada. I also read about a Canadian journalist named Pinky Fulham who was killed when a soft-drink vending machine fell on him, crushing him to death. (He was rocking it back and forth, trying to dislodge a stuck quarter.) Apparently eleven North Americans a year are killed by overturned vending machines. The next time I approached a vending machine, I did so warily. And, I thought, *this* is what I should have told them when they asked, "Isn't motorcycling dangerous?"

Seshat, Goddess of the Archive

If I wanted to push the motorcycle metaphor, I'd say it's about putting the body at risk — you have to be open to corporeal knowing. It can be a sensual experience and it can be a risk. Reading Tom Wharton's fantastical novel *Salamander* about the infinite book, I came across a reference to the goddess of the archives, Seshat. Wharton, like any good postmodernist, riddles his book with bogus references. Had he made up Seshat? Surely, I would have heard of her. I'd found myself muttering about the "gods of the archives," wanting to burn incense at a shrine when the work went well, wondering if I should burn a fatted calf in the parking lot when the archives had turned sullen and intransigent. Nothing seemed straightforward in the archives. We all spoke of solid research methods, and good detective work, but the real discoveries seemed to come from nowhere, to be handed to you, after days or weeks in which (it appeared in retrospect) the discovery had been perversely denied. If there was a goddess, I wanted her.

A quick look at the Net confirmed she was real: an Egyptian goddess of writing, libraries, archives, mathematics, and architecture. In recent times, Seshat has been taken on as the Silicon Goddess, protector of computers and software. Some view the Internet itself as a manifestation of the goddess. This was getting a bit spacey. I turned from the Net to the codex. I prefer print I can hold, and where I used to search for the latest article, now I burrow for an early book. I like to see how the ideas and their encrustations emerge. I found *The Gods of the Egyptians* (1904) by the former keeper of the Egyptian and Assyrian antiquities at the British Museum, one Wallis Budge. I learned that Seshat (Sesheta, Sefkhet-aabut, and half a dozen other spellings) was the goddess of writing. Married to Thoth, she taught him how to write and he got all the credit: lord of books, scribe of the gods, he had his own followers and his own temples, while Seshat had none.

She is pictured with what looks like a sprinkler coming out of her head, a seven- or nine-pointed star that no one has satisfactorily explained. Modern devotees on the Net have argued that this star is a cannabis leaf, but it only looks like one if you've already been smoking it. Seshat is the only female deity shown writing (though others are pictured holding a pen), and she's beautiful. Even Budge refers to the "close-fitting panther skin" she usually wears. I thought of a sultry archivist at Princeton and briefly imagined her in a panther skin. Then I thought of the formidable Lola at the New York Public Library in a panther skin, and the vision dissolved. Seshat appears to be related to Selquet, also called the "mistress of the house of books": a golden, arch-eyed goddess, with a downturned mouth, very sexy, she has a scorpion on her head. That sounded more like some of the archivists I'd known — scorpions presiding over the entrails of the embalmed. Selquet/Seshat is an apt emblem of the seduction and the danger of the archive. People have disappeared into the archive, and they have for all practical purposes never come out. Slaves to the goddess.

At my university, a colleague across the hall heard of my interest in archives.

"I love them too," she said, "but I can't go into them anymore. I did some work for a theatre historian, sifting through boxes of old programs and the like. I went for six days straight, nine to five — they always close early. I hate that. You have to wrap up by 4:45 — and I started to get hives."

"You mean like measles?"

"No, big welts, the size of a toonie and raised about a millimetre. They itched so badly I wanted to dig my fingernails into them and rake them off. The rash started first around my neck, I even had two on my cheeks, and then they popped up along the inside of my forearms."

"Sounds awful."

"And then they moved down between my breasts …"

"Yes."

"By the third day they covered my thighs …"

"Oh."

"Anywhere that was soft …"

"Horrible."

"I don't know what I'm allergic to. Maybe some kind of paper dust. It *is* horrible because I love the archives, love working with old material. I just can't do it anymore."

I told her I had had a professor who developed an allergy to the ink in duplicating machines — that old purple ink in Gestetners that smelled like the purple gum that tasted like soap. She became unable to use the photocopy machine, then she couldn't touch print of any kind and had to read with a pane of glass over her book. The last I heard she had moved to the States, and she had to live in an old house built before certain additives were included in paint. From print, she had gradually become allergic to all the world.

The inhalations of the archive are not always so dire. In *The Social Life of Information,* John Seely Brown and Paul Duguid write of working beside a library patron who sniffed the bundles of dusty letters as he took them out of the box. The man was, it turned out, a medical historian documenting outbreaks of cholera. In the eighteenth century, vinegar was used to disinfect letters to prevent the cholera from spreading:

> By sniffing for the faint traces of vinegar that survived 250 years and noting the date and source of the letters, he was able to chart the progress of cholera outbreaks.
>
> His research threw new light on the letters I was reading. Now cheery letters telling customers and creditors that all was well, business thriving, and the future rosy read a little differently if a whiff of vinegar came off the page. Then the correspondent's cheeriness might be an act to prevent a collapse of business confidence — unaware that he or she would be betrayed by a scent of vinegar.

I liked this: an olfactory subtext, a level of textual meaning generated by scent of the document. I did not realize I would soon be chasing non-textural meaning myself, not only crumbs of information but crumbs as information.

Silence of the Bike, Silence of the Book

When I hit Austin, it was 90 degrees with 90 per cent humidity. My head felt like a steamed dumpling inside my helmet. The next morning I was working through the catalogue in the 68-degree chill of the Ransom Center's reading room. (You can tell the newcomers — they sit hunched and shivering over their research and come back at noon with a Texas Longhorns sweatshirt from the bookstore.) W. B. Yeats, James Joyce, D. H. Lawrence — all the big names were there, and, equally interesting, the papers of lesser-known writers, literary agents, and publishers. At most archives, you look at one set of documents related to your project and then move on to another library. At the Ransom Center, an obscure reference in one file could lead you to a whole other archive, and then another and another, all contained in the five-floor, windowless building. It looked forbidding from the outside — a giant, white marble cube. British archivists hated the Ransom Center. Against Ransom's oil-cash reserves in the 1960s, resistance had been futile and Ransom had assimilated all the best literary manuscripts. Bad enough that the British literary heritage flowed to America, but this institution wasn't even Harvard or Yale. Texas was off anybody's cultural map. That was forty years ago. Now, for modernism, Austin was at the centre.

When I got to the archives, I expected to have trouble adjusting. Whitman knew it — his *Song of the Open Road* opens by abjuring libraries:

Henceforth I whimper no more, postpone no more, need nothing,
Done with indoor complaints, libraries, querulous criticisms,
Strong and content I travel the open road.

Now I was giving up the open road for libraries with their attendant "indoor complaints" and "querulous criticisms." How would I cope? Making miles had been my job, eight hours a day for two weeks. But Whitman is a liar. All travel writers, from Hakulyt to Kerouac, exalt their time on the road, minimize and denigrate their time in the library. The two worlds might seem opposites — the silence and stillness of the archive after the roar of the Ducati on mountain passes and desert highways — but the more I worked, the more I thought that archival work was the inverse, not the opposite, of motorcycling. For one thing, silence surrounds them both.

Motorcycling is not noisy. If you're riding a Harley with straight pipes and you crack the throttle at a stoplight in a skyscraper canyon of the city, or open it up going through a tunnel, you'll feel the roar. That's not what I'm talking about. When I first put on a full-face helmet, I have a moment of claustrophobia. I can only hear my own breathing and I feel like one of those old-time deep-sea divers. (The boots, jacket, and gloves feel cumbersome too — they're shaped all wrong for walking, but once you are on the bike, the gloves curl round the handgrips; the arms of the jacket flare out and forward, the wristbands are at your wrist instead of your fingertips; and the boots are snug onto the footpegs, reinforced toe under the gear lever.) When you hit the starter, your breath merges with the sound of the bike, and once you're on the highway, the sound moves behind you, becoming a dull roar that merges with the wind noise, finally disappearing from consciousness altogether.

Even if you ride without a helmet, you ride in a cocoon of white noise. You get smells from the roadside, and you feel the coolness in the dips and the heat off a rock face, but you don't get sound. On a bike, you feel both exposed and insulated. Try putting in earplugs: the world changes, you feel like a spacewalker. What I like best about motorcycle touring is that even if you have companions you can't talk to them until the rest stop, when you'll compare highlights of the ride. You may be right beside them, but you're alone. It is an inward experience. Like reading. In the archive might be ten other readers, each at a solitary table, yet if you intersect at all it is only at lunch breaks. You may spend two weeks or more together, in silence.

The classical pianist Alfred Brendel once told a *New Yorker* interviewer, "I like the fact that 'listen' is an anagram of 'silent.' Silence is not something that is there before the music begins and after it stops. It is the essence of the music itself, the vital ingredient that makes it possible for the music to exist at all. It's wonderful when the audience is part of this productive silence." He was speaking of classical piano concerts, but he could have been talking of the highway. Some of the best moments on a bike come when you are not moving; roadside moments. You stop, kill the engine, take off your helmet, and all is still.

On my last day I got on the road at dawn and drove for about a mile before pulling off on the shoulder. I ate my doughnut and drank some juice, and after about ten minutes, I heard a semi. I heard it coming from probably five miles away, a low rumble, building gradually to a windy roar as it passed me, and then subsiding to a distant rumble once more, leaving me the desert silence. My boots scrunched on the sandy pavement, and my leather jacket creaked as I lifted the juice bottle to get the last mouthful. The desert was fully lit now, though the sun wasn't yet over the ridge beside me. Like reading, where you lift your eyes from the page and then move back, riding is defined and punctuated by silences. What we strive for is a productive silence, a collaboration with the text in which the silence is, as Brendel says, not an absence but the "vital element." I capped and stowed the bottle, and got back on the bike. I had an empty road. This was going to be great.

The excitement at setting out is what I've come to think of as the *andiamo* phenomenon. *Andiamo* is Italian for "let's go." D. H. Lawrence calls it the most beautiful word in the Italian language. Certainly, the English "let's go" feels flat-footed in comparison, pedestrian in the worst sense. The Italian is like a whip about to crack; the throb on the third syllable marks the wave that pulses through the word. Both command and response, with a built-in exclamation mark, *andiamo* conveys the exotic, carries the excitement of taking off. It's the word you breathe inside your helmet when you finally clear traffic and the road opens in front of you. It's the feeling you get when you finally clear time and space and settle in with a new book. Heading into the silence. Not the so-called plenitude of silence, but the possibility of silence.

Grease

I felt that excitement when I called up Sylvia Beach's subscriber notebook. Sylvia Beach, the reverend's daughter from Princeton who had fallen in love with Paris and Adrienne Monnier, who ran a bookstore, had opened her own English bookstore, Shakespeare & Co, in the Latin Quarter in 1919 and had published Joyce's *Ulysses* in 1922. She followed the same three-tiered format Monnier used for works published at her bookstore, and the thousand copies of the first-edition *Ulysses* were all numbered and all on handmade paper, with the first hundred on special *vergé d'Arches* paper and signed by the author, the next 150 on good but less fine paper and unsigned, and the remaining 750 on standard handmade paper. The cost at the time for an "ordinary" *Ulysses* was not extreme, about fifty American dollars in today's currency. Now an ordinary, unsigned first edition would set you back $60,000. I had twenty of them spread out in front of me. I wanted to match the books to the subscribers and to compare the books to see if there were any clues to the responses of the reader.

I admit I was intrigued by the celebrity books. I passed over the Gloria Swanson copy, bound in soft fecal-brown leather and obviously never opened, to the copies of T. E. Lawrence. He had bought two of the expensive copies, one of which (#52) he retained in its original paper covers, unread, untouched, in pristine condition. The other (#36) he had bound in full burgundy leather by one of his favourite binders, C. & C. McLeish, with the pages trimmed and the front and back covers bound in at the end. This was a reading copy, and it was heavily read: more than one hundred and fifty pages had marginal notes, and it was read casually: many of the pages had greasy smudges on them. These marks suggested a complete lack of reverence for the physical book. Molly Bloom's famous closing monologue was the only episode without marginal notes, but it has obviously been around the block. I also discovered a shard of biscuit in the second-last episode, just as Stephen Dedalus takes leave of Leopold Bloom, as if the reader were participating in the communion.

When I showed the greasy pages to the curator in the reading room, I said, "It looks like he was eating a muffin and got butter on the pages."

"Not butter," she said without missing a beat, "motorcycle oil."

Of course, I thought, why didn't I think of that? Lawrence is famous for the fact that he was killed on a motorcycle, the very fast Brough Superior, known as the Rolls Royce of motorcycles. He had a series of seven "Bruffs" (as aficionados refer to them), one of which was bought for him by George Bernard Shaw's wife, Charlotte. It seemed obvious Lawrence was as devoted to *Ulysses* as he was to his bike, making careful, factual notes in the margin and reading it between bouts of working on his motorcycle.

However, such was not the case. When I looked at some of Lawrence's correspondence, I discovered that the handwriting was completely different from the marginalia. It turned out they were written by his friend W. M. M. Hurley, and they were mainly factual notes to do with Dublin — nothing to do with classical allusions, literary technique, or exegesis — and they may have been *for* Lawrence, who had trouble getting through the book. Though Lawrence had written to Sidney Cockerell in December 1925 that "to bring [his own *Seven Pillars of Wisdom*] out after *Ulysses* is an insult to modern letters," in May he is moaning to Eric Kennington, "Arnold Bennett ... said the perfect word about *Ulysses,* when he swore that Joyce had made novel-reading a form of penal servitude." Another month later, he is no more enthusiastic: "It is even worse to read than I had hoped. Months: and such dull stuff. Joyce is a genius, but an unlucky one. His writing has the architectural merit of Balham. It goes on forever, and needn't ever vary in spirit."

So who did read the book?

While stationed in the Drigh Road Royal Air Force base at Karachi, where all the RAF aircraft engines in India were sent for overhaul, Lawrence worked in the office of the engine repair section. There he lent books to the "book-hungry men (hungry for more than the fiction library can give them)," he wrote to Charlotte Shaw. "We are rough, and dirty handed, so that some of the volumes are nearly read to death. You can tell the pet ones, by their shabbiness." Even without other volumes from Lawrence's Karachi library to compare with, I found his *Ulysses* certainly qualified as "shabby," and its condition suggested multiple readers, readers who read the entire book. A few months later he returns to this theme:

> Everybody reads rubbish when he is tired, and isolated in camp; it would be an insult to give a good book only the dregs of our attention. So magazines and shockers are read: but my little library of queer books is almost as much used as the thousand-volume fiction library which the H.Q. maintains. It's because I tell 'em about books, and make them see them, as they reflect us.

I wondered what these airmen, on a dreary base seven miles outside Karachi, some of them obviously reading at mealtime during work, thought of Joyce. The crumbs and stains leave us only the trail of these anonymous readers, a trail leading off the map. If they'd been book collectors, they would have stolen it, and if they'd been pornographers, the smudges would have been grouped around two famous passages. Yet though we cannot track them, they *were there,* for their presence alone unsettles any easy assumptions we might make about the audience of *Ulysses.*

As for Lawrence, why did he buy the book? Why two copies?

Since 1919 he had been working on his own epic, *The Seven Pillars of Wisdom.* He would begin printing a draft in January 1922 and produce fine press copies in 1926. He had always dreamt of printing on a hand press in a great medieval hall, and he had a collection of hand-press books, from Kelmscott to Ashendene, which he spread out in his room at Oxford to compare typefaces when deciding on the type for his own book. *Seven Pillars of Wisdom* was far too large to hand set, so he opted for monotype.

Nevertheless, he not only deplored "rivers" (the vertical white spaces that run down ill-set pages), but he hated long spaces at the end of paragraphs (which cracked the page across) and large blanks at the end of chapters, so he rewrote to force his paragraphs to end in the second half of the line and to make his chapters close near the bottom right-hand corner of the page. Like Joyce, he wrote and rewrote on the proofs, sometimes fourteen times, but he did so to enhance the *mise en page* rather than to enhance the text. Given all of this, Lawrence likely ordered the fine edition of *Ulysses* not as a speculator, nor even primarily as a rare book collector (and probably not as a pornographer — since he does not appear to have read it until five years after buying it), but as a print aficionado obsessively concerned with the production values of his forthcoming book. It was something I would expect from a man who owned a Brough.

Brembo and Bembo

The boundary between archiving and motorcycling seemed increasingly porous to me. In the reading room, at first, I doodled and dreamt — that too is part of motorcycling. The guy you see working so sedulously on a report, raising his eyes to consider some fine point of structure? He's not even there. He's on his bike, crossing a high desert. That woman in accounting who's poring over her figures, twisting slightly in her swivel chair? She's gone. She's on a tight little sport bike carving through some canyon. But it was more than that. I found myself musing on Brembo and Bembo, the one an elegant Italian brake, the other an elegant Italian typeface.

Will Goodwin, the bibliographer for the *James Joyce Quarterly*, turned out to be a biker (he named his old BMW "Isobar," after ignoring a weather forecast and getting caught in a Colorado blizzard) and a printer who favoured the classic typefaces.

"That's a beautiful typeface," he said. We were looking at the immaculate cover of T. E. Lawrence's #52 *Ulysses*. "Is it Bembo?"

"Hey, that's the name of the brakes on my Ducati," I said. "But I don't know about the typeface."

"No," said Will, as if this were a common mistake, "That's Brembo."

"Oh."

That prompted me to do some research. Brembo, supplier of fine brakes to Ducati and Moto Guzzi, as well as car manufacturers Alfa Romeo and Ferrari, is located near Bergamo, a walled city whose winged lions in the piazza proclaim its Renaissance subservience to Venice. Bembo was a typeface cut in Venice for Aldus Manutius — the man who invented the first pocketbooks — to publish a piece by Cardinal Pietro Bembo in 1495 about his visit to Mount Aetna (called, unsurprisingly, *De Aetna*). In the 1920s, that decade of high modernism, Stanley Morison supervised the update of Bembo for the Monotype Corporation. With what typographer and poet Robert Bringhurst calls its well-proportioned "functional serifs," Bembo became known for its "quiet classical beauty" and "high readability."

So why would you want to look at typefaces? Why in particular would you want to look at a single letter? At a *part* of a letter, for pity's sake? Who cares about serifs (those little lines at the top and bottom of the letter, which originally resulted from stonecutters finishing the letter with their chisels)? Any motorcyclist would understand. Only the uninitiated look at whole bikes. The concept of "garage appeal" is predicated on the notion that you're not going to walk out to the garage, look in, say "Yup, she's still there," and walk away. With a bike like a Vincent Black Shadow — the Mona Lisa of motorcycles — there is almost too much to look at. To be in its presence is to risk Stendhal syndrome. (When the writer Stendhal went to Florence, he was so overwhelmed by the beauty there that he fell into a swoon.) Your gaze glides from the tank, to the engine, and to the exhaust pipes, and then works back, noting the shape of the ends of the pipes, the cylinder heads and rocker covers, and smaller details: the headlight, as important as eyes in a face for character, the brake cables, perhaps the snakeskin pattern that indicates braided steel ... You've just begun.

Before I left for Texas, I had taken the Ducati's seat off to get at the battery, and my Italian friend Pasquale, owner of five motorcycles, said, "Ah, look at that casting."

"What?" I said. He pointed to the bracket for the uni-shock under the seat. I'd seen it but never really looked at it before, and I realized that the beautiful curve of the piece echoed the lines on the visible parts of the bike. The first time Pasquale rode my Ducati, he came back, put it up on the kickstand, and stood back from it. "You know," he said, "a motorcycle looks different after you've ridden it. I liked it before, but now it's beautiful." The bike looked different to me now that I knew about that bracket; like a detail on a medieval cathedral that no one can see, if you know it's there, it changes your sense of the whole. And knowing its function made me see — of course! — that there were no shock absorbers at the back, which in part gave the bike its clean, airy line. Do you think about this when you ride? No, "think" is too emphatic and specific a term, but the knowledge becomes part of the experience, suffuses it. The machinist's and the typographer's art are not far apart, and their effects similar. The beauty, born of functional precision, is initially invisible because transparent. We look through type, past the brakes. Only later do ligatures and calipers move from ground to figure. After an afternoon of reading about typefaces and page design, I came back to T. E. Lawrence's mint copy of *Ulysses*. It looked different.

Reading the Road

A road, too, is a text. In a car you read the map, but on a bike you read the road. You look for the shiny black of tar strips; they're murderously slick in rain and they turn to soft goo in the heat and will slide you sideways. Hit one on a tightening bend of an off-ramp, and you'll be dropped before you know it. You watch for ridges clawed in the road by the machines preparing a road for new asphalt. They're usually marked, but if it's a Sunday and the road crew isn't working, you may find yourself juddering through one unwarned. The ridges do the same thing those metal grill bridge decks do — set the whole bike squirming. My dirt-biking friend Dave told me how to handle it.

"It's the same as riding in gravel. Put your weight on the pegs. Don't hold the bars too tight. If you try to stop the wobble, you'll just make it worse. Don't look down or you'll go down. Just look at the horizon, keep your speed steady, and ride it out."

"Okay, but why do I put my weight on the pegs? Do you mean stand?"

"No, just push down. It lowers your centre of gravity. It transfers your body weight from the seat, three feet above the road, to a point about a foot above."

"Makes sense."

You also have to watch out for grooves in the road. Ruts, of course, but also the worn lanes of heavily used traffic corridors in cities. There the road isn't flat; it's like the lower half of a double-barrelled shotgun. You can pull up to a stoplight in the middle of a lane, go to put your foot down, and find the road surface is a cowboy boot-heel lower than you thought. Instead of steadying the bike upright, you're staggering to keep it from falling over, worrying about scraping the tank, and looking like a fool in front of eight lines of commuter traffic. Out on the highway, the grooves fill quickly in a thunderstorm, providing wonderful potential for aquaplaning.

You learn to watch for oil slicks at intersections or anywhere cars have to stop. As you set up for a curve that runs under an overpass, you peer into the shadow, for the road can be sandy, or still wet, or even have a thin skiff of ice if it's cold out. Manhole covers, crosswalks, the white line, the yellow line, any kind of painted line; railway tracks and tram tracks; glass, sand, gravel, fruit, dung, blood — anything on the road except the road is a hazard.

If you're going to hit anything, you want to hit it straight on. If you have to go over a log or a curb, the technique is to brake just before, to compress the front suspension, then release and accelerate slightly to lighten the front end as it rolls over. Sometimes you can post, like a horseback rider rising up in the stirrups. But that's only if you have time. If you're surprised by a lump or a hole, then you just take it; the last thing you want to do is brake and swerve. Momentum is everything. But after you've had a few big potholes slam your crotch against the tank and grind dust off the bones in your wrist, you learn to anticipate. Even as you're looking at the street signs or the view, your eyes are searching, constantly reading the road.

Outside the Frame

The most repeated passage in *Zen and the Art of Motorcycle Maintenance* is where Robert Pirsig contrasts riding a motorcycle with riding in a car. You're *in* a car, he says; when you're on a bike you're outside; the frame dissolves. It's an apt metaphor for working in the archive. There you're outside the frame: you read the topography of the texts as well as the linguistic codes; you get a perceptual jolt as well as an intellectual thrill. Responding to handwriting, looking at the stamps on letters, feeling and sniffing the paper, hearing the crinkle of a heavy parchment manuscript — you're reading with all your senses. And while in a library we often pursue a particular line of thought, in the archives we often don't even know where we are going. The end is less a destination than an excuse, and the narrative that unfolds proves digressive, contingent, surprising. For me, a line on some obscure bookstores and a chance tip by a curator took me on an archival ride with as many twists as the off-the-map Highway 31 in Utah.

For anyone doing print-culture history, the axiom is this: No text is separable from its context. I began tracking bookstores that handled *Ulysses* or dealt with Sylvia Beach's Shakespeare & Co. In other archives, I found inquiries from one Jack Sacks, Bookseller, in Harlem in New York City. Who were Jack's customers? And there was the genteel-sounding Temple Bar Tea Rooms in San Francisco; and one from Gammel's Bookstore in Austin, Texas, whose folksy letterhead proclaimed,

THE OLDEST BOOK STORE IN THE STATE, ESTABLISHED 1877. THE PROPRIETOR, GAMMEL, WAS BORN IN DENMARK RICH AND GOOD LOOKING — NOT SO NOW. YOU UNDERSTAND MONEY RULES THE WORLD THE WORLD RULES YOUR GOOD LOOKS SO DON'T BE DISAPPOINTED WHEN WE MEET AGAIN. H. F. N. GAMMEL

REFERENCE: MRS H. P. N. GAMMEL HER 3 BOYS AND 5 GIRLS AND A FEW OTHER FRIENDS DON'T HESITATE TO SELL TO ME OR BUY YOU WILL NOT DOUBT MY REFERENCES. IF YOU DO, WRITE THEM. H. P. N. GAMMEL

Whew. How many copies of *Ulysses* did he sell? And then in Canada, not Montreal, but the Alexander Cigar and News Stand in Calgary, Alberta. Were there discounts during Stampede week? Like Gammel's, this store sounded more likely to cater to cowpunchers than collectors. The listing of Mitchell's Bookstore in Buenos Aires seemed less strange to me. Texas and Alberta in the 1920s were places off the beaten cultural track, dealing with a clientele that, like the air-crew workers in Karachi, scholars had not so far even imagined.

One such outpost was the Sunwise Turn. In 1916 in New York City, Madge Jenison and Mary Mowbray-Clarke opened the Sunwise Turn, A Modernist Bookshop on East 31st Street in New York City. It was one of the first bookstores in America to be owned and operated by women, and they saw themselves as cultural missionaries in the capitalist jungle of Manhattan. They chose the name Sunwise because it meant to follow the course of the sun — to be in harmony, in other words, with the rhythms of nature, and, implicitly, to provide relief from the mechanical rhythms of the city. In a talk to booksellers, Mowbray-Clarke declared they were contributing "something more concentrated than is possible in the large merchandising Book-shops where books are — may I say it? perhaps sold as ordinary commodities rather than as what they seem to us to be — food for the soul of man — tools for the pursuits of life."

They prepared libraries for company boardrooms and had a mail-order service to provide customers with the best new books on a subject of their choosing — like the Book-of-the-Month Club's featured selections. They sponsored lectures and readings by Robert Frost, Theodore Dreiser, Amy Lowell, and others; they sold paintings and sculpture; and shop assistant Peggy Guggenheim claimed her interest in art collecting came from her time at the Sunwise Turn. In the authoritative *History of Book Publishing in the United States,* John Tebbel notes that the Sunwise Turn "was probably the prototype of the small 'personal' bookshop" and states that Madge Jenison's memoir, *The Sunwise Turn,* was "an influential guide to 'personal' bookstore operation." This much I learned from published sources.

Then the curator, John Kirkpatrick, noticing my reading asked mildly, "You know we have the Sunwise Turn archive?"

"No."

"They're uncatalogued," he said apologetically, as he brought the three grey boxes.

"Not to worry," I said. *Andiamo.*

In the first box I found bills for draperies and furniture coverings:

$211.75 for 25 yds linen, 19 yds Tudor, 2 yds Damask, 2 yds
    Agra, 6 yds Gauze

$302.40 for 38 sq ft of tapestry, purple, for sofa

39 sq ft plain tapestry, orange-red for two armchairs

36 ft of plain tapestry, blue, for 3 sidechairs

47 sq ft of plain tapestry for outside covering

A purple sofa, orange-red armchairs, blue sidechairs — the shop must have looked like a Matisse painting. Five hundred dollars was lot of money for furniture coverings in 1919, but the decor was part of the project. In the typescript of a speech, Mowbray-Clarke declared,

Our physical setting has meant a great deal to us ... Even our mullioned windows and our great tiled wall sign are a protest against the mediocrity of the eternal plate-glass ... The selling of books in a derivative and imitative atmosphere would seem a crudity, believing as we do in the interdependence of all the arts.

But what about money?

"But do you make any money?" ask all the business friends, who think everything we do a little foolish, yet continue to come to us nevertheless. "No, we do not," we have to answer. We do everything but make money ... but we have not compromised our original idea."

That was in 1922. Two years later, in a heavily crossed-out manuscript for what appears to be another talk to booksellers, we find Mowbray-Clarke bitterly noting, "Those who write for the magazines on bookshops are generally people ... who write delectable moonshine about dream shops into which the shadow of the credit man never enters."

This, I would find out after further digging, was a pointed jibe at Jenison. Mowbray-Clarke goes on to rail against the non-book-buying public: "The same people who exclaim at the price of a book go from our shop to [buy] a silk shirt that fades away in a month without a feeling of extravagance." Ironically, the site of the Sunwise Turn is today occupied by a custom shirt shop. What had happened, I wondered.

I'd put off opening the boring-looking binder of minutes of directors' meetings in Box 3, but I finally turned to it. The monthly meetings charted a swift decline. In January 1922, they discussed reducing staff, lowering salaries, renting space to the Encyclopaedia Britannica, and seeking a bank loan to refinance the shop. In April, they dispensed with two positions, made another part-time, and reduced the salaries of the officers. In May, they fired more of their help and replaced their full-time bookkeeper with a part-time one. In June, they applied for a loan. Their own bank rejected them, so they transferred to another, securing $5,000 at six per cent interest.

Soon the partners had split and were communicating only by letter, then only by lawyer. While Jenison was publishing part of her chirpy memoir in *Women's Home Companion* (what Mowbray-Clarke sneered at as "delectable moonshine" and historians would refer to as an "influential guide" to bookstore operation), Mowbray-Clarke was trying to ward off bankruptcy. Her husband ran off with one of his sculpture students to Canada, and she struggled on alone for three more years, before finally giving up and selling out to Doubleday, which added the store to its chain. I found no record of what they did with the purple sofa and the orange-red armchairs.

I turned back to the text of Mowbray-Clarke's handwritten speech and found another tantalizing glimpse of readers off the map:

> Very few Yale and Princeton men read ... More Harvard men read and they keep their library up to date. Jews and Russians and young Irishmen from Ireland read — though few Irish-Americans. Englishmen seem to read most and widest with us. But in New York when all is said and done the reading ...

Here the page was torn, the manuscript stopped. I would never find out who these consummate readers were.

But the experience had changed the way I thought about academic writing. I found I liked articles that instead of nailing an argument shut instead opened up lines of thought; that laid out instead of suppressing the vexing evidence that didn't fit, the chains of reasoning that didn't work out, the trails of cookie crumbs that led to no text.

Bad Chain

"That's a *baad* chain," said Vern at the Ducati shop in Austin. "Yessir, that's the *baddest* chain we sell. You won't find a badder chain than that."

"Uh, good," I said, and shelled out $210 Canadian for the new bad chain.

I wondered what to call my old chain, which was bad in the conventional sense — I'd overtightened it on the way down, in my eagerness to perform the one act of motorcycle maintenance I was capable of (two wrenches! grease on my fingers!). It had stretched in one spot, so it would never be right again. I could have bought the cheaper one, but the weather channel announcers were thrilling to brush fires in New Mexico and snow in the Cascades, and I had three days of empty desert before I even got to where there was foliage enough for a brush fire. I knew I wouldn't have problems with a cheaper chain, but I wanted everything ticking over more than perfectly. I would be riding thirty-five hundred miles alone. I wanted a margin of error as big as the continent. I'd planned my route across to California and up the coast, but the weather was dodgy. That was okay; I'd take it as it unfolded. I would be disappointed if my journey did not take me off the map.

KATHERINE ASHENBURG

Doctors' Daughters:
Helen, Sue, and Me

The summer that I was ten —
Can it be there was only one
summer that I was ten? It must
Have been a long one then
— May Swenson

IN THE WINTER OF 2001, MY FATHER BECAME CRITICALLY ill. All five of his middle-aged children gathered in Rochester, New York, where he was in intensive care for more than a month. We hadn't spent so much time together since adolescence, and, in a period of great anxiety and sadness, we regressed. Family dinners, after long hours in the hospital, featured our mother's recipes from the 1950s. Blue Ribbon Macaroni and Cheese. Friday Night Tuna Noodle Casserole. Pineapple Upside Down Cake. Old nicknames returned, as did sibling tensions and loyalties.

Our father was dying in something like the family firm. The hospital in which he was suffering heart attacks, strokes, and increasingly heroic surgery was where he had trained as a medical student, worked as a doctor, and taught in the medical school. His picture is on the wall in the psychiatric wing. Teaching a bacteriology course for nursing students, he met his future wife, our mother. All their children were born within the hospital walls, and two of them graduated from its medical school.

Some of my earliest memories are of Strong Memorial Hospital — eating my first mashed potatoes with gravy at Sunday lunch in the cafeteria, being taken to see the narrow white cot where my father slept when he was on call. When I was about four, my mother took me to the nurses' residence, to a Christmas party that remains one of my permanent images of joy. Candles were lit on a long, dark table in a formal room. The iced Christmas cookies came in shapes I had not imagined possible — angels, trees, Santas. My mother had sewn me a midnight-blue velvet dress that, even at four, I knew was superb (my most successful party dress to date). Her former nursing professors and colleagues made much of her little girl.

In 2001, the hospital, still laden with memories, was an altogether grimmer place. My two younger sisters and I spent our days in its cafeteria, coffee stands, waiting rooms, and corridors, as well as in my father's room. During those grey February days, I lectured them with the bossiness of the first-born: "The patient has very little visual stimuli. It's important to comb our hair and put on lipstick before we go into Daddy's room." "The worst thing you can do to a patient is bump the end of his bed." "Even if the patient appears to be unconscious, don't assume he can't hear you." For a while my sisters, one of whom is a pediatrician and the other a family therapist, bore this with patience. Finally, they noted sarcastically that they had missed the years when I had become a nurse. Where was all the nursing lore coming from?

Everything I know about nursing I learned from the seven Sue Barton books, which I withdrew from the Rochester Public Library in the 1950s, probably between the ages of ten and twelve or thirteen. The juvenile novels, written by Helen Dore Boylston, covered Sue's career from her first days as a probationer at Massachusetts General Hospital through jobs as a visiting nurse in the slums of New York City, as a rural nurse in the White Mountains of New

Hampshire, and finally as a staff nurse in a country hospital. A picture of the red-headed Sue appeared on each cover, wearing in all but one a different, distinctive nurse's cap to indicate her current status.

February turned into March. We began taking turns going to Rochester and staying with our mother, who could no longer sleep alone in their seniors' townhouse. Our father had survived, but he could not talk, sit up unassisted, or feed himself. Most of the time he seemed oblivious to our presence, barely conscious and absorbed in some irritating private struggle. Still, we spent our days and sometimes nights in his room.

Dozens of nurses appeared at intervals to press buttons on the flotilla of machines attached to him, to put in lines, or to draw blood. They negotiated his perilous journey from bed to wheelchair, and fed him puréed substances so neutralized they came pressed into cunning, identifying moulds — a pea pod, a corn cob, a carrot. Male and female, they wore coloured, unironed pyjama-like outfits that would have astonished the starched-white-uniformed Miss Barton. Head coverings — the distinguishing mark of the nurse until the 1970s — were absent.

As I watched them, more and more of Sue's experiences and maxims resurfaced. Although being around a hospital brought them back, I didn't think it was nursing per se that had appealed to me about the series as a girl. The family penchant bypassed me: I was too bookish and dreamy to consider a medical career.

But I had and have a weakness for subcultures — small, complete worlds with some accompanying custom and ceremony. Most of my favourite childhood reading reflected that, from *Little Women* to Noel Streatfeild's English books about theatre schools, ballet schools, and circus schools. I remembered the camaraderie and the enveloping institutional life of, in Sue's series, hospitals and settlement houses, as I remembered (more dimly) the stage lore in Streatfeild's *Theatre Shoes*. As recently as 2001, I would have described Sue's career as almost incidental, compared with deeper attractions like tradition and idealism.

Other than the agreeably custom-soaked life of a nursing student and nurse, my main memory of the books was the dialogue between Sue and Bill Barry. A tall, dark, surgical intern who rescues a lost Sue on her first day in the hospital, Bill becomes her husband, but only after many vicissitudes and four books. To a preadolescent, the sparkle and wit of their conversation — and the sense that the speakers were equals in strength — were irresistible. It was something new in my experience, and I had the unarticulated feeling that it was both sophisticated, a word I probably barely understood, and fine.

Forty years after reading Boylston's series, I thought of it as better written, more mature, and fully rounded than the average novel for preadolescent girls. Even the vocabulary, I imagined, was superior. When I mentioned Sue Barton to women of my generation and they asked, "Was she like Cherry Ames?" (a nurse series produced by two different writers), I responded with more heat than necessary, "Don't mention that name in the same breath with Sue Barton." It was like equating a synthetic, assembly-line wallet with hand-sewn Florentine craftsmanship.

This was hardly an original bit of literary criticism, because every reading girl in the 1950s knew the crucial distinction between the Sue Barton series and Nancy Drews or Trixie Beldens or Cherry Ameses. It was that Boylston's novels were *library* books, thoughtfully written and sturdily produced, not boilerplate stories with thin pasteboard covers that had to be bought. Understanding the difference didn't mean acquiescing to the librarians' boycott, because I was simultaneously enjoying everything from Archie and

Veronica comics to *Huckleberry Finn*. In a scene that must have occurred thousands of times throughout the English-speaking world, I demanded one day that my local librarian explain why the library didn't stock Nancy Drews. "Because we don't consider they have enough literary merit," she explained gently, infuriatingly, and correctly. Although I chafed at the distinction, at some level I acknowledged its justice.

In Helen Dore Boylston's series, written from 1936 to 1952, fairly well people were admitted to hospital. They frequently walked the wards, and their mischief-making potential advanced Boylston's plots. Mostly WASP female nurses spent their days delivering bed baths, alcohol rubs, and arcane but similarly low-tech procedures like hot-air baths (a hair-raising event involving matches and blankets, thankfully obsolete).

At one point, Sue thinks of her training as involving "science as new as the hour and skills as old as compassion." No doubt true, but there was more call in her day for good bedside manners than the use of ground-shifting technology. Today, nurses of both sexes and all ethnic groups care for seriously ill people with million-dollar machines and awesomely refined drugs. But, as my father moved from intensive care to the cardiology unit and then to a rehabilitation facility, the nurses' demeanour put me more and more in mind of Sue and her colleagues. By and large, they were brisk but not obnoxiously hearty, sympathetic but not cloying. The way they held my father's hands and made contact with him when he was only reluctantly conscious, the matter-of-fact way they preserved his dignity when he could not so much as urinate independently, was impressive. "Skills as old as compassion" were still being practised.

By midsummer, with my father at home learning to walk, talk, read, and write again at eighty-three, nostalgia was reaching ridiculous levels. Not sure whether I was about to burst a bubble, lance a boil, or encounter an old friend, I called the library's main branch to find out if the Sue Barton books were still circulating. While the librarian waited for the computer to respond, she volunteered, "I loved them ... Wasn't her beau's name Bill?" The series is indeed circulating at a modest level, she told me after a few minutes, though the titles are mostly kept in the stacks rather than on open shelves. "That's true of lots of books with more historical interest than current appeal," the librarian added, placidly relegating my childhood to "historical interest." When I showed up at the library to borrow all seven books, another, younger librarian offered a somewhat contradictory summation: "Oh yes, they're very popular ... No, I haven't read them myself. I'm probably a bit too young to have grown up with them." Were they classics or period pieces? Had I romanticized them out of all recognition?

The Rochester Public Library has not kept its checkout cards from the 1950s. That's a shame, because I would love to know how many times I carried a Sue Barton title to the golden-syrup-coloured wooden counter, signed "Kathy Ashenburg" on those stiff pieces of orange paper, and waited for the librarian to stamp my due date. How often did I carry the cellophane-protected books, emblazoned with Sue's "vivid" face (a favourite Boylston epithet), out of the Edwardian Classical branch library on Monroe Avenue? From there it was a short walk down Dartmouth Street, where we lived in a big, slightly rundown clapboard house behind a porch with Ionic columns.

I read on that generous porch in the summers and more often in my bedroom, papered long before my time with blowsy cabbage roses. My parents had given me a small-scale easy chair in dark green imitation leather, placed against the window overlooking the backyard. From there, unseen, I could watch the neighbourhood kids ringing the kitchen bell and hear my mother calling, "Barbara and Mary want you to play." But when I didn't answer, finding my book more entrancing than any play, she never pressed the point. I could hear her saying "Sorry, kids, I guess she's not here," before I returned to that other, more compelling world.

It's likely I first read Sue Barton in that shell-backed chair, but I have no memory of where I was when I encountered Boylston's books, or most books. The intensity of reading made its own place. I entered the book, and became oblivious to my real surroundings. Nor do I recall much rereading in those days. It seemed improbable that the almost clairvoyant precision with which I recalled Boylston's dialogue and descriptions was the result of one or perhaps two readings, but it may well have been. Like May Swenson's exquisitely extended age-ten summer, the profound reading a child does, the time-altering, inscribing passage she makes into the landscape of certain books, may mean that a single reading is enough.

Chapter One: Probation Begins
The train began to move at last. Sue leaned forward, her red curls crushed against the windowpane, and looked back to where her father and mother and Ted stood on the station platform. Their faces were growing smaller. Sue's resolute young mouth quivered suddenly, and her eyes misted.
Sue Barton, Student Nurse

Like shrugging into an old jacket that preserved the memory of my elbows and shoulders, the smallish books with the alert-looking heroine on the cover fit neatly into my hands. I knew those thick pages with their deep bottom margins and dash-filled dialogue, even their smell — some amalgam of paper, thread, libraries, and young girls. The nursing tradition and the life of a great hospital they evoked were as rich as I remembered. The repartee between Sue and Bill, while not up to Noel Coward's standards, still struck a stylish but authentic note — and once I started reading, sizable chunks were as familiar as if I had read them yesterday.

Then Barry said, smiling, "You do like me a little — still, don't you?"

"I can bear you," said Sue, lightly. "I even admire you — sometimes — though I'm sure it's presumptuous of me, when there are so many and better nurses to worship at your feet."

He grinned. "I was hoping you'd noticed that!"

"Dear me, how you do hate yourself! And would you kindly tell me what you think you've got — except your elegant black hair? Where would you be if you were bald — or even if it were rumpled? All women would flee from you."

"You might rumple it, and find out if you want to run," he said, bending over. His dark head was very close — a well-set head on broad shoulders.

"No, indeed," hastily. "I wouldn't dream of it." She was laughing a little.

Sue Barton, Senior Nurse

Like Nancy Drew and other girl heroines, Sue has two chums, the tomboy Kit Van Dyke and the more feminine Constance Halliday. In fact, the insulting banter between Sue and Kit is cleverer than that between Sue and Bill, though it hadn't impressed itself indelibly on my preadolescent self.

In spite of mostly good dialogue, characterization, and overall atmosphere, the Sue Barton books aren't Shakespeare. They aren't even Madeleine L'Engle or P. L. Travers. Creations of their time, they come with nuance-free stereotypes. Italians, who speak pidgin English, are always excitable; Jews worried; "coloured people" willing and gullible. The Canadian Kit Van Dyke occasionally speaks more in the idiom of Edwardian Surrey ("I say!") than rural, Depression-era Nova Scotia. Boylston's skill at dialogue plummets when she leaves the middle classes, and even rural New Hampshire people, whom she probably knew well, speak like bumpkins in a bad early Henry Fonda movie. I still enjoy the prank played on a prissy, know-it-all student who is sent to procure a neck tourniquet for a thyroid case ("and hurry!"), but the plots of the individual chapters, typically a "scrape" involving Sue and her chums or an instance of Sue's developing nursing skills, are often unconvincing. Although my hunch that these were superior juvenile novels was vindicated, they are, like the curate's egg, only excellent in parts.

Some of their flaws are more endearing than others. Like many writers of serials, Boylston felt obliged to recapitulate key developments from earlier books near the start of the current volume, and these sound an awkward note. Similarly, she must have found the need to redescribe her characters through seven books a trial. As a result, Sue is perennially "vivid," with copper-coloured hair curling softly around her face (confusingly contradicted by Major Felton's cover illustrations of her hair combed smoothly back). Her nurse's cap is always "an inverted teacup." Kit's arched eyebrows and upturned nose make frequent appearances, and Bill, with his well-shaped head, is often pictured sitting, casting his eyes down the length of his long legs while he decides how to respond to Sue. Rather than bridle at them, I preferred to think of the recapitulations as aspects of a near-oral literature, as if thousands of girls from different generations were gathered at a virtual fire, listening to oft-told stories of Sue. As for the descriptions, I thought of them as Homeric epithets, a shorthand like the *Iliad*'s wine-dark sea and cow-eyed Hera.

Although I marvelled that I seemed to know these novels, in part, better than the book I read last week, I was equally surprised by the things I did not remember — or had never consciously noticed. Until middle age, I was fairly indifferent to weather and the natural features of a place, so I failed to appreciate that Boylston is a poet of climate and the landscape of the White Mountains. "At noon the sky came suddenly down," she writes in *Sue Barton, Rural Nurse,* describing a snowfall on the New Hampshire coast. "It came endlessly, falling straight, and silent except for a little pelting whisper, an interminable sigh. There was no breath of wind — only that white curtain piling downwards forever on sheeted roofs and cotton trees."

In the same book, Bolyston writes of a house in the White Mountains where Sue rents a room:

The little house had a breath-taking view of the mountains — range after range of peaks, piled up in frozen silence. Sue's bedroom window faced them — an old-fashioned room with sloping ceiling and sprigged wallpaper — and when she woke in the morning she lay watching the blue shadows creep back up the mountains as the winter sun rose. There were nearly always clouds asleep in the hollows at dawn, and these, too, departed with the sun — in a strangely lifelike manner, for they stretched themselves vastly before they crawled away. She could never bear to get up until they had gone.

But the biggest revelation on rereading Sue Barton had nothing to do with landscape. Rather, it is a current of worry that runs through the series, an ambivalent, to-and-fro rumination about a woman's difficulties in combining an independent life with marriage, and a profession with a family. Prominent as it is, it completely escaped my attention on the first reading. When Dr. Barry asks the twenty-year-old Sue, not yet a graduate nurse, if she is "still grimly intent on a career," my eyebrows (in 2001) shot up. How could I have missed that? One of the reasons was obvious enough: I was living in the 1950s paradigm, with an intelligent, contented, stay-at-home mother. As a girl, I loved Sue's devotion to her work and her relationship with Bill Barry, and didn't notice that she almost never had both at the same time. Something similar would play out in my own life and in the lives of many women in my generation. But I would not begin to wrestle with that dilemma for years after I read Sue Barton; did not even know it was a dilemma.

Helen Dore Boylston did, however, and the timing of her novels is suggestive. *Sue Barton, Student Nurse,* the first in the series, was published in 1936, when nursing was one of the few professions where no one accused women of taking jobs from men during the Depression. Almost from the beginning, Dr. Barry (whose charm I still cannot resist) wants Sue for himself. She hesitates, sure that a woman cannot combine nursing and marriage, insisting on working in the Henry Street settlements in New York after she reluctantly agrees to an engagement, delaying setting a date for the wedding. Ultimately love triumphs — temporarily — over her passion for nursing, but Boylston continues methodically building roadblocks to Sue's domestication.

Finally, at the beginning of *Sue Barton, Superintendent of Nurses,* the fifth book, Sue marries Bill. At the end of that volume, she hands in her resignation to her husband (also the hospital director), explaining that "Bill Junior" will need her attention for some time. It was 1942 and Boylston declared the series over. A married nurse was iffy at best — significantly, Boylston writes in an estrangement that keeps the newlyweds at odds for most of that volume — but a nurse with a baby was out of the question. Boylston turned to a new series about a girl, Carol Page, who seeks a career on the stage.

For some reason, Boylston returned to Sue Barton in 1949 and 1952. In two final books, written at a time when society wanted women at home and family life normalized after the tumult of war,

Sue is the mother of four children, including twins. (The heroines of girls' books — Heidi, Meg in *Little Women,* Sue Barton — have a disproportionately high incidence of twin births, no doubt because their readers considered it romantic.) Sue's pal Connie Halliday had retired from nursing immediately after marrying, despite having been a keen specialist in anesthesiology. Kit Van Dyke never married and continued nursing. Sue wavers between those two models. Doing her best to accommodate a stay-at-home heroine in the 1949 book, *Sue Barton, Neighborhood Nurse,* Boylston reduces her to helping a troubled teenager and improvising the odd tourniquet. Three years later, in apparent desperation, Boylston gives Dr. Barry a double dose of pneumonia and tuberculosis that puts him conveniently away in a sanatorium, leaving his wife to return to work in *Sue Barton, Staff Nurse.*

Of Helen Dore Boylston, I knew nothing except that she also wrote a girls' biography of Clara Barton, the founder of the American Red Cross. (I read it, as I read almost everything in the children's section of the library, but compared with Sue's, Clara's pallid but driven nature did not appeal to me.) Clearly, Boylston was no stranger to hospital life, but children's books in the 1930s, 1940s, and 1950s came unembellished with biographical information about the author. As a child, I never wondered about the writer behind the book, but now I was curious. Was Boylston her married name, and did she describe Sue's ambivalence about marriage-versus-career from personal knowledge?

A little research, which included the happy discovery of a Sue Barton home page, filled in some of the picture. Born in 1895, Helen Boylston was, like Sue, a native of Portsmouth, New Hampshire, and the daughter of a doctor. The fictional character, whose grandfather was also a doctor and whose little brother, Ted, planned to become one, never considered medical school. Boylston did, but chafed at the prospect of years of study. After a year at Simmons College in Boston, she entered the Massachusetts General Hospital School of Nursing and graduated in 1915.

Like Sue, she was curious and adventurous. Unlike Sue, whose biggest trip in seven volumes is an offstage honeymoon in the South, Boylston had wanderlust. Enlisting in the Harvard Medical Unit in World War I, she nursed in France in the British Expeditionary Force. Specializing in anesthesiology, like the fictional Connie Halliday, she kept a journal in which she tried to "catch and hold the real atmosphere of the war as [she] saw it." Events, she claimed, were easy to remember, but quick-fading atmosphere was what "really counts" (a prescient summary of her future skills as a novelist).

"Sister": The War Diary of a Nurse, first published as an article in the *Atlantic Monthly* and then as a book in 1927, does indeed capture a peculiar time and place. In a war where soldiers with bone injuries could convalesce for more than a year in the field hospital, where Boylston kept dancing dresses and her own dog while sleeping in the dunes for weeks to avoid nightly shelling, well-founded pessimism was the order of the day long before the Armistice. "The crowd at the [officers'] school will all be killed," she writes matter-of-factly of the young men taking them to tea and dances. "They always are."

The central figure in her account — an edited self-portrait, no doubt, but a self-portrait — can contrive an armchair from boards, box covers, and a fence rail ("Thank God Daddy taught me to use carpenters' tools") and falls in and out of love with dispatch. Scornful of the older officers who see women only as "a means of amusement and relaxation," she flirts energetically until the man responds too much. Then she retreats, not sure she likes him, or wants to marry at all. Although unquestionably warmhearted when it comes to the Tommies on her ward, Boylston preserves a certain *froideur,* or perhaps simply a stiff upper lip. (She seems to have found the prevailing British nonchalance a congenial stance.) She can write archly of her current beau, one of those doomed officers, "We finally parted with all the necessary drama." After a massive German attack that killed seven nurses working near Boylston, she says only of their funeral: "I begged off." Boylston's disinclination to look sorrow in the face may partly account for the absence of serious illness and death in the Sue Barton series, as the teasing hostility of the books' dialogue surely derives from the coolness of her temperament.

Post-war work in a Boston hospital was dull by comparison with life in France. When a friend told her "there is a lot happening in the Balkans," and suggested joining the Red Cross to work there, Boylston wrote in her journal, "After she left I put my head down on the desk and gave up to the waves of longing that swept over me. Daddy, I'm sure, wants me to settle down … But I'm young! I'm young! Why shouldn't I live? What is old age to me if it has no memories — except of forty years or so of blank days?"

The waves of longing won out over Daddy's wishes and on the eve of sailing for France, on February 21, 1920, she exulted, "The world is mine!" So it was for two years, while she worked in Germany, Poland, Italy, Russia, and the Balkans. Albania in particular stirred her with its near-medieval culture and abundant revolutions.

In her twenties and thirties, Boylston see-sawed between working as a nurse and magazine writer in America and courting adventure in Europe with her friend Rose Wilder Lane. Wilder Lane, in a strange coincidence, was the daughter of Laura Ingalls Wilder, not yet famous as the author of the *Little House on the Prairie* series. (In the early thirties, Wilder Lane would coax her mother into turning her diaries into books and become her most significant editor.)

Buoyed by a stratospheric stock market, Boylston and Wilder Lane returned to Europe in 1926 with plans to drive to Albania in their new Model T, build a house, and live there. The projected house included loopholes in the walls for rifles, for use during revolutionary skirmishes. Often assumed in France and Italy to be German, because "the only women who travel about alone and fearlessly are German," the Americans journeyed to Tirana with their French maid, making frequent, expert repairs on their Model T. Their letters en route, sent to Laura Ingalls and Almanzo Wilder, are as breezy and confident as any Girl's Own Adventure Story of the 1920s. It's possible to hear the tones of the yet-unborn Sue Barton, by turns flippantly ironic and zestful, and always up for the next escapade, in her creator's letters.

Boylston, who was called Troubles or Troub, lived up to her nickname. "She once made the Albanian Prime Minister carry her trunk off the boat and tried to tip him, not knowing who he was," her publishers wrote. "She was shot at for two hours in a ditch in southern Albania owing to a mistake in identity." Not infrequently, her scrapes had a physical cost. In France during the war, she slid down a hill on an army tea tray and broke two ribs. In the Albanian mountains, a kicking horse broke her collarbone. Boylston described being set upon by a Polish peasant and his dog and being forced to kill the dog to save her life. More mysteriously, but very much in the spirit of Sue's hospital pranks, she added, "Was once pursued by a groaning pillowcase in an Albanian garden at night."

The women spent two years in Tirana, entertaining visiting Americans like Wilder Lane's friend Clarence Day. (How odd it is to think of those three people, each later connected with celebrated children's books, under one Albanian roof — the authors of the *Cheaper by the Dozen* and Sue Barton series, and the shaping spirit of the *Little House on the Prairie* books.) "Drawn by the irresistible lure," as she put it, of a photograph of a baked potato in an

American magazine, Boylston returned to the U.S. On the Wilders' Missouri homestead, she rode horses, raised Scotties, and wrote the odd article or story. But she lost more than thirty thousand dollars in the 1929 crash and returned to nursing in New York City before she realized that writing could pay her bills as well or better than nursing. She wrote stories and articles for the quality magazines of the day — *Harper's, Atlantic, Forum, McCall's,* and *Liberty*. In 1936, she launched the Sue Barton series, acknowledged as a pioneering "career series" for girls. They went into multiple editions, selling hundreds of thousands of copies all over the world.

In 1942, *Current Biography* illustrated its full-page article on Helen Dore Boylston with a photograph of the forty-seven-year-old author in profile holding up a puppy. Short-haired, slim, wearing a military-style jacket, she looks rather like Greta Garbo playing Queen Christina. *Current Biography* described her as "handsome and youthful, with strong features." Living in Westport, Connecticut, Miss Boylston spent her leisure hours, according to this account, "sewing, cooking, wood carving, collecting coins, and training dogs. Her favorite sport is long motor trips. She is unmarried."

Were any of those terms — handsome, strong features, wood carving — *Current Biography*'s code for gay? A turn-of-the-twenty-first-century question, and probably a pointless one. Boylston may well have been a heterosexual who realized that, for a woman born in 1895, a yen for adventure and marriage made a bad combination.

Whatever her orientation, Boylston had a penchant for friendship with accomplished women that served her well. Also, America seems to have been a much smaller place in those days. When she came to write her series about a star-struck girl in the early 1940s, her Connecticut neighbour was the famous actress Eva LeGallienne. She invited Boylston to observe her theatre company up close for several months. Helen Dore Boylston's last book, the biography of Clara Barton, was written at age sixty. She died at eighty-nine in 1984, after some years in a nursing home in Trumbull, Connecticut. Other than *"Sister"* and the letters en route to Albania, she left almost nothing in the way of personal papers.

By the time of Boylston's death, the Sue Barton series was out of print in the United States. But British readers found Boylston a kindred spirit, at least in part because of her dry wit. Four of the Sue Barton titles were still in print in Britain in 1999, ironically packaged as adult romances.

I don't know Boylston's personal feelings about marriage, but the Sue Barton books are full of fascinating hints and glimmers. According to Boylston, she conceived of that series as well as the Carol Page series as vocational aids. "Teenage girls about to decide how they propose to earn a living naturally lean toward the romantic," she wrote. "Nursing and acting have a romantic appeal, but young imaginations conjure up the most wildly inaccurate pictures of life in either profession. I am a nurse myself, and have loved it all my days. But nursing is quite, *quite* different from anything girls imagine. The same is true in regard to the theatre. So, I proposed to give girls as *true* a picture as I was able."

But aside from her didactic aims and unlike Sue's near-contemporary Nancy Drew, whose romance with Ned Nickerson never becomes serious, Sue has a determined suitor and then a fiancé and then a husband. Rereading as an adult, I see clearly that Bill Barry's role is frequently no more than a walk-on, made the most of by what Boylston called "young imaginations." No doubt, some of Bill's appeal was due to his scarcity. The semi-joke from a devotee in the letters section of a Sue Barton home page is typical: "Reading Sue Barton thirty years ago decided me to become a nurse, which I am. But I'm still looking for Bill Barry ..."

Although the series has a hero, his presence almost always creates ambivalence. Sue, like Troub Boylston, wants to live before she settles down, and Bill is by turns patient, impatient, exasperated, and uncomprehending about this wish. The most fully expressed romance in the series is Sue's attachment to nursing. When Bill presents his well-set head very close to Sue and invites her to rumple it, the scene continues with Sue feeling something like panic. After she laughingly says she wouldn't dream of mussing his hair, Bill turns serious.

> He straightened up. "Why not?"
>
> An odd sensation, almost like fear, stirred within her. "I — I don't know," she said, and looked up at him with eyes in which there was no trace of laughter.
>
> There was a silence.
>
> Then Sue turned back to the window.
>
> "Look," she said a little unsteadily, "the lights are on in the ward now. In a little while the girls will be getting out the supper trays. It's strange, isn't it, to think how many years that has been going on? The people come and go, but they're just the same, really."
>
> "Yes," he agreed, watching her.
>
> They talked for a few minutes: of the hospital; of the work that was being done in the laboratories on pernicious anaemia; of the differences between medicine and surgery. But when Barry went away at last Sue remained, staring out of the window with a troubled face, until Miss Lee came to find her, and say that everything was done and she had better return to the ward.

It's a finely observed, even moving scene — the girl stirred but reluctant, turning in a flurry from what she may love some day to what she loves steadily, the ongoing life of the hospital. Until Bill goes away "at last," they meet on that ground and talk as colleagues.

An on-again/off-again pattern surfaces in that book, *Sue Barton, Senior Nurse,* and *Sue Barton, Visiting Nurse:* Sue and Bill quarrel because of Sue's inability to commit to marriage, then they reconcile. In *Visiting Nurse,* Bill becomes increasingly anxious to marry, while Sue is enchanted with settlement work in New York. They argue over what Sue sees as his masculine inability to take her work seriously and what he sees as her lack of interest in his happiness, and they break their engagement. After they reunite, Bill goes to see Sue's head nurse and she assures him that Sue can fulfill her obligation to the Henry Street settlement spirit by working with him in New Hampshire. It's a most unlikely scene, which can perhaps best be understood as the reassurance that Boylston herself needed, before she could wrench Sue out of New York and into marriage.

Even after Sue agrees to leave New York, Boylston clutters the path of true love. In the next book, *Sue Barton, Rural Nurse,* when the date for the wedding is all but set, the fortuitous death of Bill's father in an accident and the necessity to support his crippled brother delay their marriage once more. In addition to plot developments that echo Sue's inner reluctance, Boylston inserts odd details that a later generation finds hard not to read as Freudian. At the beginning of *Rural Nurse,* as Sue is dressing for a farewell party in her Greenwich Village house, on her way to New Hampshire and marriage, she loses her engagement ring. That's a bad sign, her protégé Marianna and her friend the Irish policeman tell Sue. Other than a presentiment of the difficulties Sue and Bill will face during that book, the scene has no point. It's flatly undramatic, as Marianna soon discovers the ring in Sue's coat pocket. But it remains, inevitably suggesting some ambivalence about marriage, at least on Boylston's part. Similarly, in *Superintendent of Nurses,* Sue and Bill sleep in separate bedrooms for the first year of their marriage. It was another telling detail I never noticed as a child, but must surely have been an extraordinary arrangement in America in the 1940s.

Books read in childhood exert a pull that is individual and not completely analyzable. Alberto Manguel, one of the world's more sophisticated readers, rereads an Enid Blyton book every once in a while and insists that their continuing appeal is not about good writing. It's about being transported back to an idyllic world of clean sheets and a quiet bedroom at the end of a day, when the boy Alberto opened the door into another reality. The literary critic Carolyn Heilbrun, discussing Nancy Drew books, agrees that they summon a pleasure separable from any literary qualities. But in the case of Nancy Drew, Heilbrun thinks the enjoyment is connected to the nature of the heroine: "that pleasure came, I wish to assert, from the adventures of a sixteen-year-old girl who took events into her own hands."

For me with Sue Barton, there was escapism of a wonderfully satisfying sort. But there must have been some rudimentary discrimination too, or I wouldn't have remembered the series as "better" than other books I swallowed whole at the time. The better the writing, the more complete the escapism. Needing to check my scornful memory of Cherry Ames, I read a 1944 volume, *Cherry Ames, Senior Nurse*. Beyond a few shameless borrowings from the Sue Barton books, including Cherry meeting her doctor-fiancé in a scary misunderstanding in the hospital basement and declining his first proposal in terms that closely echo Sue's, there were few surprises here. The psychology was more simplistic, the plots more strained, and the heroine less smart, worrying at one point, in her last year of nursing school, about the "secret masked figures" in the operating theatre, with accompanying "hints of morbid drugs and cruel instruments and lurking death." Above all, the sentences — a morass of clichés and exclamation points — gave me no joy. Helen Wells, the author, never drew a scene or turned a phrase that permitted the delicious, longed-for escape I found with Helen Dore Boylston.

Heilbrun's point about Nancy Drew is interesting, and I wonder how much of Sue's self-reliance and adventurous spirit spoke to me at a level I didn't understand. I can't avoid noticing, in retrospect, that Sue's ambivalence about work versus the domestic sphere marked my own life. At first reading, Bill's possessiveness probably charmed me more than I noticed Sue's reluctance. I imagined my life would be lived out as my mother's, except that I would get a BA in English or history rather than a nursing degree. Then I would marry a doctor or a professor and run a household, read, rear children, and read some more.

But the lure of interesting work was not possible to dismiss entirely. I remember, while attending a theatre conference in New York as a high-school student, writing to my boyfriend that I was thinking of becoming a theatre critic. He replied in the tones of Bill Barry, telling me I would do no such thing. I was to be his wife and the mother of his children. In the style of 1961, I thought it was adorable.

In 1963, when Betty Friedan's *The Feminine Mystique* was published, I argued against its thesis with my best friend. Rearing children while keeping house, I insisted, was not the dreary, unchallenging life that Friedan painted. But three years later, engaged and enrolled in a PhD program, I had gone over to the other side. Or, more accurately, I had embraced both sides. I was confident I could get a PhD, read to my children every night, cook gourmet dinners from the newly published Julia Child's maddeningly complex recipes, and in general lead my life as a paragon. If I had reread *Neighborhood Nurse* and *Staff Nurse* then, I would have scoffed at Sue's dilemma and at Boylston's ambivalence. Surely, Sue could manage nursing, husband, and children …

Predictably, my Superwoman period proved impossible to sustain. My husband and I, reared by two stay-at-home mothers, hadn't a clue how to build a home without a dedicated "wife." As we were separating, my husband remarked that a marriage probably couldn't endure two demanding careers. At that, Bill Barry would probably have looked thoughtfully down his long legs, adjusted his pipe, and nodded agreement.

Strange how potent cheap music is.
— Noel Coward, *Private Lives*

Wendy Lesser called her new book about rereading *Nothing Remains the Same*. The triangular relationship between three doctor's daughters — Sue, Helen Dore Boylston, and me — also shifts in time. Sue is the most constant of the three, though even she evolves from book to book. Boylston is the most enigmatic, because there are significant gaps in my knowledge of her. Did she ever want to marry? Why did she resume the series in 1949? Did she change her mind about the fullest life for Sue? Chances are I'll never know the answers to those questions. As for me, there is no single, stable reader of Sue Barton. Each time I open one of the books, I put on my current spectacles.

These days I read *Sue Barton, Neighborhood Nurse* and *Sue Barton, Staff Nurse,* the last two books, as social documents, smiling fairly affectionately at their less than subtly conveyed values. To my surprise, I also read them now with considerable emotion. Like the potency of cheap music, certain contrived scenes can bring a lump to my throat.

I'm still bemused that under-twelve-year-old girls would have wanted to read novels about a married woman in her thirties with children, doing a little part-time nursing — almost as if they were transitional reading between children's books and *McCall's,* the 1950s "magazine of togetherness." On the phone last summer with the children's librarian, I asked her about that, and she said, "That's just what happened in the series books. The heroines got older."

Not necessarily — Nancy Drew never gets beyond sixteen or eighteen — but Boylston allowed Sue to age, and her readers followed her into matronhood. I certainly did, but then I also read my mother's *Good Housekeeping, Better Homes and Gardens,* and *Vogue,* prepping, as it were, for the future. It's true that Boylston writes a miserable teenager, Cal, into *Neighborhood Nurse,* and a lovelorn young nurse, Margot, into *Staff Nurse,* for those readers who needed a girl with whom to identify, but Sue remains firmly front and centre.

Neighborhood Nurse has the only cover in the series where Sue appears hatless. Instead of a hospital, slums, or visiting nurse car in the background, there's a white clapboard house with green shutters. The book hails from a lost world, where doctors smoke and children ride without seat belts, where old hospital patients get an ounce of whisky at 4 P.M. and the children's ward moves for the summer into tents on the hospital grounds. It is also a hymn to family values, vintage 1949. I think of it as "The Motherhood Book." As the jacket copy explains, "This Sue Barton story tells how Sue discovered the importance of her own job" — wife to Dr. Barry and mother of Tabitha, age six, and the four-year-old twins, Johnny and Jerry.

Before Sue reconciles herself to her job, she goes to a reunion of her nursing class in Boston, experiencing again the hospital's "familiar smell of ether and scorched cloth," and worrying that she is wasting her precious training. When she explains to Miss Matthews, the principal of the nursing school, that she isn't doing much nursing because she thinks "it's a mother's business to look after her children herself," Miss Matthews catches the note of apology. Assuring Sue that "bringing up children is a matter of the highest importance," she continues, "We're always delighted when we find our graduates using their training to its fullest advantage. An intelligent, skilled nurse has a great deal to give motherhood."

That eases Sue's guilty conscience some, but not as much as the visit she and Kit make to the newfangled children's ward, where a small patient reminds her of Tabitha. She manages to soothe and encourage the entire ward with a story about how their mothers are at home, missing them. (This is one of the scenes where, fully aware of its hackneyed and manipulative quality, I tear up on cue.) Looking at the children's newly bright, relieved faces, the head nurse says, "You know, Mrs. Barry, *you* ought to be running a children's ward." She is, Kit tells her, and Sue adds, "But it's an old-fashioned one."

Nearly all the remaining fifteen chapters centre on minor miracles worked by Sue: a bit of extemporaneous nursing or social work, the discovery that her fractious son, Jerry, has an awesome musical talent that needs expression, a successful appeal to a rich person to support the local school. Even the chapter titles indicate that this is a book about a red-haired Angel in the House: "Pure Sentiment," "Home Again," "Helpmeet," "Mrs. Barry Is Most Kind," "Other People's Business." The last chapter is titled "Sue Is Not Satisfied." Still not convinced she is doing enough, she roots herself even more firmly in the home with the announcement of another pregnancy.

But before that, there is much rumination about motherhood and femininity. When Sue appeals to a rich woman to employ a widower so that he can hire a housekeeper for his children, the woman wonders why he can't take care of them himself. Sue tells her, "A man isn't equipped by nature to spend all his energies out-thinking children twenty-four hours a day."

But nature is not always reliable. Opposed to Sue is the Bad Mother, an artist named Mona Stuart who assigns her daughter's upbringing to an employee. When Tabitha meets Mona Stuart, she says, out-of-the-mouths-of-babes, "You don't seem like a mother. You don't take care of Cal, do you?" When Mona Stuart protests that the housekeeper is better at raising Cal, Tabitha tells her it's not the same, that Cal hates not having a real mother, and that she, Tabitha, has a wonderful mother. At this treacly moment, Sue swoops in, saves the day, and banishes Tabitha — but nicely, and only after the child requests, and gets, a hug. In the end, more than a little unrealistically, Sue reconciles Mona Stuart to the necessity of being a "real mother," and Cal finds happiness. Although Sue operates on her superb instincts, it is Bill (a surgeon, not a psychiatrist) who advises her on child development and who turns out to be right in the end.

All this sounds like the worst of the 1950s. I won't try to deny that, and yet at some level it *works,* at least with me at the turn of the twenty-first century. Partly it's because even when Boylston tips into propaganda, there's something too intelligent or perhaps too fair about her to render it completely in black and white. Both Tabitha and Sue, for example, as well as the faraway art world, thrill to Mona Stuart's paintings. Tabitha has walked into her studio uninvited just before the scene quoted above, and Boylston's description of a six-year-old looking at her first fine paintings demonstrates that, even if the artist has something to learn in the motherhood department, the work she does is exceptional.

Neighborhood Nurse also succeeds as well as it does because Sue, however perfect, is so unpious, so wry, so willing to laugh at herself. After a disastrous attempt to introduce the shy Cal to the local teenagers, she tells Bill, "Next time remind me to stay at home and edge the dish towels with tatting." But at a deeper level, I respond to the idyll — the happy, stay-at-home mother in the big white house, always available to decipher a tantrum, devise a picnic, haul an errant twin in from the roof. An impossible picture, but clearly one with a strong draw for someone who grew up with a nurse-mother who ran a big grey clapboard house for her doctor-husband and five children. I now see that the Barrys were an idealized, much wittier version of my own parents, just as I now accept that the medical background struck more chords than I realized in the 1950s, or even in the summer of 2001. The hospital is, after all, part of the Ashenburg family romance.

The family romance continues, only now my father has become the nurse. The wife whose Phi Beta Kappa key he pointed to proudly (his marks were never as high as hers) and the mother who sewed my midnight-blue velvet dress has Alzheimer's. These days my father cooks and cleans for her, doles out her pills, chooses her outfit for the day, makes sure she uses shampoo when she goes to wash her hair — the kind of age-old, compassionate care Sue Barton gave her patients.

So, my mother's situation gives me another reason to appreciate *Neighborhood Nurse*. But even without that motive, I warm to it now because the life it describes was a good idea. Or perhaps a good dream. The picture of family life Boylston paints, with all her ambivalence, tugs at my heart. For my mother, the choice to stay home seems to have been relatively uncomplicated; for Sue, more complicated, and even more so for me.

For many women of my generation, whichever decision was made was tinged with regret — faint or strong. Regret of some sort is probably inevitable — and no bad thing — when it comes to balancing two such fundamental things as serious work and child raising. Perhaps second thoughts come more easily in your mid-fifties — the age I am now and that Helen Dore Boylston was when she wrote the last two *Sue Bartons*. I say that without wanting to redo my daughters' childhoods with a working mother, and aware of how loaded and complicated — and unearned — any endorsement of full-time parenting would be from me.

And it's not at all clear how fully Helen Dore Boylston endorsed it. In the last of the series, she sacrifices Bill's health to get

162

Sue, now the mother of Baby Sue along with the twins and Tabitha, back on the wards. But Bill recovers. At the end of the book, before Sue knows about his release from the sanatorium, he has a conversation with Kit. She assures him Sue will quit her job on his return. He asks if staying home will be enough for her.

"I don't know," Kit said honestly. "After all, that's up to her — and you."

"It's up to her," Bill said.

And there, after a final scene of Bill's happy return to domestic mayhem, the matter rests.

MATTHEW HART

Stealing Vermeer

ON A BRIGHT JUNE DAY IN 2001, TWO MEN BOUNCED a Nissan Pajero up the front steps of an Irish mansion called Russborough House and smashed the door from its hinges. As alarm bells rang, the men pulled hoods over their heads, dashed inside, and snatched a pair of oil paintings from the walls. One was a little Gainsborough. It seemed a bold act, even a bit dazzling, and yet the robbers were not exactly breaking new ground. In art-theft terms, Russborough had become something of a corner store — already knocked off twice by thieves who grabbed a lot more than the latest ones.

For thirty years Russborough House was home to one of the richest private art collections in the world. It included works by Rembrandt, Rubens, Hals, Gainsborough, Goya, and Vermeer. Vermeers are among the most valuable objects made by humans; their rarity — there are only twenty-five Vermeer paintings known to exist — drives the valuations up into the hundreds of millions of dollars. So in the earlier robberies of Russborough, it was the Vermeer that came to stand for the importance of the crimes. The pillage of Russborough, then, bears the tranquil, radiant face of a Vermeer.

The Russborough Vermeer was *Lady Writing a Letter with Her Maid*. A woman sits at a table intent upon her task. The maid stands

165

behind her mistress, gazing out into the murderously clear light that Vermeer has poured through the window. God knows what she is thinking, for her face reveals nothing. At first glance the maid's composure, and that of the letter writer too, suggests that we are witnessing a moment of untroubled domesticity; but upon study the scene suggests great tension only just held in check. The two women share some knowledge that they are not speaking of. It seemed to me, when I first visited Russborough to write about it in 1990, that the picture and the house were perfect parallels: apparently serene, yet crackling with some veiled menace.

That feeling was stronger when I returned to Russborough in January 2002. I prowled around in front of the old mansion on a wet, January morning before the house was awake. The dark, lichen-covered stone of the south front looked as if it had been set in place when the land itself was born. This mood of calm antiquity was jarred by the sheet of unpainted plywood still nailed across the smashed-in door. I turned my back on the great façade and faced the way that Russborough faced — across a long meadow dotted with sheep to the bare mountains that rose in the distance, mountains famous the length and breadth of Ireland as the haunt of thieves.

The contest between Irish criminals and police belongs to a tradition of brigandage that stretches back through Irish history. The most famous old-Irish poem, sometimes called Ireland's *Iliad,* is "The Cattle Raid of Cooley." The poem appeared in written form in the eighth century, but its oral roots reach back as far as the second century and tap into real events. Clearly, the business of Irish kings was always to rob other Irish kings. When Norman invaders arrived in the twelfth century, their purpose was to rob the Irish, and the Irish robbed them back. The long struggle against English rule continued the chronicle of raiding. Viewed against this pageant of malfeasance, the Russborough robberies look less like simple crimes and more like the natural activity of time.

The grey granite palace of Russborough House lies in a valley by the Wicklow Mountains. Often called the most beautiful house in Ireland, Russborough spreads itself upon a celestial park that glows with the emerald green of the Irish countryside. I first saw it from a distance, rounding a bend in the road and suddenly viewing the house a mile away. Its sheer princeliness takes your breath away, as it was meant to. Built in the eighteenth century by a family of rich Dublin brewers who had been recently ennobled, Russborough was to represent their apotheosis. The house and its wings are in the Palladian style then in the forefront of aristocratic taste. The interiors shine with inlaid floors, and the lavishly decorated ceilings are the work of the Italian stucco masters, the Lafrancini brothers. Vast, marble fireplaces rear up in the principal rooms. If fate put her fingers into Russborough in those early days, it was in the matter of the fireplaces, because they are what first attracted the attention — long, long after the brewers had faded into history — of a British millionaire, Sir Alfred Beit.

Sir Alfred had been leafing through architecture magazines looking for ideas for a fireplace for his London home when he came across a picture of one of Russborough's marble glories. It was just what he wanted, and he commissioned a replica. Later, in 1952, while scouting around for a suitable home for his art collection, he discovered that Russborough itself was for sale and bought it. Sir Alfred was the inheritor of a nineteenth-century diamond fortune, and he had added to the art collection already begun by the founder of that fortune, his uncle. By the time he bought Russborough, Sir Alfred's collection had reached a size and importance that would turn the head of any thief.

All this, then, got crated up and shipped across the Irish Sea. Along with it went a treasure in silver, bronze sculpture, and antique furniture. The great lode arrived in Ireland, was transferred into trucks, passed through Dublin, and threaded its way into the lanes of Wicklow until it came to Russborough. There they unpacked it all, moved in, and settled down. It makes you wonder. At the time this treasure was probably worth one hundred million dollars, and there it was, in a drafty old house in the middle of a country with a second-to-none reputation for banditry. Not only that, the Beits were *English*. The amazing thing is that the crooks were not parked along the road with their engines idling. Yet Sir Alfred and Lady Beit lived peacefully at Russborough for twenty-two years before people started robbing them.

The first theft got underway on a warm spring night in 1974, when a maroon Ford Cortina station wagon drove out of County Kildare into neighbouring Wicklow and took the road for the village of Blessington. Three of the people in the car were IRA gunmen, and the fourth, the leader, was a thirty-four-year-old British heiress, medical doctor, and guerrilla groupie named Rose Dugdale. Their mission was to raise funds for the purchase of weapons by the IRA. When they reached Blessington, they turned south and drove two miles to their destination — Russborough House.

At Russborough, the conspirators parked in the shadows of a row of limes. They took out knives, a coil of rope, some cardboard tubes, and a spool of electrician's tape. They kept close to a line of outbuildings as they approached the house, then walked briskly across the gravel forecourt, up the steps, and disabled the antiquated alarm. Sir Alfred and Lady Beit had stayed up late. They were reading in the library when Dugdale and the others walked in, ordered them to sit on the floor, tied them up, and gagged them. The raiders took nineteen pictures, including a Rembrandt, a Gainsborough, a little Rubens, various Italian masters of the quattrocento, and the Vermeer. They rolled up the pictures and stuffed them into tubes, walked out the front door and across the court, got in their car and sped away.

Dugdale was captured eight days later in a cottage in Glandore, Cork, caught in a net cast over the whole of County Cork by a police commander named Ned Hogan. Dugdale went to Limerick jail for nine years and the pictures went to the National Gallery of Ireland to be checked for damage. They were fine, except for the Vermeer.

"It's just that it was very dirty," said Andrew O'Connor, the gallery's keeper of conservation. We were sitting in the top-floor conservation studio, under a huge skylight. O'Connor is a suave man with swept-back white hair and a confident manner. He learned his craft in Rome, and he is famous for discovering a Caravaggio in the dusty attic of a Dublin boys' school. At the time he was already famous for another discovery — the one he made with the Russborough Vermeer.

"I said to the Beits, why don't we clean it? And they told me to go ahead. So I put it up here," he said, tapping the big drafting table where he sat, "and started to have a go at the grime. The picture had never been cleaned, so there were three hundred years of accumulated dirt. I cleaned away and I cleaned away, and then I started to see the shape of something white on the floor, and I concentrated on that and then finally it came out — the letter!"

O'Connor had discovered a crumpled letter in the foreground, which art historians had not known about until that moment. The discovery revolutionized the reading of the picture. In Dutch society of the seventeenth century, where paper was a precious commodity and letters were important communications, the fact that this particular letter had been scrunched up and tossed to the floor must point to great emotion, most likely rage. As scholars see the painting now, it depicts a woman who has received a letter from her lover, possibly breaking off their affair, and in a controlled frenzy she is dashing off her reply. The maid knows everything. The picture that O'Connor sent back to Russborough had become a very different vessel from the one that had been stolen, for it now contained a narrative boiling with human emotion. You might say that it was the robbery, itself a violent act, that revealed the painting's interior violence.

But Dugdale's robbery left behind much more than valuable art-historical information. It also left the story of a bravura deed, irresistibly tinged with the fight for Irish liberty. That was just Dugdale, of course, and her ideals. The message sent to the world at large by her exploit, as it turned out, was that Russborough could be opened like a can of peas. Enter Martin Cahill.

In the 1980s Martin Cahill was the leading criminal in Ireland. He was a heap of oddities — short and fat, often hooded in public, his clothes a wrinkled, greasy mess. He was vicious and compassionate by turn, legendary for his cleverness and for the military precision of his greatest crimes.

I picture Cahill filing the news of Dugdale's exploit carefully away in his mind, reserving it for a future date. He was to wait twelve years. We now know that once he decided to rob Russborough, Cahill — "The General" to the Irish press — studied the house for a full year, driving out from Dublin and joining groups of tourists as they trooped through the rooms with guides. He may have had trouble believing that Russborough was as unprotected as it looked. After all, it was stuffed with art, especially the Vermeer. Stories in the press had placed the value of the Vermeer at fifty million dollars — absurdly low, as it would turn out. Only one other Vermeer in the world remained in private hands; it belonged to Queen Elizabeth.

Like Dugdale before him, Cahill chose a May night. His men stole several vehicles, fitting them with false licence plates. They drove out of Dublin by different routes, some of them going down the seashore to Bray and cutting through the Wicklow Mountains.

One car took the N7 to the town of Naas and came in behind the slumbering palace. Others came straight from Dublin on the N81, which runs through Blessington and past the estate.

As was his custom, Cahill directed cars to be stationed at the ready at stipulated points in the vicinity of the target. If discovered and pursued, the robbers could abandon one vehicle for another. Nothing suggests that Cahill was in a hurry as he laid his plans. Everything points to the scrupulous deliberations of a virtuoso schemer. Martin Cahill took his time, and when at last he came to Russborough on the night of May 21, 1986, Sir Alfred's pictures were as good as gone.

The road the robbers used runs above and behind the house, a half-mile from the main road. I drove up there one day for a look. It's not much more than a narrow lane between stone walls. You come to a gate on the Russborough side. I pulled over and slogged through mud to check it out; it was on a chain but not locked. That's the way they went in. There would have been about a dozen of them — drivers, mechanics, men for the alarms, and "blaggers." Blaggers are the roughnecks. In a bank robbery, for example, the blaggers go into the bank and terrify people so they don't go pressing buttons.

The men came down through a stand of beech and oak. They planted wire stakes and flagged them with strips of white plastic torn from shopping bags, marking the way for the jeep to return when they were through. A quarter-mile from the house, the woods gave way to pasture. The robbers picked their way through a herd of cows, flagging the pasture as they went. They crossed the fence that separates the meadow from the lawn. All the windows on that side of the mansion were black; the house was sound asleep. At 2 A.M. the raiders reached the broad steps of the north front, went up, and smashed a window in the tall French doors. Immediately bells began to ring inside the house.

Two things happened at once: the alarm roused the sole staff member in the house that night — Lieutenant Colonel Michael O'Shea, a retired army officer, Russborough's administrator. At the same moment, the alarm went off in the Garda station at Naas, a town on the Limerick road. Colonel O'Shea tumbled out of bed, according to his own account, and made an immediate inspection of the house, hurrying through every room. He found nothing missing. As recorded in police reports, he called the Garda at Naas and told them all was well. Nevertheless, as the *Irish Times* reported, "two Gardai from the local substation at Baltinglass went to Russborough House as a precautionary measure. The two Gardai, however, do not appear to have actually entered the house and were apparently reassured by Colonel O'Shea's belief that it was a false alarm."

This account has holes wide enough to drive a Nissan jeep through. How could anyone have missed the broken window in the door? Obviously, they did not miss it. How could a broken window be construed as a false alarm? Why did Colonel O'Shea offer this plainly wrong opinion, and why did the Gardai accept it?

O'Shea claimed that he reset the alarm and went back to bed. The Beits were in London. The thieves swept through the mansion. There is no evidence that they were in a hurry. Nothing was knocked over. The carpets lay unrumpled as before. No alarm was ringing.

"Yes, that alarm business is a bone of contention," Detective Inspector Christy McCafferty told me in Dublin. Although he had retired by the time we spoke, McCafferty had been a lead investigator on the Russborough robbery. "If the alarm was reset," he said, "why didn't it go off?"

Colonel O'Shea came to the attention of the authorities again five months after the Russborough robbery, when Lady Beit, searching her premises for some discarded statuary that she had decided to restore, failed to find it. In fact, it was no longer there, the colonel having packed it off to auction sometime after the robbery. He had shared the proceeds with the gardener, but not with the Beits. According to the colonel's "gut feeling," as he later shared it with the Dublin Circuit Criminal Court, the marbles had been his own property because he discovered them in a shed. Lady Beit claimed to have been furious when she confronted the colonel.

"For a moment or two he was quite speechless," she told the court. "He said something like, 'The statues were here,' and then blurted out, 'They were in the way, so I organized that they should be thrown into Lake Poulaphuca.' To which I replied, 'Well then, get them back from Lake Poulaphuca.' I was very angry."

The jury could not agree what happened, and the colonel went free. Nothing was proved against him in that or any other matter. What happened to the Russborough alarms remains firmly in the theatre of conjecture — another little knot in the rippling banner of Irish crime. All we know for sure is that Cahill's men swept through the mansion and took eighteen works, including two Rubens, a Rembrandt, a Goya, a Hals, a Gainsborough, and the most valuable picture on any wall in Ireland — Vermeer's *Lady Writing a Letter with Her Maid*.

Although many great pictures went out the door that night and back up through the pasture, the Vermeer forms the true heart of the story. Among old-master paintings Vermeers are rare. Rembrandt made some six hundred pictures in his lifetime; Vermeer made thirty-six. Moreover, a public appetite for Vermeer has exploded into being, catapulting the painter into the superstar ranks of art. In the last decade, his work has inspired a feature film, *All the Vermeers in New York;* blockbuster shows at the National Gallery in Washington, D.C., and the Metropolitan Museum in New York; and a best-selling novel, *The Girl with the Pearl Earring.*

The Beit Vermeer is a classic of the so-called genre pictures that form the heart of Vermeer's work. In a 2001 review of Anthony

Bailey's *Vermeer: A View of Delft,* the *New York Times* said that it was easy to understand the place these pictures had made for themselves in the modern heart: "At once dreamlike and real, elliptical and quotidian, Vermeer's luminous canvases freeze and magnify time … daily life is stripped of its clutter and noise, the commonplace transformed into something stiller and more serene." Everything is rendered with exquisite clarity. We can almost feel the texture of the carpet covering the table where the lady sits writing her letter. The world outside the window — how perfect it must be to be flooded with that light! Vermeer's flawless lines of perspective lead us here and there about the room, and extend from the picture to the wider world, into which, on that May night, the painting itself slipped away.

Now one of the great stalking matches of crime got underway. The Garda knew within days who had robbed the Beits. Yet not a scrap of evidence turned up to support their certainty. The boldest robbery since Dugdale's had gone off within an hour's drive of Dublin, and the Garda had no leads. The cry went up to recover the paintings. In fact, the Garda already had some, because Cahill's men had jettisoned seven pictures by the side of the road not far from Russborough. This rough treatment (the art was lying in a ditch) sparked fears for the fate of the rest. The police top command put a mass of detectives into the field. They found nothing. The usual pool of informants had dried up. There was only one criminal with this control of the underworld. The Garda never had the slightest doubt that Martin Cahill had the pictures, and soon the whole of Ireland knew it. The news flowed down that pipe that passes from police to press, into the reporters' pubs, and from there to every bar in the republic.

Cahill had an unrivalled place in the chronicle of public gossip. He was born in 1949 in a squalid tenement on the north side of the

Liffey. His passions were motorcycles, pigeons, curries, and cake. He was ruthless but said to have a gentle manner. He spoke with a soft Dublin brogue. He loved his wife and his wife's sister, and saw no reason not to have both. He did not drink or smoke or take drugs. He was slovenly, cruel, loyal, suspicious, immovable, and bold. He once robbed a bank on his way to court, knocking it off at 10:55 A.M. and presenting himself at the bar of justice eight minutes later, only slightly late.

Cahill was lionized in certain quarters, where his apparent untouchability and his open mocking of the Garda made him a folk hero. Others saw him differently — a semi-literate ruffian whose robberies, while spectacular, netted him far less than those of other gangs. He was, said a senior Gardai, "an ignorant, stupid bastard." Yet he was their nemesis. A year after the Russborough robbery, the Garda had their best shot at Cahill: a sting operation set for a remote location in the Wicklow Mountains. Cahill accepted the bait — a Dutch policeman posing as a buyer — and arrived for the rendezvous. But a flaw in the Garda's radio communications prevented the Dutchman from delivering the necessary signal, and Cahill escaped. The great theft remained a blot on the Garda for five years, until a soft-spoken man named Liam Hogan stepped onto Cahill's trail.

Liam Hogan is the son of Ned Hogan, the Garda commander who tracked down Rose Dugdale when she stole the Beit paintings in 1974. Ned Hogan got them back in a week. Now those same pictures had been missing, not for a week, but for five years. When Liam Hogan took over the Russborough investigation in 1991, his burning ambition was to trap and to bring down Martin Cahill, and to restore the treasure that his father had won back almost two decades before.

By the time I met him in January 2001, Hogan had become a middle-aged spy, a detective in the Garda's secretive Special Branch.

His private e-mail address contained the digits "007," the famous code for Ian Fleming's fictional hero, James Bond. It was Hogan's little joke. Unlike Bond, spies employed by the Irish state do not jet around the world festooned with women; they stay in Ireland and watch the IRA.

Hogan is of average height and weight, with a thatch of curly, light brown hair. He has a blue, unblinking gaze and signs of tiredness beneath the eyes. You might not notice this if you walked by, because you might not notice Hogan. He has a talent for observing while not being observed. I had an appointment with him at 2:30 P.M. in the lobby bar of Dublin's Westbury Hotel. I had his description, even down to the coat he would be wearing — tweed, herringbone, black and white. I came out of the elevator ten minutes early and stood where the marble staircase comes up from the ground floor into the hotel's reception area. I studied the big lounge, sofa by sofa and chair by chair. I carefully searched the traffic of people through the lobby. There was not a trace of Hogan until I decided to move into the bar to wait for him, at which point, as I threaded the tables, he appeared beside me. We shook hands and sat down and ordered tea and Irish scones. I watched him slicing them open and slathering on butter and jam, and remembered that Hogan had my description as I had his. He must have stood there watching me as I scoured the place for him.

While a piano tinkled aimlessly nearby, we settled down to discuss the string of botched operations that had humiliated the Garda for six years as it struggled to outwit The General in the wake of 1986. In one spectacular example, an FBI agent named Tom Bishop, based in Baltimore, flew into Dublin posing as a Mafioso who wanted to buy the pictures. Cahill's men met him at the airport and took him into the city. Bishop had a reputation in the FBI as a born performer, which is why they'd picked him. Soon he and Cahill's men were all drinking and swapping stories, and Bishop decided to bring out the "proof" of his identity — snapshots dummied up by the FBI that pictured Bishop with John Gotti and other known gangsters. The Irishmen were eagerly pawing through the snaps of famous crooks when a single piece of white paper dropped out of the photographs. It was a note, of a type that policemen call a "confidence slip." This one had the FBI logo printed at the top, and in clear handwriting beneath was the scrawled reminder "Tom, don't forget these." As Bishop later told a London colleague, "They gave me a long hard look and excused themselves."

The Garda had had only one success against Cahill in the Beit case — when they uncovered an attempt to broker a painting by Vermeer's contemporary, Gabriel Metsu. Cahill's middlemen were soldiers of the Ulster Volunteer Force, a Northern Ireland loyalist militia. Detectives tracked the Metsu — *Young Man Writing a Letter* — as it moved from Dublin to Belfast, Belfast to London, London to Istanbul, when they finally blew the whistle and sent Turkish police crashing into a hotel room to find the picture changing hands.

This meagre victory highlighted the Garda's larger failure. The need to break Cahill became a fixation of the higher command. Cahill flaunted his scorn for the Garda by wearing a Mickey Mouse T-shirt, and going in and out of his house in a balaclava. Detailing more men to watch the criminal, the Garda sat on him so heavily that his business finally began to falter. He missed a string of mortgage payments on his house and faced foreclosure. "So he went in [to the mortgage office] with nineteen thousand pounds in cash and got a receipt," said Hogan, "and ten minutes later two guys showed up on a motorbike and robbed it back."

Stung, the Garda piled on a crushing surveillance. If you had driven by Cahill's house in the Dublin suburb of Cowper Downs in 1991 and 1992, you would have seen Gardai sitting in their cars, openly watching the house. No member of his family, no visitor, could arrive or leave by car without a drawn-out check of documents. Cahill took evasive measures. His only extravagance in life had been his Harley-Davidson motorcycle, and he now used it to shake off Garda tails. At this time Hogan was a member of the shadowy T squad — a tactical section attached to the Garda's Central Detective Unit (CDU) at Harcourt Square in central Dublin. His boss was Detective Superintendent Noel Conroy, an officer renowned for both a titanic appetite for work and a savage pleasure in it. "Yes," said Conroy with a wolfish smile when I asked him about the motorcycle, "we put a stop to that, though, didn't we. I put a young lad on an 1100-cc Honda, and next thing you know your man Cahill lost it on a corner, and that was the end of that."

Cahill trashed more than his bike. The injuries he sustained trying to outrun the young Garda further restricted his ability to act, and his criminal business withered. The money represented by the Beit pictures gained in importance. It was crucial that he find a buyer.

By late 1992 Noel Conroy had become the detective chief superintendent in charge of anti-terrorism and moved to the sprawling Garda headquarters at Phoenix Park. Conroy's promotion meant that Hogan was no longer under his command, yet it was to Conroy that Hogan turned when he learned through a criminal source that an attempt was underway to broker four Beit pictures, including the Vermeer.

"I went to Conroy with the information and laid it all out and said, 'Let's do a sting,' and he supported that."

Conroy arranged wiretaps against the subjects Hogan had identified. Hogan moved from Harcourt Square to Phoenix Park. In effect, he set up a unit consisting of two — himself and Conroy. He reported to no one else. "I wanted to keep it tight at the time. You have to be fierce tight, because there'd be other units trying to claim it."

What Hogan meant was that the importance of the Beit pictures — the shame felt by the Irish police in the face of The General's contempt, and the massive political credit that would accrue to anyone breaking the case — guaranteed a furious competition among Garda units if Hogan's information leaked. The CDU would try to scoop the Special Branch; the Special Branch would tail the T squad; the T squad would lie to the CDU. The counter-intelligence that policemen perform against each other is the inescapable product of life in the ambit of the criminal world, where the line between lawkeeper and lawbreaker is not always clear. But if Hogan had to guard his secrets, it was nothing compared to what Cahill faced. "They betray each other all the time," Hogan said of the Dublin gangsters. "It's the first thing a man will do when he's caught."

Inhabiting this treacherous world, Cahill took pains to vaccinate himself against betrayal. He compartmentalized his jobs, inserting need-to-know barriers throughout the chain of command. He had unbreakable alibis — he was often nowhere near his crimes as they went down. But finally Hogan got a break. In October 1992, an agent tripped across a lead, and the wiretaps went on. Soon Hogan was listening in on a genial Dublin rogue named Niall Mulvihill.

Now things picked up. Mulvihill was careful, but not careful enough. Possibly his background had not hardened him as Cahill's had. Mulvihill came from a prosperous Dublin family, had idled his way through expensive schools, bought a pub, and drifted, with his sunny disposition, into associations that brought him into Cahill's orbit. Hogan discovered that Mulvihill had approached Cahill with an offer to broker the sale of the Beit pictures. Cahill had agreed. Mulvihill, with the Garda listening in, began to fish for buyers. He found one in England.

That it was taking Cahill so long to fence the goods proves an important point: he was a thief, certainly, but not an *art* thief.

Professional art thieves do not steal top paintings. They take less-well-known work, where provenance is not so firmly established. In most countries, good faith must be credibly asserted by a purchaser hoping to legally retain possession of a work subsequently proven to be stolen. With the Beit pictures, such an assertion would be laughable. This fact precludes the sale of such art to legitimate collectors. There is an urban legend that posits the existence of the rogue billionaire collector, usually resident in Argentina, who is besotted by some famous piece and commissions its theft. Art police reject this model. Instead, stolen famous art circulates into the underworld where it becomes collateralized, at a fraction of its value, as security for drug deals. This was probably what Mulvihill was aiming for.

As soon as Mulvihill made the English contact, Hogan heard it on the wiretap. He called Scotland Yard. The Irish paintings were among the most valuable stolen objects then at large in the world, and the British moved swiftly. Scotland Yard pounced on the Englishman and turned him: to avoid arrest he would act as a double agent. This brought another man into the story — Charley Hill. Hill was a member of Scotland Yard's art and antiques squad, and with an introduction from the turned English crook, would pose as a buyer for the stolen art. With Hill in place, Hogan's sting was on.

Hill is a tall, heavy-set man with curly, dark brown hair and thick-framed tortoiseshell glasses. His manner is affectionate and expansive. I met him several times in Ireland and at his home in London. He looks very English, with a silk puff ballooning extravagantly from his bright tweed jacket. But although Hill's mother is English, his father is American. Hill grew up in San Antonio, Texas, and fought in Vietnam, and his ability to sound like an American — for example, pronouncing Rs in the American way — gives him an edge in undercover work.

Throughout the spring and early summer of 1993, Liam Hogan nursed his operation. Cahill, always suspicious, distrusted Mulvihill and insisted on bringing in one of his lieutenants. Together, Mulvihill and Cahill's representative travelled to England, where they demanded from the putative buyer — Hill — a display of "show money." Such proofs are the credit checks of the criminal world — a briefcase filled with a stipulated amount of cash that the seller of goods may inspect before he commits himself. The Garda complied with the show-money demand, sending to England a briefcase stuffed with more than one and a half million pounds.

Hogan's sting played out over ten months. It ran an obstacle course of feints and missed meetings, of suddenly changed plans, of the intense suspicion of criminals alert for traps. The curtain went up on the final act on the morning of August 14, 1993, when Niall Mulvihill got into his red BMW and drove through the gates of his home in Dublin's Ballsbridge. With Garda surveillance teams tailing him all the way, Mulvihill crossed the River Liffey at Custom House Quay and drove north to the airport. He looked like any other businessman as he walked through the terminal in his dark suit, briefcase in hand, and boarded the 7:10 A.M. Aer Lingus flight to Brussels.

At the same time, three accomplices moved into place to support Mulvihill: an Irish national known to police got on a Brussels flight at London's Heathrow airport; another Irishman, already in Belgium, drove to the airport to meet his two compatriots; and a Yugoslav "heavy" — a bodyguard — drove up from Luxembourg to wait for the others in Antwerp. It was in Antwerp that the swap would happen.

"So there we were in Antwerp," Hill says, "and Mulvihill has this big Yugoslav bodyguard standing there cracking his knuckles, and his other guys are around, and he says, 'Do you want to see the Vermeer?' I said sure, and they took me to a car park in the diamond quarter and opened the trunk and there was the Vermeer." Hill paused. "There was no frame, no glass, and I picked it up and held it in my hands. I had no doubt it was the real thing. The only doubt I had was that they might knock me on the head and dump me into the trunk. But by then they'd decided I was the real thing."

Belgian undercover agents, meanwhile, were feeding details of this meeting back to Liam Hogan in Dublin. The most important detail was that the other paintings weren't there. The Vermeer was a "show" that they had the goods. To produce all of the paintings, they wanted a money show in return. This demand presented Hogan with a monstrous dilemma — should he order the agents to grab the Vermeer, or wait for the Irishmen to produce the other paintings? It is worth spelling out Hogan's predicament.

The theft of another Vermeer in Boston in 1990 had produced a much more realistic figure for the value of a Vermeer — three hundred million dollars. Moreover, the Beit Vermeer had become the property of the Irish state, having been gifted to the National Gallery of Ireland by Sir Alfred Beit. The legal work, in hand when the picture was stolen, was now complete. Next to the Book of Kells, the Vermeer was the single most valuable object owned by the Irish people, and it now lay in a trunk within easy grasp of Hogan. Adding to this pressure was the personal one that Hogan's father had tracked down the Vermeer and rescued it in 1974. If the painting slipped out of Liam Hogan's hands now, and he failed to get it back, the son would have lost what his father had won. Nevertheless, he let it go.

"I knew if I put it to Conroy he'd say 'Grab it,' so I didn't. We showed them the money, made a date for them to come back with the whole load, and let them drive off with the Vermeer."

Hogan had meant to tail them, but the Belgian watchers soon realized that the four were not alone. A fierce counter-surveillance had been thrown up around Mulvihill. Fearing that the criminals would spot continued surveillance, Hogan gave the order to cut the tail. The Vermeer vanished down the road.

In agony, Hogan waited. Mulvihill returned to Dublin. The second Irishman went back to London and the third to Brussels. Police shadowed them all. Luxembourg "minders" had the Yugoslav in sight. The date for the next meeting — August 28 — came and went. Mulvihill stayed put in Dublin. Hogan hardly left the office, and even when he went home he could not sleep. "The truth is, we weren't even a hundred per cent sure what country the paintings were in. I thought Luxembourg, but we didn't know."

At last, early on September 1, the conspirators alerted Hill that they were ready to trade. Hill told Hogan. Less than an hour later, Mulvihill drove out of his gate and headed for the airport. The exchange was set for Antwerp airport. As before, the Belgian police were in place.

It was a sunny morning, and Hill had dressed for the day in a suitably American seersucker suit. (He tapped the page where I was writing all this down, "and a really quite nice tie.") Promptly at noon three cars drove into the airport — Mulvihill and one of the Irishmen in one; the Brussels-based Irishman and the Yugoslav each in separate cars. Hill handed Mulvihill a briefcase full of cash. Back at Phoenix Park in Dublin, Liam Hogan was experiencing the last pangs of doubt as he waited to find out what was in the trunk. Hill and Mulvihill went outside and opened the trunk. Inside were the Vermeer, the Goya, a Metsu, and four fake Picassos, apparently thrown in as a gesture of goodwill. Hill says he grinned when he saw the Picassos, recognizing them immediately as fakes. He gave the signal, and the Belgians came screaming into the parking lot in a pair of 700-series BMW sedans, four cops in each.

"They were wearing their Miami Vice T-shirts and cotton sports jackets and were all tooled up with their Dirty Harry specials," Hill recalls. He was still technically undercover, so they grabbed him too and spread him on the ground and pushed his face against the pavement.

Within an hour the Irish prime minister was telling his country the Vermeer was safe. For this and other victories, Noel Conroy rose to deputy commissioner — the second-highest policeman in Ireland. The Central Detective Unit at Harcourt Square took credit for the bust, and Hogan let them. The rest of the pictures were recovered in related raids.

Mulvihill, the other Irishmen, and the Yugoslav were acquitted by a Belgian court on procedural grounds. Mulvihill returned to Dublin, where he still lives. Sir Alfred Beit died at Russborough in 1994, the same year that Martin Cahill was assassinated outside his home by members of a rival gang.

On a bright January day, just before I left Ireland, I went to look at the Vermeer with Andrew O'Connor, the National Gallery of Ireland's head conservator. We wandered through the handsome, enfiladed rooms in the old part of the gallery until we came to the Vermeer. "It was in pretty good shape when we got it back," O'Connor said. "All I did was put in that pane of glass."

O'Connor is modest about his famous discovery of the letter in the foreground, insisting that if he hadn't found it, someone else would have. In just the same way, he downplays his role in another remarkable breakthrough in Vermeer scholarship, which is the story he then told me.

As soon as word reached Dublin that the Vermeer had been rescued in Antwerp, the Garda called O'Connor. O'Connor immediately booked a flight to Belgium. Before he left Dublin he called Jorgen Wadum, a Vermeer scholar at the Mauritshuis Museum in The Hague, and invited Wadum to join him. Wadum jumped at the chance. They met the next day in the Antwerp museum and were shown to the basement. A guard admitted them to the small conservation room where *Lady Writing a Letter with Her Maid* awaited release by the Belgian courts.

Examining the painting, Wadum noticed a pinhole in the maid's left eye. He pointed it out to O'Connor. O'Connor replied that he already knew it was there; he'd seen it when he cleaned the painting nine years before. At the time he'd thought nothing of it, putting it down to a chance accident in the past. To Wadum, though, the pinhole meant something else. It confirmed his suspicion that Vermeer had achieved his remarkable perspective illusions by fastening chalk-covered strings to the canvas along the lines of perspective he wanted to emphasize. The painter had then snapped the strings against the surface, laying down a line of chalk to paint along as he organized the picture. Apparently, he had held his strings in place with pins stuck into the canvas!

After this discovery, Wadum went on to find other holes in other Vermeers, and he elaborated his theory of orthogonal lines that now helps students of Vermeer penetrate his craft, and that of other great perspective painters of the Dutch Golden Age. The story of these discoveries now forms part of the story of this Vermeer, just as the thefts form part of its story, contributing to the picture's allure and becoming what Arthur Wheelock Jr., the principal Vermeer scholar at the National Gallery in Washington, D.C., calls "part of the package."

It is somehow elating to stand in front of the Dublin Vermeer and think of all it has gone through in the last quarter-century — probably more than in its whole previous three hundred years. But my favourite anecdote is of two Irishmen, a father and son, standing before it at the fancy celebration held in 1994 to celebrate the painting's return.

"If they lose it again they can get it back themselves," said Liam Hogan to his father. Ned Hogan is said to have pondered this remark, and then amended it.

"If we get it back again," he said, "we keep it."

ELLEN VANSTONE

Post Traumatic Stress:

How I learned to stop worrying about Conrad Black's evil plan to destroy Canada's universal health-care system and love my job at the *National Post*

THIS IS HOW MY DAYS BEGAN. I'D DRIVE SOUTH TO DROP off my daughter at her public school. I'd park the car illegally, half on the sidewalk, walk my daughter to her Grade 2 classroom and suck up to her teacher for a few minutes. The teacher was one of those left-wing people who, when you said you worked at the *National Post,* felt compelled to mention that she didn't allow the *National Post* in her home, and that she quit teaching Grade 3 to teach Grade 2 because she objected to standardized Grade 3 testing implemented by *Post*-supported Progressive Conservative bastard Ontario premier Mike Harris. I'd smile back. Hey, thanks for making my daughter think her mother works for Charles Manson!

Then I'd drive to Starbucks for coffee and one of their flaky, fake croissants, the kind that explodes on impact all over the car, and I'd head east, stuffing my face, spilling scalding coffee, and cursing, because it was difficult to drive a cheap standard-transmission Hyundai in rush-hour traffic, but it was all I could afford as a single mother. Soon I'd be having my regular morning cry about all the bad things my ex did, and all the bad things everyone else did to me — me! a perfectly nice person who just wants to do the right thing!

By the time I hit the Don Valley northbound, I'd feel better — wipe my eyes, blow my nose, check my eyebrows in the rear-view mirror for croissant crumbs, and start to think about work. I had been an editor at the *National Post* for 2.3 years, which is the longest I've worked anywhere during my twenty years in journalism, which is strange, because the *Post* was a shrill, right-wing, patriarchal newspaper, and, even worse, it was in Don Mills, which means I had spent about a thousand hours of the past two years in traffic. Every day, I'd get into my car and think about two things: the character in *Repo Man* who says the more time you spend in a car, the stupider you get; and what an ass proprietor Conrad Black was to base a newspaper in Don Mills.

My job was to put out a double-page spread called Avenue each weekday, about "Arts, Culture & Society." I ran short articles and big pictures about artists, celebrities, books, fashion, science, politics, cartoons, games — anything, really — though most days I started out with no idea what to run, which used to put me in an absolute panic. But soon I realized it didn't matter. Something always came up. They weren't going to let me go to press with blank pages, right? My hour-long trip to work ended at York Mills, where I'd exit and pull up to the three-storey brick building that housed the evil empire of Conrad Black.

The 157-year-old *Globe and Mail* used to be the country's establishment, conservative paper until Black launched the *National Post* in October 1998. Compared with the good, grey *Globe,* Canada's "newspaper of record," the *Post* smashed onto the scene with a surprisingly effective package of opinionated writing, superb design, a British-style news approach (drunken lords, cats stuck in trees, Nazi history, tits and analysis), and headlines that made the paper's agenda crystal clear: "36% back two-tier health: poll" (as opposed to 64% against), or "Recycling mania: a lot of garbage," or "Be kind to the rich; they pay our bills."

I myself am more or less left-wing, that is, a sensible, intelligent, compassionate person who doesn't believe in sticking it to the poor so the rich can get richer, and I live in an apartment building where for two years the delivery man for the "nasty right-wing ideologues" of the *National Post* couldn't get past the front door. In fact, the superintendent who said this was simply annoyed because the *Post* people had lost the keys he had given them. But in the meantime, the *Globe* and *The Toronto Star* got delivered to individual apartments, while we *Post* subscribers had to traipse down to the foyer every morning. Not only was this inconvenient; it was embarrassing, because everyone could see my name clearly marked on one of the newspapers left there. I felt like telling people, "I'm not really a right-wing-nut subscriber; I *have* to get the *Post,* because I work there." Also, I wondered who the other three weirdos were in my building who subscribed to the *National Post* of their own free will.

I also, for a while, felt funny telling people I worked at the *Post*. I came from Winnipeg to attend journalism school in Toronto twenty years ago, and while I know doctors and computer programmers and normal people in Winnipeg, everyone I know here is in the media — mostly politically correct people who when they found out I was at the *Post* would ask in lowered tones, "What's it *really* like to work there?"

"Well, every day we burn an effigy of a poor person," I was tempted to answer, "and then Conrad gives us each — the women anyway — a spanking as an incentive to produce more stories that favour the rich, and we rub our bums gratefully and thank him for it."

But the truth is I never met Conrad Black. *Post* people were very nice and helpful; lots of them were smart and funny. Morale was good. The culture of the newsroom was still developing. It hadn't yet hardened into the indiscriminate antagonism and general bad faith that marked the *Globe* newsroom when I worked there four years earlier. Example: the gossip magazine *Frank* finds it next to impossible to get dirt from *Post* employees — possibly because the *Frank* fax machine is tied up all day with a steady stream of vitriolic, backstabbing missives from the *Globe*. So if you could avoid reading the newspaper itself, the *National Post* newsroom was a pleasant and interesting place to work. The only time I was really uncomfortable was at the morning news meeting.

It began at 11 A.M., when fifteen or so senior editors would troop into the boardroom and present their lineups for the next day's paper. There was coffee (the vile no-name kind — if they loved globalization so much, why didn't they get us Starbucks?). A wall of windows overlooked primo Don Mills scenery (parking lots and trees). One wall had five large photos of the *Post* newsroom as it was being built. The sixth picture had been smashed during a table tennis game in the ongoing newsroom round robin. (Note that the boardroom table is a ping-pong table.)

When I started editing Avenue, I thought the morning meetings would be fun, but people didn't get my jokes. Sometimes I pretended I was Honey, the serious short-haired girl in the Doonesbury cartoon, and I called editor-in-chief Ken "sir," as in "Of course, if you don't want the MIT Press reproduction of the Russian avant-garde poetry book on the Avenue page, I can certainly run some pictures from the cheerleading competition in Dallas, sir." I was being the good soldier, see, doing what was clearly expected in this male-oriented, market-worshipping, breast-obsessed newspaper. But after a few failed attempts at such knee-slapping irreverence, I played it straight, not that anyone noticed the difference.

The meetings went about half an hour, with the main players at the table and the rest of us standing, sitting on the windowsills, or slouching on the floor. We waited for Ken to enter from the special door that connects to his office. I spent most of the meetings trying to look as if I'd read the newspaper that day, but I usually ended up staring at shoes and speculating about sex lives. Ken, for example, wore expensive shoes, lace-up brogues in oxblood leather, very grown-up as opposed to the moccasins or Doc Martens or desert boots or runners or cowboy boots worn by the other males in the room. He was definitely heterosexual, boyishly attractive with his softly curling light brown hair and cheerful, wide-open face. His sex appeal, of course, was much enhanced by his position of power.

If I'd been editor, I suppose people would have looked at me, tried to read my mood, and worried about what I thought about them. They would have deferred to me and maybe wanted to have sex with me. But Ken had another layer of appeal sparked by the positive energy he gave off: he was *happy* to be boss. If you subscribe to the theory that people recreate their family in the workplace, and if the workplace was a patriarchal model like the *National Post,* then you might say Ken was the king, the benevolent dictator, the dad, the one the women wanted to have sex with (or at least flirt with or speculate about) and the men eventually wanted to eliminate. Meanwhile, as he sat back in his chair and put his feet up on the table, he was clearly comfortable at the top, which made the children feel secure. Occasionally, Ken seemed wilfully capricious in his decisions, killing stories or changing a section front at the last second. Personally, I never thought he was power tripping — for one thing, he didn't have the attention span.

In a quiet voice, Ken would go around the table and ask the different editors what they had. The answers would come back in half a dozen accents. A number of staff were brought over from the U.K., lured by high salaries, the adventure of a newspaper war, and the chance to score brownie points with Black, who also owned the *Daily Telegraph* in London, where they might land a cushy job after their tour of duty in the amateur-hour colonies.

The Scottish business editor talked about the stock market and mergers and takeovers in an impenetrable burr. I had no idea, ever, what he was talking about, but he was tall with big feet and therefore sexy. The politics editor was young and Irish, rather cuddly, but with a demented gleam in his eye as he described which politicians he was going to skewer that day, which made you think he'd be a mean sonofabitch on either side in Belfast, which was also rather sexy. The sports editor, a Labour-leaning Londoner who knew his lefty impulses would have him hanged in five minutes on news side, talked about Game 3 or 4 or, more important, something like Venus Williams's migrating brassiere. Typically for a sports editor, he was a sentimental marshmallow under a gruff exterior, and a lot smarter than he looked. If he weren't so shy, he could definitely get a gal into bed.

There were also a few women whose clothes were sometimes interesting, but none of them were as funny or forceful as the males, and I didn't really care about their sex lives. So, back to the men.

Deserving of special mention is the science editor, Gerald, a bespectacled intellectual who wore a moth-eaten yellow sweater and frantically bobbed his right shoulder up and down while telling us about plants that moved ("How fast?" "Well, I wouldn't ride one to work") or the latest philosophical position on sex with animals. Deputy editor Martin called Gerald the Nutty Professor, because he knew something about everything: history, tax law, Greek, Latin, American politics, archaeology, religion, art. ("OK, where are my car keys?" Ken asked him once during a stunned silence after Gerald had explained several unrelated arcane subjects in a row.)

I usually leaned against the wall at the back of the room behind Gerald so I could see what he had each day in the gaping right pocket of his ratty wide-wale corduroys — pens? a manuscript? toothbrush? a stapler? After a few months, Gerald became sexy too. I figure it was the newsroom equivalent of the Stockholm syndrome; you're imprisoned in a sealed environment in a strange country (or right-wing newspaper in the suburbs), and you fall in love with your captors.

The only editor I found sexually neutral was a Brit whose temples throbbed and who started spluttering and leaning back and throwing his hands up in the air whenever the talk turned to gays or communism. I'm not sure if that meant he was a latent homosexual or a latent commie, though I suppose it could have meant he just wasn't my type.

There was one guy in the room everyone found sexy: the aforementioned deputy editor, Martin. Martin led the meetings when Ken wasn't there, and sometimes he'd forget to ask what I was doing on Avenue, which was OK with me, because when it was finally my turn and I'd say something like "last-minute Halloween costumes" or "I've got, um, a collection of nurses' hats at a museum in the Maritimes," everyone would blank out and I would feel exposed as the corny, middle-aged, artsy-fartsy, bleeding-heart-liberal lady editor that I am. When baseball season opened, I presented an Avenue about the legendary Yankees uniform, with sidebars about other good and bad sports uniforms. "The question is," drawled Martin, "who fucking cares?" (I think he meant because baseball is so American and rugby and cricket are so much more interesting.)

Martin was Catholic, conservative, married with children, which sounds boring, but he had this animalistic energy. He'd sit at the head of the table, the boss's swarthily handsome henchman, with his short, dark hair, sleepy eyes, his thick neck and bulky muscles busting out of remarkably well-cut T-shirts. He was a sharp dresser, despite the double handicap of being British and a jock, but more like a lad than a grown-up, with his gigantic black boots, untucked shirts, and two-pound sports watch. He sometimes had a cigarette tucked behind one shell-like ear. He sometimes played with a large, shiny jackknife-type thing during the news meetings. His nails were always bitten to the quick. It was the first time in my life I understood why men behave like fools around a useless, stupid, but very sexy woman.

Not that Martin was stupid. He mumbled in a down-market British accent, as if he were in a Guy Ritchie film, though in fact he was an aristocrat from Argentina, educated in Britain and the U.S., and married to a clever lawyer (the daughter of high-class Belgians; he imitated his Belgian father-in-law for us — "Maw-teen, you haff breasts like a woo-man"). Supposedly, he at one point had studied to be a priest at a Jesuit seminary. He complained about recycling, the Germans, the bloody lefty wankers at the CBC, and he always wanted the *Post* to do a story about how fantastic it is in Canada that you can still be killed by a grizzly bear.

He mostly completely ignored me. Sometimes I wondered if it was because he was terribly attracted to me and didn't want to betray his desire, so he avoided looking at me or paying much attention to Avenue, and I imagined running into him somewhere, some day, and falling into a conversation in which he finally revealed his passionate feelings for me, but the conversation would initially have to be about politics and recycling so that I could convince him to change his reactionary ways, because I couldn't sleep with someone who believed in dismantling our health-care system — it would be too abusive to my self-esteem.

I wondered if Martin might be the exception to the rule in the who's-better-in-bed debate: left-wing boys versus right-wing boys. Admittedly, it's a spurious proposition, and I certainly would not claim any expertise in this area, and we're possibly getting off topic, but let me just say this. I once lived in a Marxist-Leninist commune, and to a man they were far more obsessed with bedding each and every female who lived on or visited the premises than with the tenets of Marx or Lenin, sharing the cooking, or admitting to their monogamous girlfriends that they were secretly pursuing the pleasures of a free-love approach to anything with a pulse. You might impugn their characters, their politics, their personal hygiene, but you had to admit they were a dedicated bunch of sack artists.

Right-wing boys seem more sanguine in their social pursuits. I offer my friend Tabatha's experience as an example. One of my Avenue freelancers, she was young, pretty, with pouffy blond hair and an enormous bosom. Alex, a *Post* writer who I think we can safely assume is a hundred per cent right-wing, judging by, say, the apologist article he wrote on Augusto Pinochet's behalf after the Chilean general was found unfit to stand trial, met Tabatha and asked her out on a date. She wanted to see *Gladiator*. "It's only the best movie ever made!" effused Alex. "Great," she said, "we can go on Friday." But, said Alex, puzzled, "I've already seen it." Poor Alex never did get to take Tabatha out, to a movie or anywhere else. "It's the greatest movie ever made? And he wouldn't go see it again with me?" said Tabatha, her blond curls bouncing, her prominent bosom heaving in pretty indignation. It does make a girl wonder.

But investigation of sexual habits on the right was not the reason I took a job at the *National Post*. It was in the spring of 1999 when I accepted a short-term contract to edit part-time in the weekend section. The money was good. I was curious about working on a brand new publication in a real live newspaper war. After my recent separation, I was too distracted to continue freelancing. And I thought it would be nice to meet new people, even if they were servants of the devil.

The arrangement was perfect. I came in three days a week and made a lot of personal calls. In my emotionally fragile state, I continued to be somewhat distracted (or drunk or hungover or in tears — or all three), but at least I had a place to go. Occasionally, I buckled down and edited a piece as requested by my boss, Harriet, formerly of the *Independent* in London. As it turned out, Harriet was getting me to edit pieces already handled by other sub-editors. So I'd edit a six-thousand-word piece down to two thousand words, and then beautiful, beleaguered Aida would come over and tell me, in her Oxford-English boarding school accent, that *she* was the editor of that piece and my cuts weren't really needed, thanks veddy much. Or literary editor Noah would politely inform me, in his patented mid–Atlantic Richler accent, that I needn't bother making copy changes in his book review section.

Yeah, sure, whatever. Believe me, this kind of mismanaged communication and mildly passive-aggressive behaviour was child's play after working at the *Globe*. (That was a very strange place — full of talent, tragically demoralized, perhaps inevitably after 150-odd years of putting a bunch of journalists in the same room. People were snide and uncooperative on principle, and even the nice ones had a hard time behaving normally. "You're from Winnipeg?" said a senior writer who apparently thought he was paying me a compliment. "You hide it well.")

And I do believe Harriet was trying her best; the bigger problem was that nobody knew who was in charge of the book review section that ran inside her Saturday section, and in the time-honoured tradition of newspaper management everywhere (q.v. the *Globe*), lack of clarity from above led to infighting below.

I returned to my daily routine of making personal calls, not editing, and sitting through interminable weekly story meetings, during which Harriet never wrote anything down or made any decisions. At the end of two or three hours, when everyone felt head-explodingly bored and also anxious because Ken was unhappy with our lack of entertainment stories — more celebrities! more celebrities! — then Harriet would say, with her plummy daughter-of-an-English-diplomat accent, "Right, then, what about pets?"

One day, in an unexpectedly sober state, I idly suggested to Harriet that she keep an updated list of what was in our next issue. What the heck, I'd start it for her. (I must now confess that I myself did not invent this idea: the concept of making a list has long been used by successful editors and other people throughout the civilized world.) Harriet was effusively grateful for my input, which led to her giving me more and more responsibility while she spent more and more time planning her escape from Don Mills. Eventually, she found a job back in the U.K. and left. On her last day, Ken stopped me on the stairs as I was leaving (early, as usual). He must have gotten wind of my superb list-making capabilities. Would I mind handling the Saturday section for a few weeks till they put the new editor in place? Why, certainly, I said. I'll do it for a month.

And so began my relationship with the diabolical genius Ken. There was no new editor of the Saturday section. I just kept doing it and hating it (it was a lot of work, and there was staff to manage), month after month. But Ken had what I now see as a particularly sleek and efficient management style: he simply ignored things he didn't want to deal with. After two months, I e-mailed Ken, saying if he wanted me to edit the Saturday section, he would have to double my salary, figuring that would speed up getting a replacement. He trumped me with a seventy per cent raise. I continued to badger him with threats, appeals, sob stories about my neglected child, all in vain. I begged him to make me a TV columnist so I could work part-time … from home … in my pyjamas. He ignored me. Finally, after five months, he waved me over as I was leaving a features meeting. "Wanna do Avenue?"

"What about the TV column?"

"I need an Avenue editor."

Since I never read the newspaper, I didn't quite know what Avenue was, but when I checked it out it looked easy. Big double-page spread. Not much type. I could probably throw it together in no time. I went back and told Ken I'd do it, but only if I could come in three days a week. "Whatever you want."

At this point, I began my relationship with Ken's unholy twin, executive editor Doug. Doug was the boyish (they're all boyish), forty-ish, harried executive editor who was supposed to balance budgets while Ken impulsively hired people behind his back. I used to think it was an acute case of one hand not knowing what the other hand was doing. Later, I suspected they knew exactly what they were up to: politely listening to employees asking for a raise, or clarification of duties, or the assistant/title/office they were promised when hired, and then putting them in cost-saving runaround mode. "I don't know — I'll have to talk to Ken about that," said Doug. Or, "Talk to Doug," said Ken. In the workplace-as-family model, Doug was the bratty little brother you wanted to kill when he was torturing you and whom you accepted, with some affection even, when you realized there was no escaping him; he was part of the family. So, after negotiating the deal with Ken, I went to Doug, explained that I'd been reassigned as Avenue editor and asked that my pay be cut immediately. I wanted no misunderstandings about my obligations — they were *part-time.*

Pretty soon, I was working six days a week. I was supposed to have a full-time designer but didn't for ten months. One reason was that I managed to burn through a couple of designers in the first month (I didn't like them and, strangely, they didn't like me). I asked for a part-time designer from the Saturday section, the brilliant wee Scotsman, Gavin. Ken and Doug's answer for several months was yes, no, maybe so. I sent e-mails: terse, funny, vaguely threatening, viciously sarcastic. Finally, Ken e-mailed back, telling me to get a designer: "Avenue needs that kind of support." No shit, sir. I had endless, pointless meetings with Doug, who gave me any number of newsroom designers for a day here, a day there — which was worse than useless, because nobody knew who was doing what, and they were all getting madder and madder at me — me! a perfectly nice person who works so much better when I think people like me!

By the six-month mark, I was spending the first hour of each day in a tear-blurred rage at my computer, writing long, savage e-mails to Doug, most of which I was prevented from sending by my friend Barry, who sat across from me. "Forget it," he'd say laconically as he trolled the wires looking for arts stories — more celebrities! more celebrities! "They've got bigger fish to fry than Avenue. Besides, why would they hire a designer when you're getting the page out every day on your own?"

Too true.

In spite of everything, Avenue was doing just fine. My baby. The little bundle of full-colour feature joy that I sent out into the world each day with a hot breakfast and the cleanest, smartest clothes I could manage, hoping its good manners and delightful personality would reflect well on Mommy.

Astonishingly, some people at the newspaper didn't like Avenue. It was expensive to produce. It was a waste of space if you thought hard news was more important than a photo essay about Hoppy the pet deer who thinks he's a dog.

But my Avenue was more than flaky features; it embodied the very essence of the *Post's* personality — larger than life, cheerfully insolent, sexy, sentimental, sensational. In this way, Avenue mirrored the instincts and interests of one person: editor Ken — *Dad* — which to me made Avenue his beautiful wife, the distaff reflection of his greatness. Avenue liked everybody — and what wasn't to like about her? She was gracious and clever, but not too intellectual, and certainly not aggressive and hard-hearted like the news and editorial pages. And though her flamboyantly sexy attire betrayed her showgirl roots, she'd learned not to be overly provocative, always remembering that her behaviour reflected directly on her husband and family.

For me — the woman (editor) behind the woman (Avenue) behind the man — Ken was the perfect boss-husband. He paid me, that is, Avenue, gallant compliments from time to time, but he mostly, respectfully, left me alone. When he wanted something on Avenue (pix from a Christie's auction of Elton John's cars, a critique of the Victoria's Secret Web-site fashion show, a photograph of, allegedly,

Hitler's skull), he told me and I was happy to oblige, because the best Avenues tended to be Ken's ideas: a fun-filled obituary of Bodacious the killer rodeo bull, famous for hurtin' (cowboys) and squirtin' (staggering amounts of the world's most expensive sperm); a tongue-in-cheek fashion critique of the gear worn by cops and activists at anti-globalization protests; a hugely popular series on how to self-test your intelligence, confidence, career, sex life, and relationships.

When I made a mistake — running coloured type on a coloured background (illegible!), or putting sexy author Candace Bushnell's face over the gutter, where it soaked up extra ink (illegible!) — he would send a short, but never sharp, e-mail telling me not to do it again. If he didn't like the Avenue I presented at the morning news meeting — a photo essay of an elderly deaf-blind man, say, or a collection of quilts by a textile-folklore artist — he'd make a little face, screwing up his nose and squinting. He didn't have to say anything. I sensed his impending disapproval, and I was quick to suggest an alternative: a heavily illustrated review of a new book about the history of lingerie, Pamela Anderson's breasts, Anna Kournikova's bum. My Avenue loved, honoured, and obeyed her husband — and she knew how to keep him happy.

But Avenue was not a doormat. (That's not what a real man wants.) Sometimes Ken made his squinchy face, and I knew he didn't want an Avenue about two silkscreen artists from Vancouver, or about prison work programs in Kingston, but I'd do them anyway, and they'd turn out just fine — or maybe they wouldn't, but he never seemed to hold it against me, because in the long run he knew it was better not to have a steady Ken diet of sports and politics and cars and bums and breasts, but to trust me to bring my own voice and interests to our joint effort with confidence and a woman's intuition.

It was a good marriage. Of course, even a good marriage has problems. In our marriage, the problem was Conrad Black.

About seven months after I started the Avenue job, the *Post* held its second anniversary party, a formal, extravagant bash at the Design Exchange on Bay Street. Conrad gave a speech, most of which I don't remember, having gotten stinking drunk for personal reasons. What I do remember is how handsome and powerful he looked in his evening wear, which made me think that the Left might be better in bed, but the Right really knows how to dress. And I remember he was talking about the Alliance Party, which the *Post* was actively supporting in the upcoming federal election, and he said something like how fabulous the Alliance was for having the "courage" to talk about privatizing medicine.

I found that so shocking that I'm still not sure I heard it right. I looked back over my shoulder at the crowd. Nobody was laughing or snickering or rolling their eyes the way we would have at the *Globe*. A sea of upturned, well-scrubbed young faces hung on Black's every word.

I could fool myself no longer. I was working for an organization that wanted to destroy the country.

Going back to work on Monday was extremely difficult, first because I didn't know how many people had seen me behave like the kind of hard-drinking party animal that gives single mothers a bad name. And, second, because I started wondering if working for the Liberal Party was a firing offence at the *Post*. The Sunday after the party, I had called my friend Tim, a card-carrying Liberal once cited in the *Post* for views symptomatic of some kind of "psychopathology." I asked Tim how I could counter the *Post*'s support of the frighteningly ridiculous Alliance leader Stockwell Day.

"You could go door to door for the new Liberal candidate in Markham," he said.

"Hmm, I don't really know anything about the issues or Liberal party policies," I replied. "But I could explain strategic voting! You know, I could tell people that we all know Chrétien is an idiot, but at least voting for him would be one less vote for Stockwell."

"Or maybe you could just put up signs," suggested Tim.

So I went out a few times after work and put up signs. Terrible work. You have to bend this sproingy wire frame and slip on the plastic sign, then shove it into a frozen lawn on a creepy, dark, empty street in a suburb even farther out than Don Mills. I did it with a young guy who was very nervous with me. We kept misreading each other's signals and bending frames when we should have been handing each other signs, and we had to keep taking off our gloves to grab the slippery plastic sleeves, then put our gloves back on to bend the wire, which was coated with black stuff, and we kept leaving the car door open (bing! bing! bing! bing!) and getting lost on the dark, winding, stupid suburban crescents and cul-de-sacs. What a nightmare. I soon decided to go back to supporting the Left the best way I knew how: baking cookies for the strikers at my daughter's school each year.

Meanwhile, what if Ken found out I was working for the Liberals? Sure, the future of Canada was important, but was it worth losing my job over? During the next few weeks at work, I found myself staring at him across the newsroom as he played ping-pong or tossed around a rugby ball or football or basketball with the guys or leaned on a partition and shot the breeze with various passersby. (His sleek and efficient management style was obviously paying off in terms of downtime.) He was from Edmonton. He had a sense of humour. He of all people must have known what a bunch of goofs the Alliance were, yet he seemed untroubled by his paper's pro-Alliance stance.

That's what I couldn't understand. Ken was a guy who blithely followed his gut instincts ("I think we should do a week-long series about John Travolta"), and he was often the voice of reason in the news meetings. For example, if a certain editor defended a couple's rights not to allow homosexuals into their bed and breakfast, Ken might say chidingly, "There are laws about that." Or maybe there was a story about Sea-Doos, and an editor wondered what angle to take. "It's a case of haves and have-nots," someone might say. "We're usually in favour of the haves," another would joke. Ken's reply: "Can't we just report on the story and be agnostic?" Or there's a kid up north with severe dental problems that have made her an outcast, and Ken would ask a few questions about the case and then kill it with a shake of the head that read, "Let's not add to her pain and embarrassment."

There were dozens more examples of how non-rabid and sensible and decent he was. But I felt like I was married to Tony Soprano. He provided, he was a solid family guy, but at a certain point you had to admit to yourself what your man did for a living: he was a cold-blooded conservative. And we were living off the avails of a right-wing agenda.

I went over it a million times in my head, mostly in the mid-afternoon. I never ate lunch, because Avenue had a 4 P.M. deadline, so at two or three o'clock I'd take a short break, which consisted of leaning back in my chair and staring into space for ten minutes. I used this time to think about how I would probably be crippled in a few years because my chair had collapsed into its lowest position a few months earlier and I didn't know how to fix it, so I had to reach up awkwardly to claw at the keyboard when I typed. Also, the left armrest was loose, so when I slumped back in my chair I listed sideways. But now, instead of worrying about my vertebrae or worrying that people might think I was keeling over because I was a drunken slut of a single mother, I started worrying about Ken.

Maybe he didn't know about all the weird stuff that got into the paper — flattering profiles of Stockwell Day, news items about gay marriages written as if we were reporting on headhunters from Borneo, or a column by Donna Laframboise saying mothers who separated from their children's father were "total idiots" for having chosen the wrong guy in the first place (which prompted one single mother to e-mail the newspaper: "The only mature response is to fuck her husband and watch the walls come a-tumblin' down"). But then I had to admit that even though Ken sometimes suggested stories that had already appeared, proving he didn't always read his own newspaper, he was probably aware of the overall agenda — that is, he was conservative, not mentally incompetent.

Then I'd think that maybe he didn't believe all the extremist nonsense in the *Post;* he held his nose and let it appear because he was a good soldier and he worked for Conrad Black, who was the real villain. But I couldn't believe Ken was that much of a hypocritical suck — for one thing, he didn't have the attention span.

Then I'd think that he'd never edited a newspaper before, and he was trained at the *Daily Telegraph* in England, and it's well known that the English are animals when it comes to journalism — vicious extremists in a culture that understands exaggeration and sensationalism are a necessary part of the soul-destroying package sold by the media, not to be taken entirely seriously.

Yes, that must have been it.

Anyway, it wasn't as if my hands were clean. I lured small children into the *Post* with pictures of pets and toys and candy and ladies' boobies, softening them up for a lifetime of Conrad-shaped world views. For adults, I made Avenue easy — full of light, useful information, presented as if we were just refreshing your memory about this or that film or book or sport or mountain or musician, so that you could feel smart and knowing without taxing your brain too much. And then — oh, clever and sophisticated reader! — then you could mosey on over to the editorial pages and gambol through the uncharitable idylls of Mark Steyn or Terence Corcoran, and it was all part of the same wildly amusing package.

Lolling disconsolately in my broken chair day after day during that long, dark winter, I began to feel like Klaus Maria Brandauer in *Mephisto,* selling his soul to the Nazis for the sake of his art, except he was doing Shakespeare, and I was working on newspaper articles about pickle recipes and "Hey, what's up with capri pants this year?"

Time passed. I chafed. I considered the pros and cons of my job. Liked the people I worked with; hated driving to Don Mills every day. Despaired over the *Post*'s politics; took inordinate pride in my darling Avenues. Hated to think I was abetting the nefarious schemes of Conrad Black in aid of the filthy rich; liked getting a regular paycheque.

As spring rolled around, I became less tormented. Chrétien had won the election handily, and the Alliance began to fall apart. I stopped fighting with Doug, who responded by giving me a designer. (Actually, he gave me a copy editor, but we agreed to call him a designer because he knew QuarkXPress so well.) Half the *Post* had been sold to a prominent Winnipeg Liberal, Izzy Asper, though editorial control resided with Black, but then Black turned around and renounced his Canadian citizenship so he could become an English lord, which possibly meant he couldn't be proprietor of the *Post* anymore, so things were looking up. I knew I wouldn't be at the *Post* forever, but maybe I wouldn't have to quit just yet.

Then, on May 3, exactly one year after taking office, I produced the quintessential *National Post* Avenue. It was a Thursday, and I had to put out a page related to the movies for our Film Friday arts section. I had nothing — but by now I knew where to turn.

Breasts.

I wandered over to Jane's desk. Coincidentally, she was wearing a tight sweater that day and a very expensive foundation garment that made her average-sized breasts look huge. She was the style editor of the Saturday section, and part of her job was to test and write about various products, so she ended up wearing a wrinkle-free suit to bed, or trying to dry clean one of her husband's suits with a do-it-yourself kit, or taking herbal anti-cellulite remedies from France for three months that made her nauseous and didn't cure cellulite. She had also tested various shape- and size-enhancing brassieres by first walking through the newsroom with a regular bra, then changing into a water bra, or whatever, and doing another walkabout. There were about two hundred people in the *Post* newsroom, mostly young and mostly men. All the brassieres had tested well with this demographic.

She had pitched me a piece about breasts the week before, something about how so many female celebrities were letting it all hang out to a ridiculous degree. I didn't really understand her point — 'twas ever thus in popular culture, wasn't it? Plus, I couldn't see how to get around the problem of running a piece that deplored the prevalence of boob shots in the media alongside a bunch of boob shots. It seemed too cynically obvious — even for the *Post*. Now, I had an idea. "I need that piece about breasts," I told her.

"It's almost done. I can check it in to you in an hour."

"It's for Film Friday. Can you make it about movie stars?"

"No problem."

I had my designer gather photos of the usual suspects — from Jayne Mansfield's dangling décolletage to Julia Roberts's push-up bra in *Erin Brockovich*. The main image would consist of Pamela Anderson's mounds bursting off the page. I threw in Lara Croft and Jessica Rabbit (for the kids). There was a minor glitch when Jane sent me the piece: it had no thesis. Jane shrugged. "You said you needed it this morning." We stared at the copy together. "Well, do whatever you have to," she said, walking away. "I'm going to a perfume launch."

After several semi-prone minutes in my broken chair, I had the solution. I reached up to the keyboard and shoved in a few sentences near the bottom: "So what's wrong with large, exposed breasts anyway?" and "Some might object to the ongoing objectification of the female form — reducing a woman's worth to the worthiness of her mammary glands," yadda yadda, that sort of thing. Then I wrote a deck that covered all the bases: "Call it a cultural idiosyncrasy. Call it a magnificent obsession. Call it vulgar, infantile or reprehensible. The fact is that breasts are now the biggest celebrities of all — and we can blame (or thank) Hollywood." As for the headline, it wrote itself the minute Jane's copy hit all that celebrity cleavage on the layout: "Booby Trapped."

In the morning meeting that day, I waited for my turn with confidence. "What's Avenue?" said Ken finally, looking around the room to see where I was.

"It's about how Hollywood's obsession with breasts is reflected in the popular culture," (sir,) I answered.

Ken nodded slowly, staring straight ahead, playing up his role as the breast-obsessed editor. "Perfect," he said. And it was — the surefire, all-purpose *National Post* story: tits *and* analysis all in one glorious package. I was clearly at the top of my game — and I could only get better.

Maybe that's why I quit. Or maybe it was just one too many trips to Don Mills. In any case, a few weeks later I told Ken I was leaving to freelance, that is, our marriage was over, I wanted a divorce. He took the news remarkably well — though I'm not so sure about Conrad. It was probably coincidental that he sold his remaining interest in the paper soon after I resigned. But one thing is certain: it was the end of the *National Post* as I knew it.

CHRIS KOENTGES

The Pedro Guerrero Principle

I wish it was the sixties. I wish I could be happy. I wish, I
wish, I wish, that something would happen.
— Radiohead

He only grows for guys he knows. And me.
— Gomez

ON A SLOW DAY IN TIJUANA.
The box. Metal. Rusted. Dial at the centre, as on the front of a
beat-up closet safe. It dangled from the neck of a silent Mexican
man like an oversized talisman. Cords sprouted from opposite sides.

Hands, not the silent Mexican man's hands, rather yours, the
gringo customer's hands, go on the dangling grips. Rotating the dial
clockwise sends something measured in volts down the cords to
each handle. Leaving only the question: Do you give pesos for the
cheeky masochism of this service — or wager that you can hold the
ends of the cords for longer than the silent Mexican man can turn
the dial?

He was a crumpled man; grey, dusty, and gaunt. He was the best of
Tijuana, which, by definition, made him the worst too. To be a

209

tourist in Tijuana, to be someone who's going to *enjoy* TJ, you had to forget that a silent, withered Mexican man with a mousy Fu Manchu, this *Señor Tijuana el Curioso* in the grimy poncho, might have been human. Easier to assimilate him as a symbol. Or, better yet, as a cartoon character named Jorge, in which the *ooor* is theatrically rolled, as a running gag, by the other characters in this, your private, animated, almost-foreign-language dystopia.

Paul, who crossed the border with me that morning, understood the premise of Tijuana as Saturday morning cartoon, but he never embraced it deep down as I did. Not even in the dark toonjoint where we waited and drank and uneasily watched the silent Mexican man with the box did Paul understand how appropriate it all was. *Look around, you gormless fuck* — there's a lone fly buzzing above shelves crammed with one brand of tequila. There's a spittoon that's stained — *from spit.* A live rattlesnake in a jar. Over there, Paul, *look* — a saloon keeper having *a siesta,* stool leaned back against the beer fridge, snoring and everything.

On a slow day in Tijuana, the young gringo male is a more aggressively sought commodity than on regular days. During a forty-five-minute lap through Avenida Revolución, we passed the donkeys painted like zebras, shooed away runny-nosed orphans hawking Chiclets, talked poontang with scarred nightclub owners in gold chains, and stopped to watch the pale, obese ladies from Minnesota pose clandestinely for photos next to blind beggars with no legs. Revolución is the anti-travel experience of visiting a leper colony on the Ganges. The squalor and human suffering is kitsch. Everybody who's allowed to goes back when the sun sets. You simply click your heels three times, wave your passport, and recross the border.

Straying from Revolución, an American marine with a giant gut had warned us when we crossed the border, was "like sticking your hand into a cockatoo cage." And off Revolución, where Tijuana is dustier and more blanched, we stumbled off the circuit. We stumbled past the Lorena Hotel, which rents rooms by the half-hour, where a scrawny American kid scrubbed blood from his collar on the curb out front. We stumbled into the nether regions of what the AAA *TripTik* called the red-light area north of Calle 1A, west of Constitución, and we were finally hustled into the sombre toon joint by an sneaky señorita who scanned the street to make sure nobody had seen us enter.

The dark room was half-filled with hard men who didn't speak to one another. We referred to them as "hombres" — we'd only encountered such men in Robert Rodriguez films. They wore crisp blue jeans, thick leather belts, heavy patterned shirts, and dark Stetsons. There was a tension as we entered. We scurried into the booth at the back and regrouped.

We drank Tecate.

We waited.

We believed we had super powers.

We weren't born with super powers. We acquired them that week, blitzing down the west side of America aboard a blue minivan on a reckless, whirring quest for what we called "character." We rolled day and night, pounding stale roadhouse coffee, eating only buns and cold wieners from the Costco in Spokane. At every turn, our eyes were peeled for a nouveau "B" American gothic. West Coast noir, we called it. Evidence of the continent's alter ego. *Character*.

I'd met Paul eighteen months earlier, but we didn't become friends until nine months after that. We worked as friends because neither of us had to resort to small talk around the other. We'd had but one über-conversation since the nine-month breakthrough. It began during Lilith Fair, after which we co-wrote a solipsistic feature article for a local alternative newspaper in which we lamented how overpackaged and characterless the day had been. It was a long conversation, our über-conversation about character, but we could always pick it up where it had last been left, even when it had been left for weeks.

As we pressed south in the van, on our search for character, an interesting thing had begun to happen: we turned, almost uncontrollably, into characters ourselves. At a trailer park in Bonners Ferry, we drank and played cards with skinny, salacious girls whose husbands were locked up in prison for armed robbery. In the checkout line at the Paso Robles grocery store, we dumbfounded Minnie Driver with accusations that she was far more stunning than the real Minnie Driver — in all likelihood ending her engagement with Josh Brolin. We Holly Golightlyed our way through greasy diners and wrong-side-of-the-track lounges. Liquor, caffeine, insomnia — we developed the super power to synthesize it into momentum. We escaped our suburban world of received stories, we became larger-than-life protagonists in a tale of our own. We convinced ourselves that every foolish twist in our unfolding narrative, every word, every thought, every shrug, and pick of the nose was being borne for our generation. We made superheroes look mundane by comparison.

And so we tried to conjure every ounce of our powers as the silent Mexican man with the homemade torture device stumbled like a zombie to our booth. He thrust the grips at the ends of the cords in our direction. And with indifference, he thrust them again. The third time, he thrust them at me.

I froze.

The Tecate we'd consumed while waiting to test our powers had clearly been laced with kryptonite. I couldn't move. Mistaking my hesitation for indifference, the silent Mexican man turned around and shuffled toward a scowling man sitting with a shot glass at another table. To my momentary relief, he was dismissed with some Spanish to the effect of "fuck off."

It had been a devastating lapse. Attempting to recoup the lost momentum of the week-long spree, I began to drink faster. I decided that we had to spend the night in the sombre toon joint to atone; to wait for another, badder silent Mexican man. Paul wanted to go back to San Diego and drink at the laid-back bar on the beach beneath the roller coaster. And for the first time since boarding the van — for the first time since I'd met Paul — we disagreed.

"Give me one good reason why we should stay," he asked.

"Character!" I answered without hesitation. Then added that "forty million people come to Tijuana every year, none of them spend more than an afternoon; if we leave, we'll have nothing on any of them."

"This isn't character," he replied with disgust. We'd left the sombre toon joint and now walked down a dirty street as the hawkers packed up for the night. There's a desperation to Tijuana at dusk, of not having sold enough trinkets or sufficiently crippled Americans on Tecate.

"This *is* character," I shot back. I had raised my voice and now swept my arm at a broad angle over the cartoon realm — then beyond it, up toward the long dusty roads that wound into bleak hills crammed with corrugated-iron shacks, as if it were all for my entertainment.

"Dude," Paul shouted back, his head following the path of my arm's kingly sweep, "*this* isn't character!"

I'd given the realm — my whole notion of the seedy border-town bender — a mythology and vividness that couldn't be sensed at that moment. My evaporating personal mythology now depended on Tijuana's reputation for sin and debauchery, and even at the end of this quiet, stupid afternoon, the realm was still going to be Herb Alpert, who named his brass after what we were sweeping our arms back and forth over in disagreement. Alpert's silky elevator music, its magical jauntiness, never lets you doubt that Tijuana could be anything but a place where, no matter what kind of potential harm you might throw yourself at, there would never ever be any real consequences to anybody.

"*This* does *not* have character," Paul said one last time, not sounding convinced. And nor did I sound sure when I again hissed, "Character!" We were being watched by five-year-olds. They tugged at our shorts, pleading for quarters.

So we left Tijuana. There were no BJs; no contraband pharmaceuticals. Our pockets weren't picked. We weren't beaten up or propositioned by a toothless hoochy-mama named Lola. The tacos didn't make us lax. We didn't get scammed on fake Rolexes. We didn't spend the night downing shots of labelless mescal. We were in Tijuana, and the high-pressure sunglass vendors tried to buy *our* bug-eyed snowboarder shades. In short, we failed to consummate any kind of significant relationship with it whatsoever.

But before we went back to the bar beneath the roller coaster in San Diego, before we even left the sombre toon joint, we witnessed the silent Mexican man approach an older and prouder-looking man sitting at the bar. He was a rancher with a weathered face and black Stetson that was less crisp than the other Stetsons. He nodded slowly at the enigmatic box. Solemnly, he placed a stack of fresh American bills atop the counter. The silent Mexican man passed him the cords, and surreptitiously, painstakingly, every head in the bar shifted to the money, then the box. My heart exploded up into my throat as we watched the hombre, almost regally, take the ends of the cords.

The expression on the silent Mexican man's face never changed as he rotated the dial. At first, the hombre clenched his teeth; then, as the dial was turned further, he manoeuvred his arms as if driving a truck off a cliff. Further still, and he was up from the stool to his feet, body tensed. And then a slow smile cracked. And then, the dial cranked, a full grin. And then he let go, shaking the pain out of his hands. The silent Mexican man grabbed the money and hobbled out of the joint. Still shaking his hands, wiping sweat from his brow, the hombre looked to a younger, tougher-looking hombre two stools down. They looked each other in the eye for an instant, the younger nodding in quiet acquiescence to the older. And all was silent again on a slow day in Tijuana.

And so we went to Nevada.

Pedro Guerrero

Think of the great road trips as performance. Think of Kerouac meandering across America (so we'd know how to dig it). Hunter S. Thompson bombing out to Vegas (fearing it, loathing it specifically for us). Humbert Humbert, motel to motel (so you and I won't ever have an excuse to). Even better than the great road trips, think of the shitty road trips. Your trips and my trips, think of them also as performance. Think about quantifying that less literary performance in the grand scheme of human expression, and think about how we might handicap that human expression in a way that makes our expression, our road trips, our stories mean something. The key is delusion. *Convince* yourself of the expression, the trip, the story's importance. Delusion and stories are highly personal. My key is Pedro Guerrero.

Pedro Guerrero played third base for the L.A. Dodgers through the end of the seventies and most of the eighties; through *The Rockford Files;* through Tommy Lasorda; through a world championship; through Fernando Valenzuela, the Mayan pitcher who breathed through his eyes; through the first generation of *Saturday Night Live* films; through the endless, glorious jive-turkey days of the bottom left corner of America — which, I believed, were the jive-turkey days of all America.

I traded baseball cards through those days. As a preteen in inner-suburban Calgary, worn down by the hobby's compulsion to categorize and organize, I craved an intangibility behind the statistics on the cards' backs and came to obsess over the wild texture of names and facial expressions and secret skills. There was Pascual Perez, who threw a circus pitch called the Pascual Ball; Rollie Fingers, who waxed his moustache; and Gaylord Perry, who would *let* people call him Gaylord Perry. Guerrero's cards, though, more than the others, came to represent the face not just of whatever a "Dodger" was, but also whatever a city that had just reached eight million people was. The shots were of what it meant to be a ballplayer in that jive-turkey era, the era when the game became at once decadent play and a melting pot; and, in my young suburban mind, not quite as unfathomably ageless.

Frozen with a bat on the front of the latest *Topps* card (*O-pee-chee* in Canada), Guerrero always seemed to be captured in various states of swagger. Born in the Dominican Republic, San Pedro de Macoris (abbreviated San Ped. De Mac on his '90 *Donruss*), #28 went from subtle 'fro to Jerry curls to 'stache to mack-goatee to high fade above the ears over the evolution of his cards. At 6'0" and two hundred pounds, he was the archetypal sparkplug-cum-ballplayer. He batted exactly .300 in a career that predated steroids, juiced balls, gutless parks, diluted pitching, and the proliferation of baseball-card manufacturers. And even though his defensive stats are, at worst, *decent,* he's ubiquitously referred to as ham-handed. He turned routine fielding episodes into full-blown hold-your-breath-in-the-bleachers escapades. And here we get a glimpse at the witch-craft behind the stats.

After hitting .218 in 1993, Guerrero retired from major-league baseball at the age of thirty-six (although some argue he was thirty-eight). An all-star four times, he left the legacy of a handful of moderately colourful anecdotes in a sport stitched together by a haphazard spectrum of anecdotes. Two years later, he signed up with the Sioux Falls Canaries in the Northern League, where he paid for his own plane tickets rather than endure twelve-hour bus rides; boasting to a *Sports Illustrated* reporter, "I am the only man in the history of professional baseball who is paying money to play." The writer followed the season, noting that Guerrero was "as carefree and playful as a kid on a sandlot, happily doing the lambada against the batting cage during BP or comically playing up his limp for the adoring hometown fans." He hit .338 and then faded from both baseball and the lesser American consciousness.

It wasn't until 1999 that he resurfaced on the bottom left corner of page seven in Sports, the B drug bust, and/or domestic violence corner of the North American subconscious. He'd attempted to buy two hundred thousand dollars' worth of cocaine from an undercover narcotics agent. After demanding that the charges be dismissed under the 1963 Vienna Convention, his attorney Milton Hirsch argued that Pedro Guerrero couldn't have possibly known he was buying cocaine. Hirsch argued that Pedro Guerrero didn't know how to make his own bed. Pedro Guerrero didn't know how to make lunch. *Pedro Guerrero was on a weekly allowance from his wife.* Pedro Guerrero, Hirsch doggedly emphasized throughout the trial, had an IQ of seventy.

Pedro Guerrero was acquitted after four hours of jury deliberation.

And so I learned that the streaky free swinger wasn't *technically* intelligent.

After what came next, the universe made sense to me for the first time. Pedro Guerrero publicly entered the O. J. narrative.

After five years as America's story — the country's quintessential protagonist, antagonist, and author rolled into one — O. J. Simpson was on the phone with Miami-Dade police. "I'm trying to get a girl to go to rehab," he jabbered to a disinterested 911 operator. "She's been doing drugs for two days with *Pay-drow Ger-arrow,* who just got arrested for cocaine, and I'm trying to get her to leave her house and go into rehab right now.

"This girl has spent the last two days doing drugs with him. Me and a friend just came over and said, 'You're going into a rehab.' She got mad, she just got her car, and now she's loaded out of her mind in her Mustang driving around town. She needs to be stopped."

On the transcript O. J. said *"she"* — his girlfriend was Nicole look-alike Christie Prody. On a tape of the call, however, I heard *"he."* A certain type of person who'd listened to that call a few times also heard "he." It was *Pay-drow Ger-arrow* who clearly needed to be stopped. Paul and I were bowled over by the notion that a human being might exist that could out-O. J. The Juice. For O. J. was that greatest of L.A. things, the proverbial man for his time and place, and he'd announced — from *Miami,* no less — in his most pathetic voice possible, that he was ceding the role. He'd never sounded whiter; never more like a victim. America's protagonist/antagonist — the sucker relished every moment as the nation's narrative — joined us in the cheap seats as a helpless spectator. Want denouement? Two police officers drop by Prody's townhouse and give him a domestic abuse pamphlet.

I began to see Pedro as a beacon, a kind of *real* superhero who could naturally assume centre stage and stake claim to a moment with little thought. It didn't end there, though, not for me and Paul.

We'd hear O. J.'s announcement over and over again on the Jim Rome show. Said to be the basis of Oliver Stone's frantic, fickle *Any Given Sunday* journalist — the symbol of all that's dubious and weird in sports media — Rome's syndicated radio persona is a religious experience for a certain American demographic. Laced with unreferenced jargon, an incomprehensible internal mythology, and a style devoid of any recognizable context, his then four-hour show would baffle the novice listener. Rome himself explained, in the gruff, choppy time-killing way that he does explain things, "If you're new to *The Jungle,* you'll have no idea what I'm talking about right now. But take my word for it, this is very, *very* funny."

Years after the Simpson acquittal, after the Calgary affiliate picked up Rome's program, O. J. riffs were still a pillar of daily *Jungle* lore. The only thing worse than Orenthal (a Jungle verb, by the way, which meant to "'melt down' and 'lop off' somebody's 'dome'") were the people who thought O. J. was innocent. I'd never heard such frank dialogue. The matter was entirely black and white.

During the course of the program, Rome begrudgingly accepts calls from what he calls his clones. Clones wait on the line for three hours to unleash what usually amounts to a twenty-second barrage of hyper performance art, which he picks brutally apart afterward. The week before we left on our mighty streak down the west side of America, Paul and I, at different ends of the country, heard a clone from New England make it for *minutes* without interruption from the host. As the caller became increasingly consumed — no doubt the apex of his life to go this far on Rome — he began imitating the 911 call (now mythic in *The Jungle*), at first in the current of O. J.'s earnest white voice, then breaking down and hoarsely screaming Pedro Guerr-*ero*. (The syllables begged for crazed inflection.)

Because of its numbing overuse, I haven't trusted the exclamation mark since the second grade. So, as a staunch, unflinching exclamation-mark cynic, I stain the following description with twenty-six such wretched punctuations. That's how much I want you to understand the senseless passion.

All but spent, it became clear that the clone from New England didn't know how to bring his epic barrage to climax. Violently, he began shrieking (vital organs hemorrhaging in the background). "War Bawston! War Red Sawx! War Providence!!!" Then he stammered for a moment. Nothing in the English language, no word, no concept, no known idea could express his state. But a framework of understanding suddenly dawned on him. His voice went vile and rasping and inhuman, like he was being electrocuted, and he began howling

"PEDRO GUERRERO!!!!!"

"PEDRO GUERRERO!!!!"

"PEDRO!!! GUERRERO!!!"

Over and over, until Pedro Guerrero was one big, scary, loud, and fast monster. Then he screamed, "OUT!!!!!" And he hung up and, I like to imagine, died at the pinnacle of delirium.

The moment we started imitating the clone's climax, Pedro Guerrero became bound to me, Paul, and our road trip forever. Performing the call would become the rug that tied our entire mythology together. For as much as my notion of Pedro was about usurping the role of protagonist from maybe the most spectacular protagonist in American history, it now also came down to the sort of raw intensity-for-intensity's-sake exorcised by the clone from New England.

How to Do Reno Definitively

The way to do Reno definitively is to walk in with twenty bucks, parlay it into a small fortune, and put a casino or two out of business. That never happens — hence the mythology of the casino heist. So we went to Reno to get it all over us. To get it inside of us. To get ourselves all over it. To filter ourselves through Reno and become reborn into the world as the type of super beings who have known a place such as Reno with absolute intimacy.

Reno had me fifteen years ago.

I always imagined Reno as a dull gnarly glow on the Nevada desert. At the centre of the glow was a rundown establishment — either the glow implied that similar establishments lurked beyond, or it was just the joint's own wicked pulsing history (perhaps a bit of both). The implication: Reno, the definitive crossroads. The image came off a yellow singlet that one of my dad's softball team-mates wore through two summers in the early eighties. It had a slogan along the lines of "Reno: biggest little city in the world." I was drawn to Reno because I felt it was the only place left that hadn't changed since the singlet. I believed that it had only grown to resemble the yellow singlet more.

We blazed through the desert in the hours before dawn. Ripping pages off the *TripTik* like windows off an Advent calendar. When we finally saw the glow on the horizon, butterflies exploded like firecrackers in our stomachs. In a reverent tone, hushed at first, we began slowly muttering — almost in chant — "Reno ... Re-no ... Reno ..." Punching the "O" in the manner of old drinkers/smokers at the end of their life. And as the desert yielded to the grail, the morning was Christmas. We didn't make a single wrong turn. We didn't double back once. We rolled past the streets and buildings right to Reno's heart, as if we had lived there — or even better, had been going to Reno — our entire life. We nodded our heads hypnotically, like pilgrims on the verge, virgins on the brim of a volcano. The Reno chant hardened. Then we stopped for a long cargo train. As it chugged past, I realized that we were "there" — *Reno* was just across the tracks. We were tense and straining and stammering and stuttering, and this fucking train wouldn't end. We could barely talk. Pounding the dash, the horn, ripping at our own hair. We'd turned the radio down and opened the windows to better hear and smell the city. The Reno yell suddenly turned into a Pedro yell, and in frustrated euphoria, as car after car inched by, I screamed "*Traaaaaiin!*" The force of the shriek momentarily startled Paul out of his trance. "You really communicated it was a train," he said. I knew. And he knew. And the train knew. And then the train was done. And we were psychopaths, haphazardly screaming, out of unison, alternating "*Reno, Fuck-, Pedro, -en, Reno, eh, Reno, Guerrero, RENO,*" and "*Train,*" eventually combining reno and train and pedro guerrero and fucking into another big, good word. It was the most exciting moment in history.

Someone once asked me to explain what we saw that morning; what Reno looked like. *Explain what Reno looked like?* I don't think we know to this day what it *looked* like, only how it felt in the gut and tip of our nostrils. In our rampage, we were never able to distinguish it as a place versus an idea. The plan had only ever been: "roll down to Mexico, stop in Reno at some point." *All* we'd wanted was to be in Reno, and now that was accomplished.

We had to have a ninety-nine-cent breakfast, because this was a place in the world where you could purchase a ninety-nine-cent breakfast. And we wanted to have it with beer. The Cal Nevada — the Cal *Nev* — was as big and old school and crusty and character-riddled as exists anywhere in Nevada. We went up stairs and escalators to what seemed like the attic of the creaky old building, then proceeded through a narrow, cramped, dark, woody labyrinth of chambers until we reached a narrow, empty compartment with a low ceiling and long slit cut out of the wall that allowed us to survey the establishment. We were conquistadors watching a hostile Inca valley come to life. After some time, a huge lady rumbled over — *exactly* what we expected from a Reno waitress. Jaded, tough, take no shit; she obviously ran a bordello on the weekends. She looked to be in her fifties (which is early forties or late sixties in Reno years). She was someone who belonged in Reno. Nothing about us could have possibly — nor did — impress her. We were pathetic and desperate and persistent enough to find the cheap breakfast; we wouldn't possibly be customers who believed in tipping.

"Can we·start with a couple of Buds?" Paul asked softly. Shortly before 6 A.M. now. She looked at us like we were fresh off the boat, shook her head in disgust, and hissed, "What?"

"Please?" I followed.

"No, we don't serve up here."

This was more crushing than it should have been, and our expressions didn't hide that. Her façade, jaded caked in overlapping layers of jaded, softened, and something close to love flashed. Paul took the opening, "We've driven straight from Canada. We're awful thirsty."

"Yeaaaah," she started tentatively. "I guess I can go downstairs — hey, you guys want beer, you can have whatever you want ... This is Reno." *This is Reno?* She had to send out some people to find the beer, but as the eggs and ham and coffee and toast drenched in butter came out, the bottles arrived. And more arrived after that.

Other people sat down in the dim compartment. People who had been up all night and like us were nowhere near sleep now. We looked haggard. But it was only a couple of days of haggard. Fresh henna, really. Haggardness that builds up over years, even after you've had a shower, is real. We began to learn about the local species and heard a line that we'd hear muttered over and over the next twenty-four hours whenever we asked people how long they'd been in Reno: "Been here a long time." It's inevitably followed by a break in eye contact and a long silence.

After Lois brought out more beer, the supporting cast blurred. Someone at another table lectured: "Money isn't money in a casino." Our compartment felt like a hovering submarine — a sub-Zeppelin tree house. The intensity rose. We revelled in the stench, the alcoholics, the super losers. In the same way an anthropologist revels in a remote tribal ceremony in Micronesia, we obsessed over the rituals of the B Nevada down and out. It was like going to a second-rate zoo, except we yearned for the line between spectator and exhibit, observing and being, to converge. We wanted to fornicate with Reno more than ever.

Outside, as the morning's first light flashed, we shuffled through lounges and casinos and 1950s-era lobbies in a search of a suitable spot to penetrate. After two fruitless hours, we were in The Fitz. (*Located in the heart of Reno, Nevada at the world famous Reno Arch Fitzgeralds Casino & Hotel Reno is Committed to Make You Lucky!*[TM]) Our shuffle had long since turned to a trudge, and we trudged as we had everywhere else that morning, through tangles of slot machines, thickets of blackjack tables. We trudged through a half-hearted luck o' the Irish motif that management had long since renounced. Pale green leprechauns, misshapen shamrocks, and an unlit pot at the end of the rainbow. One criterion for judging "modern" in Reno is to study an establishment's carpet: trod, cigarette burns, spilled pink-gin drinks, and vomit patches were the benchmark, and The Fitz was the most wretchedly futuristic we'd entered yet.

But in the corner at the back of the never-ending room, we spotted several rows of tables meant to constitute a lounge, along with a peeler-style half-moon bar. Big screen behind, just above a little stage. Layout-wise, it was an afterthought. The room was all but empty in the early morning, as a hunched Vietnamese janitor vacuumed, while a clean-cut bartender set up for a slow morning. A lone drinker sat quietly on the far right side. Paul didn't want to be there at first, but we traded the look of character appraisal we'd developed over our friendship, and he nodded begrudgingly. It wasn't the singlet. Not even the singlet was this perfect.

We sat on the stools beside the lone drinker, a fifty-four-year-old black man whose backpack was slung over his chair rest. The bartender brought us a couple of Buds. We spoke with quiet uncertainty at first, then with enough volume to seduce the drinker.

"You boys came all the way from Canada?" he asked.

We nodded matter-of-factly.

"I worked on a fishin' boat in Alaska."

"Wild country," I said, trying not to sound eager.

"Gonna get back up there one day," he smiled and nodded to himself. "Build me a cabin and fish and hunt."

He wore a dirty blue ball cap. Smoked at a pace gently beneath chain. Drank gin and tonic; sipped bourbon from a two-ounce shot glass on the side. But when you looked at Fred, the lone drinker, your focus inevitably came to rest on his teeth. They were twisted; the roots barely hinged into the gum. His chafing lips curled down into a contemplative frown. He was sad because his radio had been stolen. So sad that he decided to take the day off from work. (Fred lived and worked as a carpenter in Sparks, but he came to drink in Reno, which I felt was an appropriately old-school thing to do.) Sam, the clean-shaven bartender originally from Jalisco, would periodically whisper to us, "Fred, he's been here for *days* ... Fred, he can stay here for *days* ... Fred can *sit* here for days." He said it with so little concern for Fred that I didn't immediately understand why he'd said it at all.

Sam was the best bartender I'd ever had in my life, so I would carefully weigh everything he said. I spend time sizing up bartenders. (I once worked behind a bar in a nightclub.) It was a slow morning, but Sam kept the tumblers filled with ice. He'd rotate through lines of them, making sure there was always fresh ice. He had a towel folded neatly over his left shoulder. He never leaned against the wall. He was smooth, attentive, active. He was in his early sixties and vain as hell about how good he looked for his age (the opposite to Fred). He liked to say that he went to school with Carlos Santana (although their ages don't jibe). Fred would chime in with the handful of B-Motown figures he'd grown up with. When asked what we did back home, Paul and I looked at the carpet and mumbled, "Writer."

Something in Fred immediately assumed that we were a certain type of writer. To Fred, there was only one certain type of writer, and that writer was Ernest Hemingway. We wrote. We knew about fishing and hunting and Alaska. (We didn't, but he *felt* we did.) We wanted to have the same occupation as Hemingway. Beaming, he began, "Now *Heming-way*" — the word "Hemingway" could only leave his lips in a wistful boom — "*There* was a writer."

Fred's inflection and 1960s inner-Detroit cadence tightened when he got excited; loud and melodic, his head bounced to the rhythm of his voice as he summed up Hemingway. "*Old. Man. And. The Seeea.*" A long, thoughtful Motown pause; an acknowledgement of marvel for the work. "*The. Sun. Also Righ-zesss.*" Another such pause. "*Old. Man. And. The Seeeea ...*" Fred's style was infectious. Never in our lives — and Paul and I are both homeboys — had we ever achieved such pitch-perfect Ebonics as those hours we spent drinking with Fred. Fred from *real* Detroit. Us as black as he was. At one point, Paul started jiving his shoulders and wiping his nose with his sleeve and grumbling, "Fre*hd*. Fre*hd*. Fre*hd*. What about that Miiiil-es Daaaav-is?" Fred remembered who he was talking to — the only moment he ever called us out — and shrieked back: "Miles Davis ... Miles Davis ... a little white boy from Canada gonna talk to *me* about Miiiiiles Daaaaavis. Shi-it!" And *that* was Fred's move. He would look at you, brush you off verbally, turn away in mock indignation, and mutter under his breath — sometimes for five minutes. "Imfromdetroit michigan hegonnatalk to *me* aboutmiles-davis." Until he'd stumble back to Hemingway.

I'm a Fitzgerald guy.

I wasn't sure I wanted to be a Fitzgerald guy that day. I started slowly, watching myself lean in, taking on Fred's gruff enunciation, "Yah, *that* Heming-*way* sure is a good writer." (A good writer, a guy who could write, or a dude who went to Africa — never a great writer.) "But what about Fitzgerald?"

"Fitzgerald?" Fred shot back in surprise. He said it quickly and curtly. Dismissive. He rolled the concept of F. Scott Fitzgerald around in his mind in the time it takes to get through the three syllables of the last name. He rolled it around in a way meant to imply he'd rolled it around for longer in the past and had long since come to a conclusion. And neither of us said anything else on the topic for a Bud and two bourbons.

It was eerie how easily we slipped into the fray of a Reno lounge at seven-thirty in the morning. Fred would sporadically scream, "Hey Sam! *Sam!* We need some *shots.*" Sam would pour big two-ounce shots of Jim Beam. In real life, the mere smell of American whiskey is enough to make me vomit; even *thinking* about the shock at the nostrils makes me shiver. But like the weak American beer, it felt nourishing consumed beside Fred. The lights from the video poker built into the counter warmed my forearms like sun. He'd drop his voice to an avuncular tone. "Hey, you boys need some beers?" Round after round, all morning, he kept buying. We'd protest. We wanted to buy Fred a drink. And when he wouldn't listen, we'd plead, "Sam, can't we pay for this one?" Sam's voice would take a savvy edge — like a spy talking to another spy with the secret greeting line — that suggested we ought to understand some hidden implications. "No. It's OK. Fred's got it. *Fred's got it.*"

But we persisted, "No way, we can't be taking all these free drinks from Fred. We can pay for these."

"No, no, it's *gooood,* my friends. Fred gets comped a lot." Fred's wallet looked like the sort of sandwich Dagwood Bumstead once packed over three panels on Saturday afternoon. Hundreds of multi-colour complimentary drink tickets spilled out, as he'd throw three times what was needed to cover the round on the counter. Not even the most vengeful alcoholic could drink as fast as the drinking resources he possessed. "Fred plays a lot of *Keno,*" Sam would whistle. That sounded even more like a code for something else that we couldn't quite wrap our minds around — for we sat there with Fred a good ten hours, and Fred didn't play a single game of Keno.

As we drank, the lounge gradually filled. We learned that Sam led a ten-piece mariachi band. Played all the instruments. Coached Little League. Was active with the neighbourhood council.

Whenever we'd give Sam too much attention, Fred would yell: "Sam, Sam, *Sam*. Play that *San-tan-a* song, man." Sam would saunter to the VCR, put in "Smooth," the song in which Rob Thomas from Matchbox 20 went old school with Santana. (It's *all* Santana, of course.) Fred would bop in his seat as the duo came up on the big screen; we felt like we were sitting at a spayed peeler bar. Sam must have played it twenty-five times that morning.

Fred always got back to Hemingway ("*Old Man and the Sea, Sun Also Rises ...*").

"*Hemingway* can write," I nodded. "But F. *Scott* Fitzgerald — huh?"

"Ah, Fitzgerald." He dismissed Fitzgerald again with a shooing motion.

And there was more Hemingway and more Fitzgerald, mostly whose name sounded better to say in a drunk, raspy Motown voice. (At one point, I attempted to recite part of the last page of *Gatsby*, which I had memorized a year earlier to impress girls.) Eventually, though, Fred made what has come to be known to me and Paul as *the point*. "Yah ... OK ... you *see* ... the thing with Fitzgerald is he never had nothin' but only that *one* book." And he flung his head around and muttered righteously.

As we discussed literature, Sam would periodically disappear and Chuck, the relief bartender, manned the wood. Sam was smooth, Latino, diligent, clean-cut; Chuck was burnt-out, speedy, useless. He loved working this bar, and you could tell Sam hated to cede it whenever he came down. Chuck was somewhere in his thirties, had blond helmet-hair (tinged ungracefully grey), a meek wispy moustache, some days of stubble. He blathered non-stop for the fifteen minutes or half-hour that he was the relief bartender. He inhaled coffee non-stop. He'd fix it like a Looney Tunes character, relating entire anecdotes about playing football with Lawrence Taylor at North Carolina as sugar spewed into his mug. He'd say things like "Yah, I like a little coffee with my sugar." It struck me that he drank sugar and coffee so he could say things like that. He'd start sentences with "Dude, I'll tell you what" — but would seldom tell a dude what.

Fred, of course, *hated* Chuck. We knew that Fred hated Chuck because when Chuck had been standing behind the bar riffing, Fred would lean over and mumble, "I. *Hate*. Chuck." The Ebonical Wayan brother Motown richer than ever against Chuck's sharp honky Carolina rushes. Fred would follow it up with, "I'll tell *you boys* what. One of these days I'm gonna *kill* that Chuck." His shoulders would surge up like a Halloween cat and a mischievous grin broke that meant he was *honestly* going to kill Chuck. This was a man who had done two traumatic tours as a marine in Vietnam — the first such veteran I'd ever met — and he'd been forced to kill people he didn't even hate.

It seemed to me that Fitzgerald wrote more than one book. When I explained this to Fred, he shook his head. "See *Heming*-way … had … old man and the sea, the sun also *ri-zez*." Sometimes Paul would throw in *For Whom the Bell Tolls*. "For whom the bell tolls!" (The Hemingway canon acquired depth as the morning waned.) "But Fitzgerald just had that *one* book."

And it became abundantly clear that — *yes!* — Fitzgerald only had that one book.

"So, Fitzgerald only had that one book," I started in a new tone that made Fred tilt his head suspiciously. I paused, took a long sip of whiskey, and waited for his gaze to plug into mine. I was a fifty-something black Detroit castaway, lasered and missing teeth. Slowly, trying to squelch my excitement, I squinted and continued, "So what if you say everything you gotta say" — long pause … then fast, so four short words blurred into one that somehow seemed even shorter than each as a component — "INTHAT*ONE*BOOK." I made a long gesture that indicated I had blown my own mind, then turned away dramatically, muttered for a while (hemingway-had-to-take *awl* them-books …), got up and left. (Sam had given us the code to the VIP toilets.)

Fred was agitated when I returned. We drank some more; he thought deeply about what it meant to say all you had to say in a single book.

"So, let me get this straight," he started earnestly, his words crisper than I'd heard them. "If you say all you got to say in that one book, then … you've said all you got to *say?*" He turned away. Muttered.

"Well, yah," I replied when he turned back. "Because, see, you've said *all* you got to say in that one book." Turn, mutter.

Back and forth, back and forth, back and forth, until finally Fred, in admiration at the notion of a writer saying *everything* in a single book, stated: "You're saying that *one* book, if you're saying everything you got to say —"

"— no, that one *two-hundred*-page book."

"That *one two-hundred*-page book can be worth as much as *all* them books Hemingway wrote?"

And I made an overly slick point-from-the-nose gesture. Fred nodded. His forehead furrowed in the way of a man accepting a nice cognac into his personal vernacular of worthy taste. "Yep, I can see that … *Damn* that Fitz-gerald, man."

Later in the afternoon, following another of my trips to the VIP restroom, Paul had moved beside Fred and their conversation had deepened. They were both in tears. We'd been talking about Fred's Vietnam tours and were now onto why he wasn't happy with life. The room had turned spinny. I had trouble concentrating. "How can I be happy," I heard Fred lament, "when there are starving kids in the world?"

After hours of prodding, he agreed to come for lunch. He hadn't eaten in days. Sam seemed disappointed when he left the stool. We went out a back door, across an alley, through an unmarked door into the rear of The Nugget. Fred's gait was slow and shaky. People were astonished to see him — everyone knew Fred — and the crowd parted as the three of us entered. Someone gave us a table; the guy behind the counter yelled for our order. We were immediately handed a plate of fried chicken sandwiches and fries — a good twenty minutes before the people who had already ordered. I had the swelling sensation of what it meant to be a local, more local than I'd ever been anywhere at home.

As we ate, I attempted to assimilate the crowd into my changing identity. I allowed myself to wonder if we were copulating and being reborn, or simply slumming. Reno, that afternoon at least, was the West Egg of Nevada. The people were uglier and heavier than they were on the other side (in Vegas). They possessed mild physical deformity (from bad teeth to hunched shoulders). Chubby, middle-aged white women seemed to run it. Old ladies and waitresses called you "Hon." They drank free Grand Marnier and ground down hours at the dollar blackjack tables. Nowhere else in America had I seen people so optimistic about such modest prospects. Driving through B Nevada, south from Oregon, a hierarchy of counter staff had unfolded. Unlike struggling actresses who dream of getting the big Hollywood break, the waitresses in McDermitt only dreamt of waitressing in Winnemucca. In Winnemucca, Reno. And Reno, Vegas. To see beyond the next step was impossible — to even speak of the next step seemed to be putting yourself on an imaginary hook. They gushed about the move, but they would ultimately be content with anything. Most hadn't *ever* been to Vegas. I felt privileged and spoiled and, at times, something like a real superhero whirring through the desert, one place after another. The waitresses were all so candid. Open. Pure.

Beautiful. I wanted to stay and live out my days with each one I met. It *could* work. With a little bit of whiskey each day I could be happy. But which would you choose? They were indistinguishable sirens; a spectrum of sandy colour that changed too gradually to notice.

At the lunch counter, those who knew Fred were stunned when he ordered food. He picked timidly, taking it in a doggie bag, which he would later give to someone passing through The Fitz.

At the end of the afternoon, as the early evening waitresses started their shifts and the tables filled with retired couples and losers played the video-poker machines built into the bar, I told myself that a tourist makes the locals feel like animals at a zoo, but superheroes make them feel like stars. Fred/Sam/Chuck (the quintessential unimaginative one-syllable American names seemed exotic for someone nurtured in a multicultural suburban school system) were more than exhibits; their narratives became ours. I hadn't wanted the Nevada of Burning Man or the bastardized legacy of Mark Twain, Howard Hughes, the Rat Pack, and Vince Vaughn. I abhorred the popular lore. There was nothing hip about my Nevada. Nothing quaint. Nothing scholarly. Nothing witty. Nothing historic. We sensed a crust; I've tried to give it a name — Western American noir, old school, character — it's not kitsch, though. Texture, maybe. Burning Man and Vegas represent horrible colonization. Smug contrivance. The death of crustiness and isolation. They represent the hope of a certain type of civilization. It's a cookie-cutter vitality, where Reno and the B towns that string to and from it are an abiding stagnation. A failure even. When we'd get to Vegas, we couldn't find a trace of that abiding character. The city was so immense and sterile, we didn't even know where to begin. We fled after only a few hours for a town called Stateline. I wondered what it was about people so burnt by life. What was it about crust and haggard?

At The Fitz, the morning after leaving Fred, we slunk back in with dread. We'd have been devastated to see him again; his shakes and bad teeth and starving kids. It had meant a lot to him that we make something of ourselves. That we do good work in our lives. That we tell good stories. He believed good stories could change the world. That's my last memory of Fred. Thank God, he'd gone home.

As we passed one of the smaller side bars on our way out, Sam yelled, "Heeeey, my friends!" The tourists along the wood looked at us enviously. We were natives. We were Reno. Can a passerby stroll through a place and know it better than the place knows itself? You could inhabit your body for seventy years, but a family doctor who gives you an intense physical ultimately knows it better. Differently, at least. Pure euphoria comes from barrelling through a place that seems unfathomable, through a place you don't totally understand. Salman Rushdie wrote about his journey into the Australian outback looking for Bruce Chatwin. He succumbed to the high to which travellers barrelling recklessly through a desert succumb, imagining they're the only ones to ever experience such esoteric glimpses. He rattles off a bunch of exotic-sounding cities, then asks: "Do you know that places only yield their secrets and most profound mysteries to those who are just passing through?" The basic premise of wandering — of conducting narrative — is paradoxical; we intentionally seek out places we can't possibly fathom — on the sole basis that we can't fathom them — only to do everything we can to try to understand them, in the process stripping away the wonder that attracted us in the first place. We strip away too much, kill the mystique, and must move on. Along the way, we do the same thing to our personal identities. Paul and I knew all we wanted to know about Reno. Had we stuck around for weeks or months, we would have shattered the delusion of what Reno was. We had our story. Like Rushdie, we achieved delusion. We need to believe we're super.

I wanted to tell the tourists at Sam's bar about *being* Reno. I wanted for the tourists along the bar to ask how long I'd been there. But nobody asked. Had they, I would have answered: "A long time." Then broken eye contact and fallen silent.

Perhaps a Chase

After Reno, we picked up three different personas in Sam and Fred and Chuck. Crossing the wasteland to Vegas, we incessantly relived the Reno lounge. The image was still crisp; it felt as if we might be able to exist in that day forever. To initiate conversation, you had to begin: "Dude, I'll tell you what" — or "I'll tell you what, *Dude.*" Depending on what the first guy said, the other would reply, "No dude, I'll tell *you* what — or "I'll tell *you* what, Dude." And if there was nothing fresh to add, you'd follow up with, "Fred plays a lot of Keno," which might lead to "I'm gonna kill that Chuck," which would segue into "Heming-*way*!" by which point an original thread of conversation had hopefully emerged.

I always pictured Reno as a couple of hours out of Vegas, but there were still *pages* to get through on the *TripTik*. The I95 runs parallel but crooked to the famed S.F. to L.A. #1, five hundred miles west, along the Pacific Ocean through Big Sur where America geographically runs out. In the Nevada wasteland, it zigs east and west like a river through a jungle, and America pathologically vanishes. We made slow progress down our map. We didn't speed. We revelled in the barren terrain; sagebrush with a smattering of cactus. We felt like we were driving on a treadmill.

"It looks so familiar because you've seen so many movies about the desert," said Paul. He thought about this for a while. "It's never occurred to me that I haven't been in this type of desert before, in the desert of the western U.S. It's landmarking something I already understood. I don't think I've ever been in a limousine either, but I can swear that I have. If I was ever in a limousine, I would never think to myself, this is cool."

"Sometimes it works the opposite way," I pointed out. "Like if you've never been to —"

Paul interrupted me mid-sentence: "Yankee."

As I continued "Fenway."

"Stadium."

"Park."

Day fell through Fallon, Shurz, and Walker Lake. By Hawthorne, it was twilight. A pair of ten-thousand-foot peaks cast a shadow west of Babbit. By Luning, it was dark. Then, almost equidistant between Reno and Vegas, came Mina. We passed a gas station that was closed, then ninety seconds out of Mina, we passed another that was open. We'd spent days extolling the virtues of moving seamlessly and were not about to double back. But we proceeded to dissect the decision for a few minutes — as we drove farther away. There was a solid quarter-tank, but the impending dots on the *TripTik* didn't look any bigger than Mina, they were more spread out, and it was getting late. Turning back felt awkward; it cost us time and pride and momentum. That something could go wrong hadn't even vaguely dawned on us up to this point. We felt soft to acknowledge that something could; that we could be anything other than indestructible.

A pair of vintage pumps stood in front of a crumbling garage. As Paul cleaned the windshield, I pumped. We were loose. On a continuous road trip, you develop an arrogance about what you can and can't get away with at a gas station. I filled it up dead on thirty dollars, then squeezed so it went just past $30.02, a very deliberate act on an old-fashioned pump. Entire seconds elapsed as the digits turned. My benchmark at the time was three cents, but even two seemed far too long on this pump. It seemed invasive and intentional.

"You don't have to pay when it's cash and less than three cents over an even number," I reminded Paul as I jerked in the two and a half cents. That was maybe the fourth time I'd said it to him in the last seventy hours. "Actually, it's quite Machiavellian because it's an unmanly act." He knew what I meant. Stopping even is one of those unspoken skills between men, like choosing urinals or distance pissing or knowing to order eggs sunny side up.

As we walked to the garage, I continued: "Look, if we drive all the way to Tierra Del Fuego, and squeeze an extra two cents out per gassing, that's going to come to at least three free gassings." We sauntered in like we owned the world. Didn't we? We were captains of the craft on which we'd come down. We made definitive pronouncements about all we saw and did. We critiqued our performance — always generously — at every bend. We'd even generously critique the critique.

The station had the hue of a place in which people only grabbed for things with greasy hands. It was unusually bright, but the light was neither comforting nor ambient. The bulbs weren't where they would have been in a rational building. Not in the Texaco sense. And in stark contrast from the precisely calculated merchandising of a Texaco, most of the shelves were empty. There was bare space where there should have been more empty shelves. They sold miscellaneous merchandise: hunting magazines, tobacco, "garb" — stuff that you'd carry for scattered members of a militia. The proprietor, as Paul noted, possessed a J. T. Walsh, Hoyt Axtonish quality. It was the quality of the bad guy you vaguely recognized in a suspense movie. He was in his forties, forty pounds over his ideal weight. Deceptively tall at 6'2", 6'3". The counter was low for a gas-station counter, which accentuated his size. He had a sloppy moustache, and he wore tinted glasses, a trucker cap with mesh back, stained jean jacket with a flannel shirt underneath, and wrinkled jeans that didn't hang properly from his waist. The ends of his hair were dark; curly, unkempt, and greasy. He was drenched with sweat. In a way that would gnaw at me afterward, he seemed ever so slightly off. Not threatening — not at that moment, at least — just somehow "off." His strained grin struck me as a permanent expression, a mark of inbreeding, but I slowly realized there was more to it than that.

How did he see us? We rolled out of a family van with Alberta plates. We were in our early twenties. We were kids pretending to be savvy and haggard. How would *you* see us?

Because it didn't seem remarkable until we left, I don't remember the conversation explicitly. Our MO was to excessively engage everyone we met. We'd take an overly animated, unnatural patronizing tone. He sensed this. He'd dealt with "us" before. We told him what we were doing, where we were going. Subtly, he kept us babbling. He asked about our route, where we were heading that night, if anyone was waiting for us, who knew our travel plans. (If we suddenly went missing, would anyone come make a fuss?) It didn't seem entirely harmless, but we were confident and excited and eager to interact with the only human on such a long, lonely, dark stretch of road.

And then talk somehow got onto our mothers. "Your moms are probably wondering where you're going."

Paul, who had phoned his a few hours earlier, answered, "We haven't talked to our moms in a long time."

The owner talked about his mom who won forty grand in Vegas a few days earlier. "She goes down and wins a lot and loses a lot." He shrugged, then asked if we were going to gamble — "By the way, how much are you guys carrying to gamble with?" — and Paul answered, "We're not like your mom. Your mom's a bit of a roller." A picture flashed in my mind of a guy raised by a wheezy, unstable, cruel old lady whom he was yearning to please.

It seems to me, looking back, that his tone turned sharp when the door behind us opened. It went from friendly to business, as if he'd procured all the information he needed from us; as if to say, "I have what I need. I'm going to charge you for the fucking gas now."

The kid who opened the door — the front one through which we entered — wore a camouflage cap, jeans, and a black leather jacket. He'd pulled up in a dusty navy pickup. Might have been chewing tobacco. I can't remember for sure. He looked at us, then to the owner for a reaction. It didn't seem like he worked there. They weren't father and son or uncle and nephew or brothers. Why would they know each other? He walked around behind us and leaned against the long side of the counter. I felt him sizing me up out of the corner of his eye. We must have both felt it, because there was thirty seconds where we tried to be more earnest; to show them both a more human side.

"$30.03." The owner said it in a voice that implied he'd heard every word I said outside. I noticed a well-thumbed *Hustler* beside the register.

We each took a fast glance back on the way out. The owner had already moved down the counter. They were whispering, quickly and urgently. He was telling the kid something about us. And the kid nodded. The look sent shivers up our spines.

Hitchcock said that suspense plays better than action. Tommy Lasorda, Pedro Guerrero's manager with the Dodgers, said that "the difference between the impossible and the possible lies in the person's determination." I now realize that to find Pedro Guerrero is to exist in an original story outside your frame of reference — in such a way that out of however many billion humans inhabit planet Earth at any moment, you are, if only for that moment, numero uno with a bullet. The longer you can stay there existing as Pedro Guerrero the better. Tragically, most of us don't find Pedro in our read-the-paper, listen-at-the-water-cooler, surf the Net, watch TV on the couch, read a novel, inhabit the second-third-fourth-fifth-hand-narratives-of-others existence. And you clock the moments of those who accidentally do in nanoseconds. There's a small group who seem to know how to channel the dude for *minutes* at a time, though. As we barrelled through the Nevada wasteland, I realized I wanted to be such an individual. How significantly, I now wonder, must we inhabit fresh narrative to reap its secrets?

As we drove, the night took on ominous qualities. Our most minute action, or lack of action, could alter global history. If we didn't interact perfectly with such and such a local, there'd be an earthquake in Bangladesh. Let someone else take the cords at a dive in Tijuana, a teenage girl would be raped in Tasmania. I had a vivid, swelling déjà vu. The eeriest song lyrics arose in my head. It was dry, for instance, but it was a "Riders on the Storm" night. It was a "Riders on the Storm" meets "Ghost Riders in the Sky" night. What happened in the gas station with the redneck and his creepy sidekick was the equivalent of giving that proverbial stranger a ride — despite the visceral karmic warning from the universe — and now sweet Emily would die. A dead man with a lightning bolt had already taken her.

The radio only turned up static. Scratchy AM radio on a long-abandoned stretch late at night comes to sound like the devil's thought pattern. There were lights on the horizon, as well as back where we'd come from. We monitored them quietly, but nothing neared nor drifted farther away. It had been hours since we'd seen another moving vehicle. The wasteland arced unevenly in the moonlight from the side of the road. We were cut off from anything.

Paul was driving. We hadn't talked about what had transpired right away; in hindsight, lulling each other into a sense that all was well. "Was that a little weird?" I eventually asked.

"*Yes*," he answered, then exhaled loudly. We were relieved for a moment that the other had sensed it, too, but only a moment. We were dudes who had analyzed every single mundane instant of the trip, and now we ripped apart the Mina gas station. "This guy knows a *lot* about us," Paul concluded nervously. "That's freaking weird."

And the more we talked about it, the weirder it got. Tension would go up in jagged fits, then whenever we'd reach a level of safety in our understanding, dire and speculative thoughts became too dense and incited another flurry.

"You ever see ... umm ... what's the name of it ... that movie with Kurt Russell?" I knew the name, but, brain squirming like a toad, I wanted to draw the moment out. "The couple's from Boston, driving that new Jeep Cherokee across the desert ... Those creepy dudes kidnap Kathleen Quinlan ... Those creepy dudes *really* knew what they were doing."

We'd both been thinking about that movie and promised not to bring it up again. But I wouldn't be able to stop myself from blurting out, "At this very moment there are people locked up in closets in compounds that you *know* are just over that hill." We spooked each other to higher levels. "They invite their fat tattooed friends over and torture you."

There was an ultimate futility when it came to anything we could do, though. We had Paul's brother's cellphone, which didn't work. I rounded up a Swiss Army knife and Leatherman from the back of the van. We talked scenarios. The kid would ram us off the road in his truck (if he hadn't already sabotaged our engine at the station); they'd radioed ahead and a roadblock was being set up at the top of the next hill; a semi would suddenly light up on the side of the road. "If it comes down to a sheriff pulling us over," I asked, speculating that they'd be hunting buddies, "we're driving the speed limit, and our lights are working. Is he in on it and what do we do?"

I imagined having to lie naked, bound in rusty barbed wire in front of the redneck as he locked jumper cables to my testicles. I imagined the look on his unshaven face. I imagined having to be subservient to a serial killer like the kid who came into the garage. Just having to face him on his playing field stirred a poisonous feeling. I processed that feeling differently than Paul. We goaded each other into *believing* the delusion that we were being chased — to a point at which he finally cracked and soberly demanded, "Look, I know you're fucking with me now and that's fine. *Whatever.* Don't stop, I don't care. Just give me your absolute straight as honest as you can be answer. This is a weird situation."

I was shocked by how grave he'd become.

"Is this happening?" he continued, panic and confusion in his voice. "Is this just our minds and too much coffee and too little sleep coming down, and we've spun this tale and worked ourselves into this froth? Or is this really happening? Because I don't really know where I'm at right now. I have *no* idea and I need you to help me. Give me a percentage. What is it? Don't mess with me. Is this happening or not?"

"OK," I replied, matching his grave tone. I scrunched my face and pretended to work through a detailed, incomprehensible set of primordial calculations. I drew a long breath. I had an answer. "A God's honest answer?" I asked nervously.

"A God's honest answer," he replied, the pupils of his eyes bulging. At the last second, I adjusted the number to be conservative. "Twelve per cent."

A half-second passed, and I wondered if I'd said something too low. Then he took his eyes off the road and his expression broke in a way that I subsequently saw people react to news that the Trade Center had been hit by airplanes. It was so outside the spectrum of anything anyone could imagine *actually* happening. There was an instant of terror — two instants of total terror. Something else snapped in his face. He flashed that kind of giddy disbelief for about thirty seconds. We both cackled nervously. Then he got serious.

He had expected me to say, "OK, Dude, get over it. This ain't happening." Because I *seemed* more composed, he wanted to believe that I somehow understood better. He knew that part of me *really* wanted it to be happening. The potential consequences were not yet direct enough. We were on our own. We were scared. When I was younger, I was mildly tough. Bruised. Sunburnt. Frostbitten. Sniffly. Bloodshot eyes. As I matured, I grew delicate; the tissue around my wrists got thin. My only mettle test was hatha yoga. *Hatha yoga.* I went out of my way not to put stress on my body, not to live hard, not to live real. I lived delicately, to avoid disease. I desperately need-ed what was happening right now. And the fact that I enjoyed it only made me enjoy it more. As I became more excited, Paul grew increasingly irritated.

"Now is *not* the time," he ordered. "You can't have an iota of your being being the cold observer. You gotta be in the moment and not anywhere else."

"Oh, I'm in the moment," I replied. "I didn't say one hundred per cent. I didn't say eighty per cent. I said twelve."

"Think about this," he pressed. "This is a situation where there are guys you have met in a gas station who are part of a weird freaky Nevada cult that kidnaps people and twelve per cent — that's more than *one in ten* it could happen *to us*. I was thinking either fifty/fifty — or more. I believe this. The only thing that is kind of helping me is that I know you're goading me."

The pitch of our voices peaked and dropped, and we talked around the fear we both felt, each testing the other to gauge the validity of paranoia to which we were instinctively succumbing. The closer to the truth, the greater the delusion turned out to be. We'd crossed truth (fact, at least) and didn't know where the delusion ended. And maybe that's what fear is; when you don't know if a nightmare is real. We weren't male friends who bonded in a world war or Vietnam. We'd solidified the first phase of our bond on the grounds of Lilith Fair, and this was our battlefield on which it was ultimately consummated. Men desperately need to share harrowing narrative. They need to share shocks.

I wish that life could come down to routine moments of reckoning (to which we'd all *actually* reckon, like action heroes). Here was ours: It had been two hours since we'd seen another car. We could still see headlights — in the distance up front, and in the far, far distance behind. "Are they closer?" Paul would ask. But nothing materialized. Nothing passed. We plowed through a small town called Coaldale, the perfect spot for anyone who might have been called to make an assault from (but not in). We drifted through without incident. We drifted through another dark, anxious hour to a bigger town called Tonopah. We agonized about stopping, but it felt too dangerous. I had the sensation of being watched. It wasn't inconceivable that all of Tonopah could be in on our abduction. A few miles past, powering up a hill, not far from Area 51, we felt more certain that the block was going to be there. That late at night, it would have taken them this long to organize what they were going to do. The sheriff was *definitely* involved.

The terror surged past anything we'd yet experienced. And an idea came: to turn around. "I mean, what's stopping us?" I asked. We were about an hour from blowing out of whatever territory or jurisdiction the killers operated. We believed, though, that what was going to happen would be just over the hill. "The last thing they'd expect is that we'd power right back at them." Because of the minivan's tight steering, it was a clumsy four-point turn. But once we picked up speed again, we were on the attack. It seemed like the greatest plan ever. The hunted was suddenly the hunter.

After boomeranging back to Tonopah, Paul clenched his Leatherman in his pocket as we left the van and marched cautiously across the parking lot to a rundown casino called The Station House. Inside, to the right, were blackjack tables and slot machines, to the left what felt like a deep sunken rectangular pit. It was dark and smelled like the end of the 1950s. We descended a dozen abrupt steps, past four or five tables of hard people, drinking short-neck Buds, then sat at the scratched-up counter. The bartender was big; he wore a white cowboy shirt with the buttons undone. On any other night, we'd be intimated to order anything from him. We sat at the far end of the bar so we could see the door. I ordered scotch. Paul looked the bartender in the eye. His voice didn't waver. He said: "Get me an ice water." No tip. No gratitude for bringing the water. No acknowledgement that his hairy-chested narrative counted whatsoever.

If they show up, I remember thinking, they'd show up in the form of people they'd called ahead to. I scanned the lounge looking for anyone who might be looking at us. It was busy. We said nothing, just spasmed with intensity. "What do we do if these guys come in and sit down behind us?" I whispered to Paul.

His eyes went berserk. There wasn't a trace of sarcasm or false bravado. Slowly, succinctly, he uttered, "I'll kill them." Emergency room doctors, to determine how genuine a potential suicidal patient is, will ask if the patient has a plan. They take the ones who have it planned seriously, because it's more than just a vague jones. I knew Paul had it mapped out. And I stopped worrying. It was his problem, and I could focus on the ambience.

The place was an anti-modern Wild West saloon, full of mysterious characters in varying states of desperation. It was something that Disney would pattern a ride after; where Warren Oates in *Bring Me the Head of Alfredo Garcia* gets another head. Had every light been on, it would have still seemed dark. Old dark. Red dark. Smoke dark. Déjà vu dark. The place exuded nothing but the fact that there wasn't a place like it anywhere else; and no one gave a shit if anyone else knew it existed. There was a bona fide *bar act* onstage playing what sounded like an AM car radio church-pipe organ run off a wheezing alternator. The singer swayed in front of long, rich, crimson drapes saturated with decades of non-stop nicotine. Phantom notes plowed through the darkness, slowly, steadily, echoing off one another. And "Downtown" is the song I remember. It wasn't a rendition of hope or solution; it wasn't anything Petula Clark could have intended. A bordello owner — or so I like to think — with a couple of young, tight women literally on each arm, screamed: "Come on, you skinny little bitch. Play some George Strait."

For the first time in our lives, we were permitted to sit in a dive with a sense of purpose. It was the most vivid mood we could ever hope to discover — and it was only background. I realized the inadequacy of all those other experiences. This was a functional experience. We weren't voyeurs; we didn't have to wonder if we were slumming; we were an actual part of the scene. We were *characters.* And I remember thinking how right it felt to be there. The story we were living felt valid in the scheme of others stories. We were Pedro Guerrero. Such was the intensity of the delusion, at least.

My problem on every other night of every other year is that there's just no flow. There's so little flow left anywhere. Purity has a component of continuity — or irregular lengths of interval. Modern existence, on the other hand, is uniform segments. Eight hours of sleep. Nine to five at work. One hundred and nineteen minutes at a movie theatre. Conversations that take the length of a cup of coffee. A baseball game. Back-to-back *Simpsons* reruns. The commute. The one-page memo. The shower before breakfast and quick fuck before bed. Paul and I, in achieving a near–Pedro Guerrero state, were also discovering continuity. We were, however temporarily it might have been, going though life *A, B, G, X, L,* instead of *A, B, A, C, A, D, B, A, C, D, A.* (You need to get down into the bowels of the alphabet to have stories and make life count, because it's not meant to be episodic or so excessively compartmentalized; it's flow predicated on self-perpetuating conventions.) Thus, purity is a three-day bender. Extra innings. Kinky one-night stands (or week-long love-making sessions). A novel read or written straight through. A road trip with no point. Lots of coffee. No stopping. No sleeping. Working on projects, not until noon, but 'til they're done. Jagged texture is purity.

Sheer want does not get you those minutes of narrative purity; those Pedro minutes. It rarely happens when you press. But throw yourself into the right types of situations and anything can happen. Our yearning to be Pedro highlighted our sleep-deprived transmogrification into a different version of the Chris and Paul who existed only days earlier in Canada. As we got farther away, we'd become freakier men. Madmen capable of killing other madmen. In our opinion, better men; repurposed products of perhaps the most intense forty-eight consecutive hours of our sheltered, boring lives. This was a near-flawless performance. It was near-perfect wandering. It was a succession of unparalleled moments of existence. Unparalleled anywhere else that night.

After the act, the bar emptied. It didn't seem safe to leave, so we wandered across the casino into a diner, which had just turned on its lights. It slowly filled as we sat there. "Holy Christ, we're pounding coffee right now," Paul remarked.

A nearby booth filled with a rowdy group who'd been out cruising a half-dozen streets in Tonopah. I caught snippets of the conversation. A big dare was about to happen. (Bravado before a big, insignificant bet is so B Nevada.) Someone pulled out a straitjacket. Before the straitjacket, we had casually attempted to ignore them — for we sensed their moment was about to usurp ours. The bet was something like "get out of a straitjacket in fifteen minutes." You knew the guy couldn't do it. He looked like rabies-inflicted Trent Reznor. You knew he'd never attempted it, but he simply wanted to have a story for fifteen minutes. He was inhabiting the delusion that this was something he could do. This was something he did back in his "amateur days." He wanted to believe he was the type of person who could get out of a straitjacket. And he almost convinced himself that he could. He asked us if we happened to have any handcuffs. With what little Pedro Paul had left, he rolled his eyes.

But someone, a stranger at another booth, had already pulled out not one, but two sets of handcuffs. Another table deftly helped him put on the jacket and fix the cuffs. And after an hour, he had to acknowledge that he couldn't do it — and proceeded, because his act lacked substance, to clown for another twenty minutes. His girlfriend fed him cocktails. On our way out, we saw him dealing blackjack, his speech slurred.

Our fear, our edge, our worth to humankind had dissipated. I saw myself in the clown's straitjacket, trying to invent a story that stood out from all the movies, television, water-cooler conversations, breaking news, comic books, and songs he'd lived through. The difference between me and him was that his straitjacket wasn't an illusion.

Is that the personal story spun as thriller? Suspense with no pay-off. That's this story, at least. That's Pedro Guerrero too. It was only the idea of what he did that I cared about. I didn't mind if he rocked the girl or OD'd on cocaine or had sparkling conversation in the Mustang along the way. I wanted the experience without the voltage. It was only the idea of being involved in something authentic; it didn't have to be plugged in.

What's character? Nick the Greek said that it's "the only difference between a winner and a loser." My *Oxford Paperback Dictionary* with the broken spine cites eight definitions including "all those qualities that make a person, group, or thing what he or it is and different from others." Or "a person in a novel or play." Character is what manifests itself in the dark, when and where nobody's watching. Nobody watches B America, the alter ego, whereas the jones for validation is all that allows Vegas to be seen from the moon.

Character is the overlapping stains from narrative that life leaves behind. It's the old bus station instead of the new airport. Fred, not Josh Brolin. Old-school Reno, not modern Vegas. Pedro, not O. J. Hunted and hunting, not watching. Shocked, not wondered.

What's character? Character is the gaudy thread that holds together the human delusion.

DOUGLAS BELL

The Accidental Course
of My Illness

In matters touching on death, the clinical and the moral are never so far apart that we can look at one without seeing the other.
— Sherwin Nuland

All your life you think you have to hold back your craziness, but when you're sick you can let it out in all its garish colours.
— Anatole Broyard

MEMORIES OF JUNE 10, 1974, START WITH breakfast. Later, when I threw it up in the emergency room, a nurse who was cutting my clothes away remarked on how lucky I was to get scrambled eggs. "Those must have been delicious," she said cheerily. It wasn't luck. It was habit. My dad, a creature of military routine, served the same breakfast every morning: eggs, half a grapefruit, two rashers of bacon, toast (no crust), juice, and milk. The blue-and-white plate always sat on top of a solid placemat depicting an Audubon nature scene. The twelve- to fifteen-minute meal, which never varied in duration, was measured by the sections of the *Globe and Mail,* delivered to me as my dad finished them: front section, sports, comics (Blondie, Rex Morgan, Pogo). Then he'd fold up the business section and march down the hall to the john for his "morning's morning." I'd saunter along behind, past the closing washroom door, a right turn into my room, loiter over something or other (*Sports Illustrated,* CFL player cards, Helmut Newton's latest shots in *Photo* magazine), pick up my knapsack, and drop the rest of the paper off to my night-owl mother still lolling in bed. Kiss goodbye, back past the john.

"See ya, Dad."

"See ya, Sunny Jim."

This day was the same, except I left the house with only my history text attached to the back of my Raleigh ten-speed. I had an exam — Mr. Kidell's Grade 9 British history class. Two hours. I wasn't exactly full of confidence. I unlocked my bike, pulled my chain-side grey sock up over my grey flannel trouser leg, rolled the bike around to the front of our house in the Forest Hill district of Toronto, and took off along Lonsdale Road toward Russell Hill Road. From there, it was south past St. Clair Avenue, sailing down the long hill of the old Lake Ontario shoreline and under the railway bridge to Dupont and Davenport. Then, a right turn past Tony Sisca's Esso station, where my dad got his car gassed up (and where, as a result, I was able to gather extra Esso NHL power players), ride west along Dupont past Loblaws and past Spadina, negotiate the wiggle in that otherwise straight-arrow street, and turn left down Howland Avenue two long blocks to the Anglican boys' choir school, St. George's College, I had attended for five years. Twenty more minutes to bone up, then bring on those Anglos and those Saxons. That was the plan.

I passed Loblaws in the warm morning light and approached the corner of Spadina and Dupont. I was aware of a truck to my left as I approached the intersection. I felt its steamy presence. I went past the passenger-side door high over my left shoulder. The light was red. Then it was green, and without a backward glance I started to walk the bike between my legs across the intersection. At the same moment, the truck started to turn right up Spadina. As it moved into me, I started to hop-waddle-walk, trying to turn with it. But the bulk of the truck began exerting a gravitational force, drawing me and the bike under the rear wheel. I felt an increasing pressure, and I remember thinking as the truck turned around me, my body falling gradually between the right rear tire, the curb, and a lamp post: "I'm in trouble." Then an odd thought: "This is what it would be like if I were mashed by the big freezer in our basement." There was a crushing sensation, and then the pavement, stretching down Spadina Avenue to the horizon, rose up and pounded me. I didn't fall to meet it. It rose to meet me, and it loomed far and wide and black ... blacker ... blackest.

It was like waking up in the morning, with a momentary sense that what had just happened might not have happened. Next, some-one — a policeman as it turned out — was asking me questions. My eyes opened onto a huge du Maurier cigarette sign looming over me, and I responded in peppy rapid-fire as much to reassure myself that everything was going to be fine as to satisfy the cop. I rattled off my name, my address, my phone number ("foureightsix-eighteenthirty"), and my parents' names ("Cicely 'n' Norman"). I mentioned that I was going to be late for my history exam. Not that I thought my lateness was a negative thing. Far from it. More time to study. I knew I was woefully ill-prepared. The cop laughed and said I wouldn't be writing anything any time soon. "But I'm going to be OK, right?" "Sure, probably a couple of broken ribs." I don't remember any acute sensation of pain at that stage so much as a dull, pervasive ache that indicated something was the matter. As a precaution, I was lifted on a hard stretcher into the back of the ambulance. I remember thinking that my back wasn't the problem. Shortly after the ambulance started to move, the pain opened up like a blossom, and I asked the attendant for something to kill it. No, he said, if we give you something, the doctors will have a more difficult time figuring out what's the matter. By now, the pain was like a pulsating sensation of white, everywhere, inside me and all around me. It wasn't something that was happening to me. The pain was me. I kept asking where we were, as if my knowing would relieve the relentlessness.

Then we were there — the Hospital for Sick Children. As I was wheeled into the emergency, I found myself cursing the truck driver — swearing a blue streak — "fucking bastard, if I ever get my hands on that cocksucker …" I thought maybe I should be angry — after all, it was his fault — so I was. Later, a resident on the medical staff met my mother in a waiting room. "Nice kid," my mother remembered his saying, "but he's got a mouth on him like a stevedore." Meantime, the pain had subsided, and I began to feel not much at all. I'd later discover this numbness was a clear indication of shock; the body's way of turning the pain volume down (and, unhappily, often a way station to the hereafter).

At this point, my effort to recount the history of my trauma takes on a slightly more respectable cast. My medical records come into play, and the history of my accident and subsequent illness gets tied in with the efforts of those who succeeded in saving me.

On a clear spring day in 1996, my mother called me around to the house on a leafy cul-de-sac in southeast Rosedale. Dad met me at the door, then disappeared. Mum was waiting in the living room surrounded by shelf after shelf of eighteenth-century porcelain sauce boats. Her face is my face; a prominent jaw takes it past beautiful nearer to handsome. She told me she had "a spot of terminal cancer." If my mother were to describe a mother and son exactly like us, she'd point out that "they get along after a fashion." Which is to say, it's like politics, or war carried on by other means. That's who we've become. But when I was a little boy, Mum would read me C. S. Lewis's *The Lion, the Witch and the Wardrobe,* and by a flick of the eyebrow or a turn of the lip, she could make me laugh or cry, sometimes on the same page. For that, I loved her unabashedly.

So when she said she was dying, I felt the craziest curry of thought and emotion. I wept, which is rare, and my mother said she didn't want me to feel bad. Then she told me she had recently tried to commit suicide. The way Mum described it, she walked out to the garage in her nightie and slippers with some duvets, pillows, and a book of Cecil Beaton's photographs, shut the garage door, turned on the engine of Dad's car, then curled up on the concrete floor in her duvets with her Beaton and fell asleep. "The only problem," she said, "was that your father's car ran out of gas."

We both laughed — because the situation was funny and because Dad's so scrupulous that he never lets the car get below half a tank. Mum even added an apocryphal grace note to her story — a confrontation with Dad the next morning, a how-could-you-do-this-to-me scene.

At that moment, I thought I'd better tell my mother how I loved her — just saying that I loved her wouldn't do. That would be the sort of sentimental imprecision she and I mocked in others. I found myself thanking her for the way she had cared for me after the accident. And to the extent I could afford to dole out the unconditional love so beloved of therapists and preachers, that was it. Later, walking home in the clear air, I noticed every blossom on every bush and tree, and I thought I better get on with writing an account of that accident or Mum would die and with her death would go her crucial contribution to this story, to my story. I'd miss yet another opportunity to square myself with myself. I needed to understand, and to excise the accident and its aftermath. I needed a new way of thinking; one that didn't assume the course of my illness was, and would always be, the signal event of my life.

The first step was to go over to the records department at Sick Kids' and apply for the record of my hospitalization. Two weeks and seventy-five bucks later, I was sitting on a bench just outside the hospital's old front entrance on University Avenue hungrily leafing through a five-inch stack of photocopies. I was surprised to find at the top a record of my tonsillectomy (November 25, 1963). It indicated that I weighed thirty-nine and one quarter pounds and had ginger ale before the operation. I remember the strange sensation of waking up in the evening light and vanilla ice cream running down my throat. I looked for that on the chart. Not there.

And then I saw it: my admission record for June 10, 1974. "Multiple trauma," it read. From there, the record was a litany of medical terminology chronicling my ups and downs (the progress report), a record of every order given by the doctors charged with my care, and technical reports indicating the results of a variety of blood tests. As I read, I became increasingly discouraged by the distance between what I felt and what they wrote. For instance, one passage referred to having 5.7 litres of fluid drained out of my abdomen. That's it. One declarative sentence. Having 5.7 litres of fluid drained out of your abdomen, I thought, deserved more telling than that. In fact, in pursuing the story of my illness, I sensed that all these events deserved more telling. It's certainly how I felt at the time. I wanted to tell people what was happening to me, but doctors and nurses and friends and relations and parents weren't all that interested in letting me talk (or at least listening to me), because I was a patient sick unto death. The big thing was to make me better. I remember as I left the emergency room on my way to the intensive care unit, my dad, 6'2" in a crisply pressed grey checked suit, appeared beside my bed as it rolled toward the elevator. Like most teenagers who've screwed up, I needed to explain myself. So, as was — and is — my wont, I babbled about who knows what. Dad pleaded with me to keep quiet and save my energy. And I remember feeling pissed off — "He never lets me talk."

The accident stayed with me by way of a series of acute pancreatic illnesses in 1977, 1987, and 1990, each resulting in extended stays in the hospital. The guy I wake up to be every day is, for better or worse, the guy who got run over by a truck. The scars deeply embedded in my midsection always remind me of that. Nervous dad, nervous writer, nervous guy. Me. Every so often I meet someone from the small circle of WASP Toronto in which I was raised, and we'll do the "oh-do-you-know-so-and-so?" waltz. Inevitably, it will be interrupted by "Oh, you're the guy that got run over by the truck." Blood, bile, puss, puke, scars, stitches, Demerol, IV, needles, sodium pentothal, catheters, nasogasritic tubes, laparotomy and jejunostomy, and every other goddamn thing that happened to me that summer and subsequently — more than anything else I am that guy.

At any rate, before I could hope to address these matters, I had to go back and reconstruct things. Apart from my medical records, I figured the best place to start would be with my parents and the doctors who treated me. Save one major exception, the main players were still around. Dr. Sigmund Ein, who'd been responsible for my case while the surgeon in charge was on vacation, still practised general surgery at Sick Kids'. Dr. Mark Greenberg, a medical resident at the time, was now head of pediatric oncology. I remembered him as a decent fellow, often willing to talk to me as opposed to talking about me. Dr. Adelaide Fleming, my pediatrician at the time, was still practising. All agreed to see me.

Dr. Clinton Stephens, the senior surgeon in charge of my case, had died of cancer in April of 1990. My mum and I had gone to a memorial service at Timothy Eaton Church. As we left, she turned to me and said, "Well, that was a good deed in a dirty world." I had the vague feeling that I'd missed something by not keeping in touch with Dr. Stephens through the years. In a tribute to him, published in the *Journal of Pediatric Surgery,* Dr. Ein and two others in the

Department of General Surgery wrote: "He was a precise, gentle, definitive technical surgeon, and always taught conservative surgery. His patient care was simple, easy, and impeccable. His knowledge of pediatric surgery was encyclopedic; his recall for patients and their problems was both accurate and uncanny."

In short, he was as heroic as I remembered him. Speaking laconically if at all, Dr. Stephens radiated charismatic calm. He would always ask how I was doing, and I was always ready with a report that would daunt a Royal Commission. As I spoke, he would palpate my belly with his large callused hands in a manner that I found immensely reassuring. I would prattle on and he would respond, "Uh hhuuuh, hmmmhh, uh huh." Then he would check my chest with his always chilly stethoscope, look down with amused blue eyes set wide beneath a high patrician forehead, and say, "We'll come by again a little later." And off he would go, a gaggle of sober residents and interns trailing behind his slow certain gait.

The record of my first day in the hospital indicates that, as a general observation, my condition was "pale, clammy, apprehensive, conversant, cooperative, intelligent," which is me most days. (If only that last observation meant something more than its clinical definition of "having or showing understanding.") The more specific notations were encouraging. Despite abrasions on my right face and right orbit, there was no "boney [sic] tenderness." Despite "rapid respiration" and "a slight paradoxical movement of the left sternum" (indicative, I discovered later, of a punctured lung), there was no "lateral chest tenderness." And, wonder of wonders, under the heading "genit" were the words every fourteen-year-old boy, whether he knows it or not, longs to see: "normal male." Yeah, baby!

Reading my charts for June 10, 1974, I looked like a slightly overwrought kid aiming to please. Of course, it was all much worse than that. My blood pressure when I entered the emergency room was 80/0; my pulse was 140; my respiration 60 and shallow. These three readings taken together represented a physical catastrophe in the making. My heart whacking away at over twice its normal rate was compensating for severe internal bleeding. The blood loss was starving the brain of oxygen, so the brain responded by trying to up the intake. But the punctured lung restricted the power of my bellows. Hence my breaths were as shallow as the shoreline. As for my blood pressure, suffice it to say that any time a zero shows up in the reading, it's cause for concern. I was a mess. Just how much of a mess was made clear to me in two sobering exchanges during interviews with Doctors Ein and Fleming.

I caught up with Dr. Ein, who bears a striking resemblance to the U.S. Federal Reserve chairman Allen Greenspan, at Sick Kids'. His office is an event unto itself, with photographs everywhere, mostly of doctors standing around at medical gatherings. Balloons and streamers hang from the ceiling and litter the floor. Bumper stickers, diplomas, and a Michael Jordan mask plaster the walls. Draped across the back of his chair, was Hulk Hogan's torn tanktop signed: "To Siggy, best wishes, the Hulkster."

During my stay at the hospital, a lot of rumours went around concerning Dr. Ein's wild temper and his propensity to pitch scalpels around operating rooms, occasionally stabbing unwary residents in the foot. One thing I knew to be incontrovertibly true: he and his wife, an ICU nurse at the hospital, had adopted six kids, all of whom Dr. Ein had operated on. I remembered two things about his manner: while moving around my bed during an examination, his head swivelled like that of an agitated turtle, and he brushed off my questions in a manner meant to discourage any further queries. At one stage during the month he was charged with my care, he restricted me to two questions a visit. "Make 'em count," he said. I asked him what his favourite baseball team was. "Cincinnati Reds," he said without missing a beat. "That's one."

In my interview with Dr. Ein, I tried to get a sense of exactly what had happened to me that morning twenty-four years earlier. I remembered the term "hematoma" being bandied about. "A hematoma's a big bruise," he said. "It's like if I give you a big smash in the arm. I'll burst the blood vessels, and bust the muscle, and you bleed into it and you get a hematoma. The liver's got a very fragile capsule, that if you give a good shock to it, it'll break." Dr. Ein's eyes grew wide as his explanation gathered momentum. "Have you ever seen raw liver? Take your fist, next time you see it, before your mom cooks it, and pound it like this" — he smashed his fist on his desk-top, BANG — "and it'll tear apart. And that's exactly what your liver looked like."

Later that week, I went to speak with Dr. Fleming at her home office on Dunvegan Avenue in Forest Hill, just around the corner from where I'd grown up. Once inside the door, I was hit by a smell that I remembered exactly — a powerful combination of disinfectant and Pledge. Dr. Adelaide Fleming shared the same comfortable, WASP background as my mother. She was puzzled by what exactly I was up to. "Why do you want to explore this in such detail?" she asked. "I mean the detail of the operations and your course in the hospital. I could see how you could write, say, about the powerful influence this had on you psychologically, but I'm surprised you want to relive the agony." I ventured something about being like a litigant wanting to inform himself as well as possible of all the details so he can make a convincing argument. I'm not even sure I bought that one myself. Then we got down to it.

"I remember that those first few days were very intense. Stephens wasn't very happy with the situation."

"When you say he wasn't very happy," I asked, wishing I was very far away, "what do you mean?" Her face composed itself into a matter-of-fact cast. "Well, he thought you were going to die; that's what he kept telling me. I was more optimistic. I felt that if we could just keep you supported you'd be all right."

Right then I had a clear recollection of asking my mother whether I was going to die. She was sitting bedside on one of those first few days. She turned her face to profile and said, "No, you're going to get better. You're very, very ill, but you're going to get better." As she spoke, she looked out the window, across University Avenue, maybe catching a corner of the newly minted Mount Sinai Hospital across the street. I'd always known that I'd been very sick. I probably even knew that I'd almost died. But hearing that Dr. Stephens believed I would die …

Dr. Fleming continued to speak, but she seemed to be moving away from me down a long tunnel. I could see that she was talking, but her words weren't reaching me.

Because of the "extensive disruption of the right lobe of the liver," blood, bile, tissue fluid, and intravenous fluid poured out of my liver into my abdominal cavity. As a result, my abdomen increased eight waist sizes to 86 centimetres from a regular girth of 62. I remember the nurses coming in every hour or so and measuring. I couldn't even lift my rump to let them pass the tape measure under my back. But I learned just what the word "distended" meant. The sensation is unpleasant in the extreme. Push out your abdomen as though you're trying to create the impression you have a bowling ball lodged in your gut. Now push hard, strain until your belly starts to quiver. Hold that position for seventy-two hours, and you'll have some sense of it.

I noticed on the charts that in these early days they were giving me doses of valium, presumably to keep me in a rested state. As a result of my immobility, nurses would come and beat gently on my chest trying to make me cough to keep fluid from gathering in my lungs. The record says that I developed a pneumonia. Within two or three days, I was severely jaundiced, my skin turning lime green as the liver failed to remove pollutants from my bloodstream. I remember the whites of my eyes turning the shade of egg yoke.

The ruptured liver, as it turned out, wasn't the problem. The fluid pouring out was. "Once you were stabilized and on intravenous and the blood was starting to transfuse, the chances of you dying from that injury were pretty small," said Dr. Ein. "After that, however, bile and blood mixed together in the belly, and the risk of infection was significant. Especially when this stuff stays in your belly. It stays in an area or pocket that's stagnant, just like water in a pool. There's no circulation, and it stagnates, it pollutes. And organisms grow very well in blood and bile, which is very nutritious."

In other words, I was a prime candidate for septic shock, the leading cause of "late death" — death days or weeks following trauma — in ICU patients across North America. Septic shock is a deadly chain reaction triggered by the infection to which Dr. Ein referred. One organ fails, and the rest follow along like so many horses pulling the hearse.

To remedy this situation, Dr. Siran Bandy, a poker-faced East Indian, turned up at my bedside five days after the accident and inserted an angio cath No. 14 into my right side and proceeded to withdraw 5.7 litres of fluid from my abdomen. (There are, in fact, only around 5 litres of blood volume in a fourteen-year-old boy's entire body.) Down the length of my trunk, I could see the maroon fluid running out of me the way water flows freely from an outdoor tap. Now and again Bandy mopped his brow. The stuff reeked. At that moment, I began to feel myself changing from a guy who'd had something happen to him like a bad cut or abrasion to someone else. "Look at all that shit pouring out of me," I thought. For whatever reason, I found that thought funny. I tried to say something to Bandy about how weird it was to be someone with a spigot punched in his side draining all that fluid from his body. Bandy's dark eyes stared back at me over his face mask. "I'll be finished soon," he said.

In that moment, I like to think I was taking the first baby steps toward developing what Anatole Broyard calls a style for my sickness. "I think," writes Broyard in *Intoxicated by My Illness,* a posthumously published chronicle of his bout with prostate cancer, "that only by insisting on your style can you keep from falling out of love with yourself as the illness attempts to diminish or disfigure you. Sometimes your vanity is the only thing that keeps you alive, and your style is the instrument of your vanity. It may not be dying we fear so much, but the diminished self."

The degree of my diminishment was very much on my medical team's mind in those first few days. There was, in fact, a delicate minuet being danced by the doctors. Dr. Ein remembered there being "a lot of pressure that you should be operated on right away." Dr. Stephens, however, disagreed and solicited a consultation from a senior surgeon at Toronto General to support him in what Dr. Ein described as "his conservative approach."

Other surgeons would have moved much more quickly to remove the damaged part of the liver. But in my case the damage was so extensive — "such a big mushy thing," as Dr. Ein put it — that Dr. Stephens decided to proceed "nonoperatively" for the first couple of weeks. (This course of action has since become much more the rule in treating massive liver damage.) If he expected me to die anyway, I'd like to think that, in pursuing this course, Dr. Stephens was executing a bold two-part plan. First, he was doing no harm, which, as my later experience with medical care would bear out, is the true genius of its practice. Second, he was leaving room for a miracle.

Twelve days after the maple-tree tap job, and after a further 2.6 litres of fluid were drained from my abdomen, I was taken into surgery to have drainage tubes inserted above and below the damaged portion of my liver. I read in the surgical notes that I was returned to the ICU after the operation on June 22 in "fairly good shape." I remember waking up and having no idea whether it was day or night and wishing that it would all be over.

As the days went by, my chances got steadily better: the leakage from the liver reduced, and the cocktails of antibiotics and nutritional supplements began to take hold. The arrows scattered throughout my progress notes started turning in the right direction. Hemoglobin, blood pressure, respiration, pulse, all to the good.

During this period, Dr. Mark Greenberg's remarks started showing up in my records. He was the only doctor who referred to me by name. His first entry was on June 26, 1974. In his carefully drawn script, on a single line at the top of the page he wrote, "Douglas looks better today." For whatever reason, I remembered feeling enlivened whenever he came around. Last June, I managed to elicit a one-hour interview with Dr. Greenberg. Given that his secretary has him scheduled in fifteen-minute increments, that was a coup. He's among the most sought-after cancer consultants in the world, and his time is precious. He was just as I remembered him: a tall, toothy, gangly South African. When he saw me, his face broke into a huge grin.

"I never expected one of my former patients to come see me at age forty-one," he said. I couldn't help myself — "I'm actually thirty-eight." The smile faded slightly. Did he remember meeting and talking with me? "My sense was by the time I came in contact with you, you had progressed to the point where you had a severe but not life-threatening illness. You had gone from an acute to a long-term chronic problem." How did he know it was potentially a long-term problem? "Because the location of the injury was around the pancreatic duct and the pancreatic head. I understand you have a history of obstruction around that area. You were a candidate for that condition. That was one of my concerns in treating you."

Really? I thought, why the hell didn't anybody mention that to me back then? And why was it that each time I had a pancreatic attack — four over the next sixteen years — nobody ever linked the pancreatitis to my accident, especially when one of those attacks

262

came as close to killing me as the truck did? No, they all opted for medicine's favourite free pass, referring on the record to my attacks as idiopathic, meaning a condition not preceded or occasioned by another.

I managed to hold my anger in check and asked Dr. Greenberg what he recalled about perking me up. "I remember talking to you when you took a nose-dive — emotionally frustrated and depressed — sitting and chatting to you." I recalled something about an accident he had as a kid. I asked him about it. "I had an injury playing squash. We actually talked about it. I had a head injury and had to have a craniotomy. I was very sick after, so I had a perspective on what it was like to be sick. I have often talked about the term that applies to sick people — "invalid" — as deriving very concretely from the words that comprise it: in valid. Becoming dependent or being dependent is particularly hard for young males."

I asked if he remembered the course of my depression. "As I remember, you were very sick, though quite bouncy and cheery, and then became less sick and less bouncy. I kept coming to talk to you after I was no longer responsible for your medical care. Fourteen and dealing with an illness, that's difficult — too old for Mother Goose and too young for Kafka. Fourteen-year-olds are moving forward developmentally; they get sick, they regress, and you're left with this sort of boy-man. You were in a twilight zone. If you know you're never going to get better, you have to come to terms with a new reality. Your problem was the uncertainty. I don't know why it's so vivid in my memory of you that you were not self-correcting; you were confused. The hard part was that you weren't quite sure where the end would be. I think that's what you were thinking."

After that interview, I was both heartened and put off: heartened because Dr. Greenberg seemed clearly the kind of doctor who treated me as opposed to treating my condition; put off because I hadn't been the laugh-in-the-face-of-adversity mensch I'd always thought. Especially after I left the ICU for the first time on July 9th, I saw myself cracking wise twenty-four hours a day. I remember watching the movie *M*A*S*H* and identifying with the characters played by Elliot Gould and Donald Sutherland. "I'm a pro from Dover too," I thought. Maybe the flip side of my situation was more of a problem than I'd imagined. I'd always thought the wisecracking had countered my sense of physical diminution, which was ongoing until the end of August.

A couple of days after I'd gone to see Dr. Greenberg, I picked up some photo albums at my parents' place. I hadn't seen any pictures of myself from that period in a long time. There they were: shots from '71 to '74. Two from the fall of '74 were awful to contemplate. In one, my smile seems attached with staples, and my eyes belong in formaldehyde. In the other, except for the acne, I look nine. As I studied them, I flashed back to a moment when I was looking at myself in the mirror of my hospital room shortly after the worst of the danger had passed but with a month or so still left in my incarceration. My ribs were sticking out of me like a med-school skeleton. My neck looked like a flower stalk holding up a bowling ball. I turned away. I'm not sick, I'm ugly. There were gorgeous nurses everywhere, gorgeous, healthy, strong, vibrant women. I watched them, and though I knew they were caring for me, I feared that somewhere in the back of their mind they were thinking "that poor, ugly, skinny bastard."

So I joked. I teased all the time, or at least all the time I wasn't depressed. I did imitations of Dr. Ein's turtle-headed manner, the residents, the priests and ministers, who came around looking to save a lost soul. I made the nurses laugh. I owned them. I killed them. Why? Because laughter is power, power in the face of diminution. And part of that power is rendering the other powerless in the face of your humour. They're helpless when they're laughing. That was the style of my illness. I was helpless and ugly, but I was funny, and for a few seconds, that made me powerful.

My relationship with my parents was altogether different. With them, it was a lot tougher to get any traction. I was their only son; my mother's only child. My mum, I remember, was a constant presence. First thing in the morning till last thing at night, looking out for me every way she knew how. Our relationship was complicated by my mother's desire to, well, mother me. All she saw was a very sick child who needed her constant attention. The jokes, the imitations, the barbs were lost on her. Not because she didn't have a sense of humour; she could be hilarious. But her will was attuned to making me well, when there wasn't much she could do. Still, she had to believe there was something. To make me well, she brought little pillows, big pillows, down-filled pillows, and pillows for the small of my back. She bought special foods when I could eat, and any books I wanted (the entire James Bond series, which must have nearly killed her). She organized my friends and relatives to come and see me. When I was too tired, she read to me (reams of get-well cards, not from my friends so much as her friends and friends of friends, *Sports Illustrated,* Bond, the comics from the British kids' magazine *Look and Learn*). She even read the report of the 1974 Toronto Argonauts intersquad game as it appeared in the *Toronto Sun,* a newspaper I'm sure she had never opened before and has never opened since. When I was well enough, she would wheel me outside into a small courtyard behind the old nurses' residence, where we would tilt our exhausted faces toward the sun. She was, in short, one mother of a mother.

As for my dad, it's a much shorter story. He came every day at noon on the dot for half an hour, walking from his office at King and Bay, a yard to the stride, fifteen minutes to the mile, as certain as sunlight. Later in the evening, he would return to collect Mum and stay another half-hour. His job was clear. Like the resourceful officer under fire he had been at Ortona or Monte Casino, he deployed his emotional resources to ensure a successful campaign. He rarely referred to my illness directly, but rather always asked, "How are you doing?" I would always reply, "Better." He seemed full of confidence and power. At the time, he was chairman of Sunnybrook Hospital in north Toronto, which he had helped transform from a veterans' care hospital into an acute care hospital. Tall, cool, and commanding, he scared the nurses, and I got treated with a good deal more deference whenever he was around. At one point, he told me that he had gone through his war and now I was going through mine. Later in my teens, I sneaked a look at his journal. On a couple of occasions, he comments on how courageous I was.

These things taken together make me believe in my dad in a way that his aloof stoicism never could. In the summer of 1995, on the anniversary of VE Day, I did a radio commentary for the CBC in which I talked about how my dad never let me down that summer, "not even once." What I didn't say was that I let him down more than once, mostly by bitching at Mum about embarrassing me in front of the nurses. Dad would scold me right on the spot — a cold look, a curt "pipe down," followed by something about "having to help Mum get through all this."

There's a photograph of me and my cousin Geoff taken at the cottage the summer after my accident. I look healthier but still painfully thin. I seem to remember that I had my shirt off just before that picture was taken, and Dad insisted that I keep it off for the photo. I remember angry tears springing from my eyes as I refused his badgering requests. I knew Dad meant well, so I tried to swallow the humiliation I felt, lump after lump down my gullet to a place where rage sits for a lifetime.

On July 30, Dr. Stephens and a team of six assistants, in a six-hour operation, rewired my entire digestive system (hooking my stomach directly to my bowel to bypass the damaged duodenum), drained several abscesses, and inserted a feeding tube directly into my belly. I was readmitted to the ICU, in a separate area designed to prevent post-operative infection. The rooms were glassed in. I had no contact with the other patients, but I could see them and hear them through the glass walls. At night, the place was full of electronic bleeps and blips emanating from various monitors tracking heart and respiration rates and regulating the flow of intravenous fluids. Every so often, the darkness was pierced by the harrowing sound of children in deep distress. Every so often, that sound was me.

In the room next to mine was a young girl, eight or nine years old. She was dying. On several occasions, alarms rang in her room, and a team of doctors and nurses would rush to revive her. Each time I looked over at her, she was either unconscious or gasping for air. When her parents visited, they brought balloons and other little knick-knacks for her room. Then they would sit by the bed and hold on to each other. The mother would often reach out to stroke her daughter's dark brown hair or caress her cheek.

One day the catheter in my penis started to bother me, so I asked the nurse if she could either remove it or in some other way make me comfortable. She replied that it would take at least two nurses to deal with my problem, and that everybody else was tied up "next door." "Why do you bother?" I heard myself asking. "She's going to die anyway." The nurse, her back to me, shuddered and spun around. "How can you say that?" she asked with genuine disgust. The enormity of my selfishness struck me straightaway, and after a couple of feeble apologies, I shut up. Later the same nurse came to visit me on the ward. She asked how I was doing. I asked after the little girl. "She passed away." However tempted I might be to moralize retrospectively on this incident, the brute fact remains that the will to live trumps whatever feeble efforts I might make to either justify or condemn my behaviour. One kid died and another lived. It's as simple as that.

Ten days after the operation, I suffered what amounted to a heart attack. I had managed to get out of bed for one of the first times since the surgery. It had taken two nurses to move me three feet from the bed to the chair. I had just settled in and was working a Laura Secord sucker (green, I think) when my heart suddenly began to gallop. "Oh shit," I said. "Oh fuck, my heart's going too fast." In a moment, my mother was right in front me. "Douglas, what's wrong? Are you choking on that sucker?" But what she meant was more of a command: "Stop choking on that sucker." Whenever my mother panics, it's always a mix of rage and fear. Her expression always changes in the same way — she draws her cheeks in and bites down hard on the flesh on the inside of her mouth. She never fails to provoke me into a similar rage. She was looking at me that way now as I struggled to get air into my lungs.

"Are you choking on the sucker?"

"No," I said, my voice rising. "I'm not choking on the fucking sucker." As my heart raced to nowhere I winged that sucker with everything I had, and it shattered on the porcelain sink over on the other side of the room. Suddenly, nurses and doctors were all around me, placing an oxygen mask over my mouth and nose, taking my electrocardiogram. I kept asking if I was having a heart attack. One of the residents, Dr. David Hitch, a drawling po-faced Carolinian, answered, "Yeaaassss, it's possible." Dr. Mark Bleisher, his fellow resident and a hard-faced New Yorker, asked him in a stern voice to step outside, where I've always hoped he pounded Hitch's brains out through his ears. I felt my eyes roll back in fear and panic, but just at that moment I caught my mother's eye. "You see," I thought. "You can't wish this shit away, can you?"

My "progress" report for that day noted that I was readmitted to the ICU and that I'd had a pulmonary or air embolism (a blockage in the artery), "although there was definitely a component of anxiety state in the patient's response." In subsequent years, this anxiety state played out again and again like a leitmotif. One time I staggered out into traffic in front of several thousand dog-racing fans, my pants falling around my knees, along the main highway between Palm Beach and Fort Lauderdale. I thought I was having a heart attack. Later, after I had humiliated my friends and caused our car to be searched for drugs, a Cuban doctor looked at me straight-faced and said, like Ricky Ricardo, "Maybe you need a vacation." Even so, even knowing all that, I was still put off by the doctor's description of my "anxious" behaviour that August day in 1974. "Fuck off," I thought. "You try having a pulmonary embolism in front of your mother."

Shortly before I started writing this piece, I went to see my mother to collect her memories of my illness. She's bedridden now, her left arm a big bag of cancer wrapped in dressings and bandages, which are changed twice a day by a Victorian Order nurse. She was tired and her eyes drooped under the influence of her painkillers. Still, twenty-four years after that miserable summer, her clawing, snapping, snarling will was still on display.

We started out discussing chronology.

"On July the 9th, I was let out back up to ..."

"The survival unit."

"No, no, I went onto a ward."

"That's what I call a survival unit."

"Why?"

"Because, as far as I was concerned, that's what it was. There was no care, no attention, no nothin'. You were lucky you survived."

"Right, well, there were some good nurses and there were some bad nurses."

"There were some really bad nurses, really bad. I mean they had no training. They knew nothing from nothing. Ignorant peasants is what they were."

I tried to get her off this. But she wouldn't quit.

"Did they hate me? Boy, oh boy, oh boy, did they hate me, and I hated them. You know what they used to say to you? The darling things, they would go and see you in the morning before you got out of bed, before you woke up, and say, 'You'll never be part of this floor because she's so neurotic.'"

Christ, I thought, she's right. They did say that stuff.

"I mean such bitches, such bitches, I could not believe. I did it their way, or I didn't do it at all. And they did it wrong quite a lot of the time. I'm not making that up."

"What sort of things?"

"They wouldn't turn up on time; turn up with your medicines on time. They were careless and stupid and overbearing."

"Mother ..."

"Those women were beyond description."

"Yeah, well ..."

"Cruel, wicked, evil, vile, filthy creatures."

I asked Mum if she was sure those were the words she wanted on the permanent record.

"I can use some more if you like."

"No," I said, laughing. "I think that will do nicely, thank you."

Mum's blunt vitriol may have belied a complex and subtle attitude toward those who cared for me. Every year since the accident she has taken an enormous fancy food basket and left it for the ICU staff working through the night on Christmas eve. Some of the nurses on that shift were barely born at the time of the accident. Like much that powers my mother's life, this act is born of both gratitude and obligation. Irrespective of the bile she'd just let loose, the fact remains: I was saved and, duty bound, my mum goes every December 24 to thank those responsible.

Mum flagged and her eyes dropped shut. I touched her good hand and wandered out of her bedroom. Whatever I might write about my experiences and Mum's role — good, bad, or indifferent — in them, no matter how embarrassed she made me, her fearsome, angry, ineffable love is like gravity. So long as I'm walking, my steps rise and fall with her.

Lately, my mum's been getting worse. I go to see her at my parents' new apartment overlooking Allen Gardens and the church steeples down Jarvis Street. There's an absorbent pad resting on top of her sheets beneath her bottom. There's a walker beside the bed. I find it hard to visit her. We talk on the phone all the time, but going to see her is another matter. I'm often impatient, picking up copies of the *Spectator* strewn around her bed, wandering about, looking at her books, picking out the wonderful *petits objets* my mother has collected over her lifetime. She's wasting away to nothing, and there's nothing I can do about it. When I get back home, I'm often irritable. I snap at my wife and ignore the kids. I steal away upstairs to watch television because, as an occasional television critic, "that's my job."

But I'm going to do better. I've promised my wife I'll stop yelling in front of the children, and I've promised myself that no matter the circumstances, I'm going to go see Mum at least three times a week till the end. And I'm going to sit and listen and try to be entertaining and engaging in a way she would appreciate. She has it coming.

Now that I've written about my accidental illness, I'm left with a paradoxical thought. Am I the guy who got run over by that truck, or am I past that? Up till now that question would never have occurred to me.

Whenever our kids bellyache about what they're eating for breakfast, lunch, or dinner, my juridical wife whips out a terrific admonition that clams them up every time: "You get what you get." This bit of home wisdom in no way vitiates free will or any of the other helpful illusions that get us up in the morning. It simply suggests that once the cards are dealt, get on with the game. And though I've promised myself to do a better job of living up to that sentiment, I also know even that's not enough. I need a way forward.

I've been thinking about that basket my mother takes to the ICU every year at Christmas. Pretty soon someone else is going to have take it. It might as well be me.

Author's note: Special thanks to Don Obe.

JOHANNA KELLER

Nocturne:
Remembering Pianist Samuel Sanders

So your hand moves, moving across the keys,
And slowly the keys grow darker to the touch.
— Donald Justice, "Sonatina in Yellow"

THREE MONTHS AFTER THE PIANIST SAMUEL SANDERS died of complications following his second heart transplant, on the evening of October 14, 1999, I stood backstage at The Juilliard School's Paul Hall. The violinist Itzhak Perlman was preparing to go onstage alone for the last musical performance in the memorial program. Sam had been famous as an accompanist to many of the great musicians of our time, such as cellist Mstislav Rostropovich, soprano Beverly Sills, cellist Yo-Yo Ma, and violinist Pinchas Zukerman. Most often though, Sam accompanied Itzhak.

Sam and Itzhak had been musical partners for more than thirty years. It was disorienting not to see Sam's nervous, slight figure hovering over Itzhak, who sat in his wheelchair (he had been crippled by poliomyelitis at the age of four). Itzhak's head was bowed. Beneath the greying curls on his head, the thick features of his face wore the expression of concentrated withdrawal into that inner space where musicians retreat just prior to performing. Before he died, Sam had chosen the memorial program's three speakers —

Juilliard's president, Joseph Polisi; the noted cardiologist Valentin Fuster; and me — and we spoke between performances by flutist James Galway, the Lark Quartet, pianist Stephen Hough, and tenor Robert White, among others. The audience of around six hundred comprised members of the music community along with Sam's family members, the doctors who had cared for him, close friends from other walks of life, students, and fans.

I stood near Itzhak, half-enveloped in one of the velvet wing curtains. Moments before, I had read an elegy I wrote for Sam — and I felt drained. I knew that Sam had designated me as one of the three speakers because, aside from being a poet and music writer, I would bring the perspective of being a close friend. But at that moment I felt it had been impossible to put into a short elegy all that I knew and felt about Sam. We had met professionally through the music business and embarked on a rich eighteen-year friendship that extended, as friendships do, into a web of shared relationships. The evening had been wrenching for the fifteen participants, friends of Sam's, and the atmosphere backstage had been subdued as we exchanged silent hugs, condolences, and memories.

Everyone onstage and in the audience knew Sam's life had been an ongoing miracle. His health problems had been the subject of profiles in the *New York Times* and on *CBS-TV Sunday Morning;* the evening's tributes by Dr. Fuster and President Polisi attested to Sam's courage in the face of daily physical pain. Born with a defective heart valve, Sam had not been expected to survive infancy. Or childhood. Or adolescence. And on it went, for sixty-two years of borrowed time, through six major heart operations including two heart transplants. Later, Itzhak told me that he thought Sam was like a man who had to cross a precarious bridge over and over; just as he reached the other side, the bridge collapsed behind him — and then he had to cross another. Despite that, as if trying to make the most of every precious minute, Sam kept a schedule of concert touring, recording, and teaching that would have exhausted an energetic twenty-year-old.

Itzhak called over a stagehand and instructed her to carry his violin onstage, where there stood a Steinway grand piano, lid up and full-stick, the leather-covered piano bench at the ready. In front of the piano, downstage centre, stood two more benches, and he told the stagehand to place his violin and bow on one of these. Itzhak grimaced as he hoisted himself upright out of his chair and slid his arms into the rings of his metal crutches. With a sideways stagger, he swung himself through the curtained alley that led onto the stage and into the bright lights. He lowered himself onto one of the benches, adjusted his braced legs, took up his violin, and, after a long silence, put his bow to the string. In the printed program, following Itzhak's name there had been no composition listed. After a few familiar notes, I heard the murmur and vague rustle as the audience recognized "Liebesleid" ("Love's Sorrow"), a warhorse for violin and piano by Fritz Kreisler. It was a piece Itzhak had performed countless times with Sam, usually as an encore. Itzhak stretched the familiar phrases of the melody like taffy, into the sweet, heart-catching phrases for which he's known stylistically.

As the violinist sat alone onstage, the piano bench stood empty; it was the musical equivalent of the "missing man" formation flown by fighter pilots. He seemed to be playing for himself alone, for comfort and for succour. He appeared the embodiment of loss, the solitary fiddler hunched over sobbing notes, drawing his bow arm back and forth, rocking slightly as though davening in a synagogue while reciting Kaddish, the prayer for the dead. Only the single line of the violin sounded, and yet the familiar accompaniment that Sam would have been playing — had he been with us — was uncannily audible in memory. I heard, with utter clarity, the echo of Sam playing the "Liebesleid" — his characteristically vigorous attacks when his spidery fingers crashed down on the keys; his restless driving rhythms; the elegant and tender arcing of the treble lines; and, above all, the crystal phrases of a lucid and acute mind.

If Sam had been only a pianist who achieved so much despite ill health, he would have been notable. What made him extraordinary was that despite his overwhelming fragility — physical and, in a profound sense, psychological — he dedicated himself to the point of obsession to helping friends and students, reaching out and being of service to others. Dr. Fuster, who was in charge of Sam's cardiac care for fifteen years and who became one of his close friends, saw a direct connection between Sam's physical vulnerability and his generosity. In his analysis, Sam's illness created an incredible need for psychological support. That need transmitted a personal intensity and engendered a trust with others that Dr. Fuster found fascinating. He considered Sam a unique character who, while living life competitively as an artist, was still able to remain open to others. "That was what made him great," said Dr. Fuster.

At the crowded reception after the memorial service, a middle-aged woman from Taiwan sought me out because of the elegy I had read and introduced herself as a student of Sam's who had flown halfway around the world just to come to the service. For at least ten minutes, she recounted the lengths to which Sam had gone to help her with her career as a pianist — not only teaching and coaching her whenever possible, but introducing her to people and helping her find engagements. From time to time, she ducked her head and wiped away the tears surreptitiously with the back of her hand. As well as I knew Sam, he had never mentioned her name, but I knew she represented only one of many he had helped, one of many with whom he had an intricately intimate friendship.

Itzhak told me that when Sam was at Columbia Presbyterian Hospital for his first heart transplant in 1990, he'd gone with his wife, Toby, for a visit. As arguably the foremost cardiac surgery unit in the world, Columbia Presbyterian attracts many internationally famous, rich, and powerful patients; consequently, the staff is not easily impressed. But that day, a nurse pulled them aside. "The adjoining room is *completely* full of flowers people sent," the nurse told Itzhak. "I've never seen so many for one person. I mean, who *is* this guy? Is he *that important?*"

When I asked Itzhak what characterized Sam most for him, he answered without a pause: "Loyalty. Sam would do anything for you if you became his friend. I mean anything. There are some people — well, they may be lovely and all, but when the crunch comes, they are not there. With Sam, no matter how inconvenient it was, he always came through for you."

A year after Sam died, I saw his ghost walking up Broadway. It was a biting autumn afternoon, and I was hurrying between errands on the familiar streets of my old neighbourhood — and Sam's — on Manhattan's Upper West Side. All at once, through crowds of pedestrians, I spotted Sam's thin, loping silhouette. I started to call out, then stopped as the figure changed into a stranger only vaguely resembling Sam. I was left with a sense of confusion, followed by the distinct sensation of Sam's presence. Over the next few months, after another half-dozen sightings — on Lincoln Center's plaza, at a movie theatre, in the audience at Carnegie Hall — I knew Sam was haunting me.

My thoughts had often turned to him since his death. There were those unique components of his character that had made it possible for him to survive — to cross the bridge again and again, as Itzhak said. But Sam's willpower, his generosity, and his rage (he had that too) had a profound effect on everyone around him. After many years of knowing Sam and his professional life as an accompanist, I began to understand that his ability — and need — to play a supportive or collaborative role (not only at the piano but in so many other ways) was one of the psychological keys to his physical survival. By being there for others, by developing deep and rich friendships — onstage and off — he assured himself that when he became dependent (as he had been in his childhood and would be again and again during his health crises), his friends would come through for him.

The heart — that fist-sized muscle that beats around 45 to 120 times a minute — is our most essential organ. Once it ceases to beat, we cease to be. Its distant thud is the subtle rhythm that accompanies us all our lives. It's no accidental metaphor that we locate love in the organ of the heart, since love is essential for our survival as human beings (so say psychologists). We cannot survive physically without the beating of our hearts; we cannot survive psychologically without love. As the symbolic seat of our emotions, this physical heart is markedly susceptible to them — we have all experienced the heart's flutter of passion, the pounding of fear, the stabbing constriction of grief. Just as our hearts are vulnerable, so are we vulnerable in love. How paradoxical that, for Sam, the heart would be his greatest threat and — through the generous love he gave that was returned by those around him — his survival. "Let me open my heart to you," we say. "Let us speak heart to heart." There is a subtle debt inherent in the transaction of love; over the years, through giving and receiving, we build a bridge and become linked, duty bound to those we love deeply and well. This is how it had happened to me with Sam.

I first met Sam in 1981 when I was in my mid-twenties. After finishing a music degree and deciding that a performing career felt too risky, I established a small public relations firm that specialized in classical music. In the same way that Sam found a kind of fulfillment and frustration in being an accompanist, I experienced a similar paradox in my work as a publicist; I saw myself as a kind of accompanist to my clients. And one of my first clients was Sam's fledgling project, the Cape & Islands Chamber Music Festival on Cape Cod, for which I and my two assistants were hired to handle the press. I'd heard Sam perform on many occasions, but we were brought face to face by the festival's administrator to discuss publicity plans. We met at a West Side greasy spoon with leatherette booths and mould-ed chrome fixtures.

Sitting in the diner booth, with his thick glasses and curly hair, Sam bore a striking resemblance to Woody Allen (though Sam was taller and his lush black hair turned iron grey in later years). His wide smile showed buckteeth. He stuttered a little, especially when carried away with excitement or nervousness. ("Uh — uh — uh," he would say rapidly before a sentence.) And when he directed his gaze at you, his brown eyes were piercing. Disconcertingly so.

I find it hard to explain why we had such an instant and easy rapport. There was the kind of immediate trust in one another that happens sometimes at a first meeting. Over the next few years, as I became more closely acquainted with Sam's health problems, we found common ground in the experience of chronic physical pain. In my adolescence, I'd developed severe scoliosis, a curvature of the spine, and had worn an apparatus called a Milwaukee brace that could best be described as a portable torture chamber — the pain was excruciating and unrelenting. I've never forgotten how that pain and frailty isolated me; my well-meaning family and friends had a difficult time coping with my ordeal because they couldn't make it stop. It left them helpless. So I learned to hide my pain, min-imize it, joke about it — not uncommon behaviour. Although I have been pain-free for many years, I know the effort it costs to rein in rage and despair; to fend off debilitating self-pity. I recognized all this in Sam.

Two years after we met, my spine began to deteriorate and I decided to consider surgery. When I happened to mention it to Sam, he expressed his concern. Then he became positively excited, almost gleeful. "You *have* to talk to Yo-Yo," he said, referring to the cellist Yo-Yo Ma. "He's had the exact same surgery and he'll know all the best doctors. Let me call him and tell him about you. Really — let me call him right now. And, Joanna Simon," he added, referring to a mezzo-soprano (the sister of Carly) who was also a friend of his. "She's had the operation. I'll get her to call you. She and Yo-Yo will be very helpful ..." And they were.

A year later, on the last day of May in 1983, I was at Columbia Presbyterian Hospital, where Sam would later have his two heart transplants. Because of some complicated pre-operative procedures, I had been lying in the hospital bed for two weeks. I had asked only my closest friends to stop by, and now everyone had gone home. Visiting hours were over. Sunset filled the window, the apricot clouds faded to grey over the George Washington Bridge. My operation was scheduled for the next morning, and, for the first time, I felt real fear. Added to the anticipated hazards of major surgery was another concern. That week, *New York Magazine* had reported the news that the mysterious illness called AIDS had just been proven to be transmitted through the blood supply. But there was no test to prove that the units of blood I would receive were not infected. (They later proved to have been safe.) My surgeon had given me the option of cancelling the surgery or proceeding, and I had decided to take the risk. Only ten hours before the operation, I was lying in bed wondering if I'd made the right decision.

Sam popped through the door with a big grin, like some kind of clown-doll made of strings. He found me with tears in my eyes. As I told him my worries, I felt self-conscious — he'd been through so much worse. The thought never seemed to cross his mind. He sat on the edge of the bed and listened until I'd talked myself out. Then he told a joke — I wish I could remember it, but I never remember jokes. Then he told another. And another. I'd never laughed so hard. In retrospect, it seems odd that Sam was with me that night

— I had family and other, closer friends at the time. But I'd learned that as much as some people may love you, they may not be easy or useful at the side of your hospital bed, whereas Sam showed not a trace of awkwardness, embarrassment, or fear. He kept up the comedy monologue for two hours, charming the nurses who tried to evict him. I was exhausted with laughter when he left — and I got a great night's sleep.

Sam was born in 1937 in the Bronx to a working-class family with no obvious musical talent. He had the blue lips characteristic of those afflicted with Tetralogy of Fallot, commonly known as the "blue baby syndrome," caused by a misfiring heart valve that forces blood backward into the heart with every beat, depriving it of oxygen. At that time, "blue babies" — if they survived infancy — died by the onset of puberty. During his early years, Sam was frail and his physical activity severely restricted. His father carried him around in his arms. Sam desperately wanted to be active and play baseball, an aspiration prompted in part because the family's apartment — at 243 East Mount Eden Avenue — stood virtually in the shadow of Yankee Stadium (a happenstance Sam delightedly included in his professional bio). To keep him at home and off the playground, his mother bought a piano and enrolled him in lessons. At the age of nine, his heart began to fail. He underwent a pioneering operation at Johns Hopkins University in Baltimore, with the insertion of a Blalock-Taussig shunt (named for the two surgeons who developed and performed the procedure on Sam).

Afterward, his heart function improved, he gained a degree of strength and independence. His musical talent blossomed and his ambition for recognition and acceptance found an outlet in the piano. Only two years later, at the age of eleven, he performed his first professional recital and made appearances on radio.

On the fifth floor of The Juilliard School, where Sam taught for the last fifteen years of his life, is the library where I had come to look over the papers Sam bequeathed to the school's archives. After giving me an overview of Sam's collection, the library director, Jane Gottlieb, showed me a box of private recordings on 33⅓ rpm, in brown paper sleeves. The discs were thick vinyl dating from the late 1940s and early 1950s — recordings of Sam's solo work from when he began performing in public. I had no idea these recordings existed. The LPs had been transferred onto two CDs. Eagerly, I carried them upstairs to the library's audio carrels.

As I put on the earphones, I didn't know what to expect. How would Sam sound as a child? The first track was the first movement of the Bach Toccata in G Major, BWV 916, recorded in 1949 when Sam was eleven. From the assured chords, I was astonished to discover how much Sam sounded as he did later — there was the same energetic attack on the keys, rhythmic propulsion, and astutely elegant phrasing. And, on the negative side, there was the slight tendency to rush through thorny passages, to press the rhythm at times unnecessarily.

The Scarlatti Sonata in E Major followed, and I expected a similarly propulsive interpretation, but he surprised me. Instead, he made the sonata tender, the turns bell-like, the trills featherlight; the martial dotted chords in the second theme (that so often fall as ponderously as marching feet) here sounded as delicately precise as toy soldiers. The sonata was full of emotion and a sense of nostalgia, almost as if recalled in memory — it was a startlingly mature interpretation for an eleven-year-old musician. Works by Handel, Ravel, Chopin, and Liszt filled out the discs and made it evident that Sam had thought through every phrase and already possessed a remarkable grasp of idiom and gesture.

The fifth track was a radio broadcast on March 15, 1949. First came the applause of a studio audience. Then a man's stentorian voice.

Interviewer: Two years ago, nine-year-old Sammy Sanders was only a few steps from death. A blue baby, he had to be carried around wherever he went. A few days ago, eleven-year-old piano virtuoso Samuel Sanders made his debut at New York's Town Hall. Tonight, composed and smiling at our microphones, sits this citizen of the Bronx. Piano virtuoso at eleven, Samuel Sanders. [The sound of applause.] Sammy? Come over here and tell the audience the story you told me.

Sam: [His high-pitched voice is that of a remarkably assured, chatty kid, eager to please, talking very fast.] Sure. I'm Samuel Sanders. Up until two years ago, I had to spend most of my time in bed, because there was something wrong with my heart. My fingernails and lips were blue all the time, and I would die if I moved around. But I always liked the piano, even when I was a little baby. My sister played it and I listened in bed. And then after I had my operation, I wanted to take lessons.

[After a few more questions, the interview concludes.]

Sam: I'd like to thank my teacher, Madame Rosenthal, and the nurses and doctors down at Johns Hopkins, where they operated on me and saved my life.

Interviewer: Sam, that was a pretty tough operation, wasn't it?

Sam: I wouldn't know. I was asleep!

Interviewer: [Laughs. The audience laughs.] I see what you mean. But you're all right now, aren't you?

Sam: Sure. I can play the piano and listen to the Yankees play on the radio when the summer comes. And maybe I can go see them. You want me to play now?

By the age of fourteen, Sam had performed a solo recital at Town Hall (then a major New York City venue) and, at sixteen, appeared as a soloist with the New York Philharmonic as part of the Young People's Concerts. "He disclosed decided talent, having made unusual progress during the brief period he has devoted to his art," said a review in the *New York Times,* while the *Herald Tribune* noted his "natural facility and sensitivity." It was clear Sam was headed toward a professional piano career.

Another child star of the 1940s was Robert White, who appeared on *The Fred Allen Show* as Little Bobby White, the boy Irish tenor. He and Sam met when they were both students at Hunter College in Manhattan, and they remained friends and musical collaborators for forty years. Robert, with his light lyric tenor, has a busy musical career with a specialty in the repertoire made popular by Irish tenor John McCormack. We decided to spend a summer morning together talking about Sam. An affable, sophisticated bachelor, Robert is solidly built, with a handsome face like a younger version of Patrick Moynihan and a penchant for natty dressing. (He wore a well-tailored summer tweed jacket.) Robert told me about his student days at Hunter College when he considered himself the school's star talent. One day he needed an accompanist and was told there was a new pianist who might play for him.

"In walked this wonderfully gawky, self-effacing kid, who was so apologetic," said Robert about his first view of Sam. "I took one look at him and thought, 'Oh no.' He had never played my piece before. I insultingly pointed out that even though it had three sharps, it was *not* in A major, but in the relative minor key. Then Sam sat down to sight-read it and — of course, it was absolutely perfect."

Sam began to accompany Robert regularly, and, given Robert's Catholic background, their first gigs were (as Sam once quipped) "Communion breakfasts and the Cardinal's Christmas party." Then he and Robert received scholarships to study at Fontainebleau in France the next summer with Mademoiselle Nadia Boulanger, one of the century's most legendary — and formidable — pedagogues.

Renowned for her ability to terrorize modestly talented students (some of whom, rumour had it, never performed again), Boulanger had been the teacher of numerous important musicians as well as composers such as Aaron Copland, Virgil Thomson, David Diamond, and Philip Glass. According to Robert, Boulanger considered Sam "blessed."

"She always had this mystic side of her," Robert recalled. "And she used to say Sam was one of the chosen. With his heart problem and all, he came from another world. She saw him as a fully formed and mature musician."

Musically, Robert said, Sam was a gifted transposer (in other words, he could play any piece in another key at sight — an advanced skill that used to be expected among the best musicians but is now rare), and he had an ear that made it possible for him to fake anything.

After graduating magna cum laude from Hunter College in 1959, Sam enrolled at The Juilliard School and finished a master's degree in 1961, under the tutelage of another legendarily difficult teacher, the accompanist Sergius Kagen. Sometime during those years, Sam had made the choice to concentrate on becoming an accompanist or collaborative pianist, a term he preferred. Years later in a press interview, when asked why he didn't continue with his early solo career, Sam answered, "I didn't get as much enjoyment from that as I did from collaborating with other musicians."

One of his favourite analogies was to liken the role of the collaborative pianist to the catcher in a baseball game. In an article Sam authored for *Keyboard Classics* magazine in 1984, he wrote about the accompanist, "He's in on every single play. He has an overview, and that's what you get at the piano because you are looking at all of the parts simultaneously, controlling many aspects, just as the catcher controls the flow of the game." This facile spin on the accompanist's role was something I think Sam only half-believed. He certainly had the drive and facility to have attempted a solo career. But while he took a genuine pleasure in the process of collaboration, it did always put him in the secondary position. His motivation to be an accompanist seemed to be a compensation for the terrible isolation of his childhood when he was ostracized and physically unable to play with other children. Sam had chosen a career in which he would never be alone; he could play — music — with his friends.

Being an accompanist may also have distracted him from his pain, allowing him to push himself harder than he might have otherwise. He was known for almost never cancelling a performance except when he was in the hospital. In an interview with Eugenia Zukerman on *CBS-TV Sunday Morning,* Sam said, "This feeling I always had was that I had a responsibility to those I played for. If I were a soloist, I could have cancelled. But I had rehearsed this program with them and they depend on me and I have to come through for them."

Beginning in the 1960s, he gradually established himself as a collaborative pianist and received international recognition. With Itzhak, he toured worldwide and made twelve records and CDs that won two Grammy Awards. He performed and toured with a veritable who's who in the music world, founded and directed the Cape & Islands Chamber Music Festival, received honorary doctorates, and performed seven times at the White House for five presidents. During these decades, he married the painter Rhoda Ross and had his only child, Sophie, with whom he was very close.

Another day, back at The Juilliard School Library, I read through Sam's papers (four cardboard cartons and a shopping bag of materials that had not been sorted and catalogued yet). I donned a pair of white cotton archivist's gloves and opened the first box. A jumble of letters, artist contracts, biographies, flyers, press kits, press clippings, photographs, and concert programs: here was the detritus of a life in music, a midden of documents, the material remains. The newer documents were on top, and as I dug through the layers, the newspaper clippings changed from yellow to brown. They brought up so many memories — concerts I had attended, interviews I had arranged for Sam.

Sam's significance to classical music performance in the latter half of the twentieth century went beyond his performances and recordings. His ambition led him to champion the role of the collaborative pianist. Historically, the accompanist was considered little more than hired help. Although in so much of the standard repertoire the pianist plays a musically equal role with the soloist, the "star" nevertheless held all the power. In recent decades the situation had changed, due in part to Sam's efforts. He insisted that his name be included in all paid advertisements (a practice not common at the beginning of his career but widespread today) and that his name appear in the same-sized typeface. Believing that learning to play piano with other musicians was a unique skill demanding a particular kind of training, he lobbied for and helped design degree programs for collaborative pianists at Peabody Conservatory in Baltimore in the 1980s and at The Juilliard School in the 1990s. As I examined the interviews ranging over three decades, I noticed how many articles were devoted to the growing influence of the accompanist (features in the *New York Times, Wall Street Journal, Washington Post, New York Times Magazine,* and music journals and newspapers around the country). Sam was inevitably quoted, if not the main focus.

But advocating for more prestige for accompanists — and for himself — was not always easy. Sam often complained about how little money he was paid (the soloist determines how much to give the accompanist, and the money comes out of his or her fee) and sometimes his performance was ignored by the critics. But in Robert White's view (based no doubt on their long professional relationship and a friendship that was sometimes strained by competition and professional disappointments), the "real tragedy of Sam was that he railed against the realities of the accompanist's lot in life."

"He could have saved himself a lot of anguish by not acting in high dudgeon over the slights that go with the profession," Robert told me. "It's a horrible situation for a pianist to be in the hire of his colleague. And I had to bear the brunt of it, sometimes in ways Sam might not have acted it out with someone like Itzhak." As an example, Robert described the time they played at the White House for President George Herbert Bush.

"I was just getting ready to walk out onstage to sing for the president," Robert recounted, "and Sam came up in hysterics. He waved the program in front of my face. 'My name's not on it,' he said. '*You* should have seen to this.' And then I had to walk on and sing." The incident still rankles after so many years — I could hear the indignation in Robert's voice when he told me about it. And it nearly ended their friendship. Robert threatened never again to perform with Sam if he upset him like that before a concert. "I said, 'Sam, even if they put insulting remarks about you and your family in the program book, I don't want to hear about it just before I have to walk onstage.' I doubt he would have done that to Itzhak. But Sam and I had a long and cozy relationship that gave him permission to step over certain boundaries. We used to almost come to blows, and that was the other side of the coin with Sam."

Meanwhile, Sam's heart was not his only physical problem. Because of his weakened condition and the many drugs he had to take all his life, he was beset by chronic and debilitating conditions. The worst was gout — caused by a blood thinner — that brought him excruciating pain as the crystals of uric acid formed in the joints of his feet and ankles. At times, because of drug reactions, he would swell alarmingly and his cheeks puffed out like a squirrel's. Once when I knew he was having trouble with his legs, I asked how they were and in answer he pulled up his pant leg. His shin was mottled violet, the skin so swollen it looked as if it would burst; he could only fit his feet into huge unlaced tennis shoes.

Sam was always underweight. He often looked like an AIDS sufferer, so much so that once a false rumour raced through the tightly knit music world that Sam had contracted the disease during one of his operations. He had his concert suit jackets tailored with padding so that he would look more robust onstage. From time to time, he changed colour. Usually, his skin was an unnatural red, but he would sometimes turn yellow with the accumulation of toxins in his blood. When he flushed purple, it was a sign his heart was failing.

You couldn't be around Sam for long without seeing him go through his pill-popping routine — in later years, he took seventeen crucial pills every day. "Let's see," he would say, opening his briefcase to reveal dozens of bottles of prescription drugs. "Did I take *this* one yet? Oh, where is *that* one?" he would ask casually, while your stomach turned because you knew that a forgotten pill could be serious or perhaps fatal. Feigning indifference, he would unscrew a few caps, swallow a few pills, and shrug. It was many years before I realized he always knew exactly what he had taken and, in fact, kept two or three bottles of the same drug with him just in case he ran out. The comedy routine was his way to relieve his anxiety by prompting the anxieties of those around him.

Sam was almost a parody of a diehard New Yorker. He lived on Manhattan's Upper West Side his entire adult life, read the *New York Times* religiously every morning, was a lifelong statistics-quoting Yankees fan, a rabid liberal, a non-practising but self-identified Jew, a voracious reader who seemed to have always read the latest literary best-sellers, and a devoted denizen of the food emporium

Zabar's, the Thalia movie house (in its glory days), and sushi bars (where he always ordered chicken teriyaki and a Coke). He was ironic, self-deprecating, neurotic, and fast-talking. Eugenia Zukerman (Genie, as she's nicknamed), who is also a flutist and performed often with Sam, was a long-time friend and called him "the funniest man in the world."

As is so often observed, humour is rooted in suffering. Genie remembered that among the funniest stories Sam told were the painful accounts of being put into special education classes as a child. He was the target of taunts by other children who often asked him if he'd just eaten blueberry pie. In an Associated Press interview, Sam was quoted as saying, "We called ourselves 'the misfits.' It was an experience I treasure." You can hear the sarcasm dripping from every word.

"Imagine being a very bright and sensitive boy in a class with kids who were mentally deficient," Genie said. "But he could tell it as a story that would make you fall down laughing. Nevertheless, he was one of those rare individuals with a very profound sense of himself. He maintained the ability to make deep connections with people. And he was such a sensualist. When he was young, he was crazy about women and they were crazy about him. He was Woody Allen–esque and he had such an obvious and large talent."

At a cocktail party in Ann Arbor, Michigan, I met Elena Delbanco, the daughter of Bernard Greenhouse, founding cellist of the Guarneri String Quartet. We fell into chatting about musicians and the talk turned to Sam. She had known him in the 1960s. Although she had been a young girl at the time, she remembered him as wild and fun-loving, with an aura of talent and sex appeal, the quintessential swinging bachelor. This was a side of Sam I never saw, since by the time I met him, he had settled down.

In the mid-1960s, Itzhak and Sam first met. They read chamber music together casually one afternoon at the home of cellist

Stephen Kates. Itzhak was impressed by Sam's propulsive playing, which he found so different from other pianists. But just as important as the musicianship, Itzhak said, when choosing an accompanist, he weighted heavily the factor of what it would be like to travel together. And, Itzhak said, when things went wrong on the road, as they inevitably do, Sam made everything hilariously funny.

"That was an interesting relationship," Genie has said about Sam and Itzhak, "because they were both handicapped. Because of that, they could be brutal to each other in a way that no one else could be brutal. It was like a very noir comedy to be around. They fought like the Bickersons, particularly later. And yet they were devoted to one another."

Their antics spilled into their performing as well. "No Perlman-Sanders program would be complete without some hijinks at the end," Olin Chism wrote in the *Dallas Morning News* after one of their recitals. "They played four encores and entertained with some pretended confusion about the music and what to play. For regulars, it's familiar, but the audience always loves it …"

The two of them would joke — with one another and with the audience — about their infirmities. Once, when one of Sam's feet had swollen so much that he had to wear one tennis shoe and one dress shoe, Itzhak pointed it out to the audience and made up a story that brought attention to both their problems. Itzhak explained that Sam had been so mad with him that he'd tried to kick his shin. But he'd hit his brace instead and damaged his shoe.

Performing musicians find various ways to alleviate performance anxiety. Practical jokes — those thinly disguised acts of mild aggression — are rampant onstage among seasoned performers. Sam often told a story about performing with Rostropovich at the Kennedy Center in Washington, D.C. Before going on, the cellist severely cautioned Sam not to fumble with the music because he wanted to rush out onstage, sit down, and launch into playing immediately (a favourite trick of his). They hurried on, Sam seated himself at the piano and opened the score to discover that Rostropovich had pasted a *Playboy* centrefold across the first two pages. Rostropovich sat onstage, glancing back over his shoulder and pretending to be waiting impatiently for Sam as he frantically tried to pry loose the centrefold without tearing the music. The audience, meanwhile, had no idea what was going on.

Other times, the expected unexpected was no joke. One night, Sam played for a soprano who began to sing flat in the middle of a piece. She turned pale and Sam helped her offstage. He returned to the stage and had to play an impromptu solo recital for the audience while the doctor tended her backstage.

"Let's face it, anything can happen out there," Itzhak said. "All of us are nervous before a concert. It never goes away, you just learn to manage it."

One of the ways Sam managed his anxiety was to rehearse everything ad infinitum. For some musicians, this seemed like a waste of time and Robert often found it irritating. "If we were doing 'Danny Boy' for the 3,189th time," he said, "Sam wanted to rehearse it *and* he wanted to mark his score again. For Sam, there was always hanging over him the onus of performing that he approached with a lot of self-inflicted horror."

Unquestionably, Sam was highly strung and perpetually anxious. He was inevitably late to appointments (even doctor's appointments, though never performances). He had the self-punishing perfectionist's habit of procrastination and before a concert he would frequently stay up most of the night practising obsessively. This approach only added to the usual stresses of the performer's life.

"Sam was very insecure," Dr. Fuster said. "Not personality-wise, but because of his medical condition. Also, there was his role as an artist who was almost at the top but always still under somebody else, and that was also a chronic anxiety. In terms of playing with Itzhak Perlman, he would feel always, he had to do it perfectly. And he was a last-minute person, doing everything fast at the last minute. Put together his health, his second-man position in terms of being an artist, and being a last-minute person, and you have a man who is anxious by definition."

Many highly-strung performers are known to vomit before every concert. Sam was a more nervous performer than most, and, like many musicians, he developed bizarre rituals that he *had* to carry out before each performance. No one else was allowed to touch his music or his hairbrush: he lined them up just so. Any musical score he was not playing that evening had to be hidden away. He absolutely had to eat the same thing before each concert: a Hershey's chocolate bar, a Coke, a cheese sandwich, and a cup of tea with lemon. He also had to wash his hands three times in succession.

Sam's performance anxiety contributed to his infamous treatment of page-turners. Once Itzhak's manager received a letter of complaint from a page-turner who wrote that she had a black and blue mark where Mr. Sanders had slapped her hand. When Itzhak asked Sam why he'd hit the page-turner, he replied indignantly that she was about to turn too early.

In the early 1980s, at Sam's festival on Cape Cod, a page-turner did not show up for a performance in the church at Wellfleet. I volunteered. I had turned pages throughout the four years of my bachelor's degree in music (I often said I held a major in music and a minor in turning). It's harrowing at best. You have to be a good score reader, prepared for sudden cuts or repeat signs that demand you flip back several pages without fumbling. And while some pianists will give you a nod when they are ready for a new page, more often you have to do some mind reading (a form of close observation). Above all, you have to figure out how far ahead the pianist is reading the score. A musician reads music much the way you are reading this text — not letter by letter (or note by note), but in whole words (or entire musical phrases). However, each musician reads ahead to a different degree and usually farther ahead at faster tempos; so you have to be sensitive and adjust the speed of flipping the pages.

That night, the work on the program was the Brahms Piano Quintet, not a particularly difficult score. However, the last movement, marked *allegro non troppo,* is symphonic in its proportions and complexity. Sam and I looked over the score backstage before going on.

"Uh — uh — uh, I marked where the page turns should be," Sam said, stuttering as he always did when he was worked up.

"No problem," I assured him. My assurances weren't enough, and he insisted on going over the page turns and his markings, one by one. When we got to the final movement, he pointed to one of the last page turns as a particularly difficult one. "No problem," I repeated. "You've marked it on the third beat." (I was thinking to myself that as fast as the measures would be flying by, a page turn *on* a particular beat would be a fantasy at best.)

"No! No! No!" he shouted at me. "Not the *third* beat! The *second half* of the third beat!"

That was even more absurd. I couldn't resist tweaking him a little. "Oh, of course!" I said. "But, Sam, do you want me to *begin* the page turn on the second half of the third beat? Do you want the page turn half done by then? Or the page fully turned?"

He knew I was putting him on and flashed me a furious look, one of the only times he got mad at me. However, once we were onstage, the turning went fine.

Dr. Valentin Fuster is director of the Wiener Cardiovascular Institute at Mount Sinai Medical Center in New York City and has served as president of the American Heart Association. One of the leading cardiologists in the world, he is renowned for research, patient care, and administration. His days are packed with meetings and clinical consultations. He gets home from the hospital at 8 P.M., sleeps four hours a night, and arrives back at his office at five each morning. I arranged to speak with him by telephone at 6:30 in the morning. Born and educated in Barcelona, he speaks with a strong Spanish accent.

Dr. Fuster recalled that Sam was recommended by a colleague and showed up at his office without a formal appointment. According to the notes he took that day, Sam had the audacity to say to him, "You came highly recommended, but I want to be sure you are knowledgeable about my illness. If not, recommend somebody else." After their first meeting, Dr. Fuster wrote the following description of Sam: "Very determined and strong personality, genuinely sincere. Courageous life, brilliant, and compassionate person." Sam being Sam, the two became close personal friends.

"Sam was a pusher," Dr. Fuster said, in a tone that let me know it amused but did not particularly bother him. "He would just show up. Or, if he had an appointment, he was always late. Secretaries get very uneasy when you have a pusher coming in, the kind who says, 'I want to be seen right now.' But because of the other side of Sam's personality, they could somehow always accommodate him. After so many years, people knew him in the hospital, and they were very kind to him and accepted this behaviour."

Many of Sam's doctors had become his friends, but the friendship with Dr. Fuster was of particular importance to Sam, his lifeline during the two heart transplants. "The issue of psychology and being attached to a doctor was very important to him," Dr. Fuster said. "He was a very loyal person, and he always needed somebody he could rely on entirely, for him to feel psychologically safe and relaxed."

Long before I met Dr. Fuster, Sam had told me about him. He related (several times with great relish) how Dr. Fuster wanted to surprise his wife, Maria, on the occasion of their twenty-fifth anniversary. He asked Sam to organize a secret concert for her in a medieval church in her native town of Cardona, Spain. It clearly meant so much to Sam to be able to do something for the Fusters. He told me how Dr. Fuster brought his wife for a walk through the town that day and then seemingly just happened to go into the church where an audience had gathered. Onto the stage walked Sam and Robert White. After Sam died, Dr. Fuster also told me that Sam would not accept money for the performance and said he would take care of Robert White's fee and expenses. (Robert remembered getting "a very handsome honorarium" but seemed not to know it had come from Sam's pocket.)

By 1990, I had closed my public relations firm to have time to write. Sam followed and encouraged me all the way, asking to read my stories and articles, recommending new books he'd read and enjoyed, and confiding that he had always wanted to be writer. He had come through a string of bad years. His marriage had explod-ed in an acrimonious divorce. He was in serious debt and worried about making money so he could help his daughter, Sophie, then a teenager. He was living alone in a small studio apartment on West End Avenue. His heart had been weakening steadily, and, partly as a result of his lack of energy, his performing career was in a slump. Then he was told he would have to have a heart transplant.

When I arrived at the hospital, the intensive care nurse asked if I were a family member, and I felt justified in saying yes. I found Sam strapped into a bed that turned on a huge wheel so they could stand him upright or at any angle to assist his circulation. All around him, monitors clicked and beeped, buzzed and burbled; a green line drew a range of mountains over and over; red and yellow lights winked on and off. Sam's thin arms were bruised and taped with IVs. His hair was matted; his eyes were taped shut and leaking tears; his lips were cracked and the nurse swabbed them with Vaseline. Above the tape on his chest, I could see the blood-caked terminus of the incision.

Leaning over the coils of tubes, I put my mouth to his ear and said his name; said my name. "Mmmmm," he answered. Touch heals, so I touched Sam's hair. I stroked him wherever I could find some bare skin — his arms, his neck, his forehead. "Mmmmm," he said. Anything I could think of to say seemed so irrelevant and trite.

It was autumn and I had just returned from a trip to the Outer Banks of North Carolina, where a hurricane passing far to the south sent magnificently black waves crashing against the shore. I told Sam about walking on the beach; about the power of the surf. I described the strange shells and seaweeds scattered on the strand, the angry white froth far out against the horizon, the low bruised sky skudding fast. "Mmmmm," he said from time to time, and, when I had run out of things to say about the ocean, he mouthed the words "Thank you." For years, he would occasionally tell me how clearly he remembered that visit and how I had brought the stormy sea to him and gave him something to think about during those long hours of isolation and pain.

"There are people for whom the quality of life is important, and others for whom it is quantity," Dr. Fuster told me. "Sam was the latter, and it helped him get over the hard times. He was just buying life, year after year. He had an incredible urge to survive."

Whenever Sam was in the hospital, Itzhak would visit every day. He told me about going to see Sam right after the operation. At the time, Itzhak's daughter, Navah, had just developed rheumatoid arthritis. "There was Sam, looking like hell," Itzhak recalled. "They had his eyes taped shut so they wouldn't dry out, and he was all hooked up with tubes. I said, 'Sam, it's me,' and he kind of groaned,

'Oh, yeah.' Then after a pause the next thing he said was 'How's Navah doing?' He's hanging there, just came back from the dead, and the first thing he thinks of is how my daughter is doing. That was so Sam."

Following the heart transplant in 1990, Sam enjoyed a few relatively carefree years. With his renewed energy, he revitalized his performing career and achieved some financial stability. He fell in love with Susan Rothwell, an estate lawyer. Attractive and energetic, Sue enjoyed the bustle of Sam's life and also had vast reserves of patience to meet his intense needs. It was a happy match. They set up an apartment together, and he settled into a new life. He was full of plans for a twentieth-century retrospective concert series at Juilliard and even developed an idea for a television sitcom based on a behind-the-scenes story of a performing arts centre. He had never been more happy or creative. He said at the time that they were the best years of his life. But as a result of the anti-rejection and blood-thinning drugs he had to take, as the decade progressed, Sam's new heart began gradually to fail.

One evening in 1998, when he had started the long slide toward his final heart operation, I arranged to meet him and Sue for sushi. I was eager for them to meet my new partner, who would become my husband, and for him to meet them. When we arrived at the restaurant, a glance told me Sam was not in good shape — his face was flushed purple and he was tense, his shoulders edging up toward his ears. The painful gout had swollen his ankles and feet again. We lowered ourselves into the pit of a private dining room, the waiter brought us drinks and closed the rice-paper screen. For the next two hours, no matter what anyone said, Sam was ready to pick a fight or make a cutting comment that shut off any possible response. Sue and I kept the conversation going, but inwardly I felt irritated and let down. My partner looked at me questioningly —

this was the wonderful man I'd told him so much about? Afterward, though, I found myself thinking about Sam's illness, more concerned for him than angry. His aggression was beyond his control, I told myself and my partner. I knew what it felt like to try to manage pain and how sometimes it just got the better of you. You began to hate and want to hurt the people around you who were not suffering.

That evening was a reminder of how difficult and irritating Sam could be. Long after he died, Sue told me about a young Juilliard student Sam dubbed "The Crier" because she wept at every lesson. When Sue asked Sam what in the world he was saying to her, he replied: "I ask her, why is she here? Why is she even playing the piano? Why is she wasting my time?" No wonder the girl cried. But at the end of the school year, Sue remembered, Sam came home one day and said in astonishment, "I can't believe it! The Crier played *beautifully!*" And he looked so proud of himself. Sam evidently believed that his harsh treatment had led to a musical miracle. But there was no question that there were times Sam's impatience crossed the line to outright cruelty. He left behind more than a few enemies.

When Sam told me he was going to have a second heart transplant, I tried to keep my thoughts from showing in my face; a terrible abyss opened inside me and I could tell by the tone in his voice that he didn't believe he was going to live through this one. It was the spring of 1998 and we were sitting at a corner table in Edgar's, a West Side café that stands on the site where Edgar Allen Poe once lived in a farmhouse. One by one, Sam was meeting with his close friends to let them know about the upcoming operation. Underneath his offhandedness and the jokes ("My heart is so strong that when I die, they'll have to stomp on it to make it stop beating" — an appropriately Poe-like image), I knew he was scared this time.

Since death was on both our minds, I decided we should just go ahead and talk about it. We did, for hours, as the sun slid across the tiled floor and the tables filled and emptied and filled again. We talked about faith. (Sam was a firm atheist and no believer in the afterlife — I believe some form of consciousness or energy outlives our physical existence, but in what form I can't say.) We debated that awhile. We talked about people we had in common who had died. I told him I'd read that Native Americans concentrate their minds by singing their death chant, a personal mantra they rehearse all their lives in preparation for the final moment. We talked of how Blake died singing hymns and about Goethe's "*Mehr Licht, mehr Licht*," and what the final moment must be like.

After that day, every meeting seemed a goodbye. Sam kept a beeper with him twenty-four hours a day, even when playing concerts. If it went off, it meant a suitable donor had just died, a heart was available, and he would have to rush directly to the hospital. Sam waited through one long, stressful year, with several close calls as his heart condition worsened. A story in the newspaper told of a critical organ shortage nationwide. He decided to take the step of checking into the hospital and letting himself be put on a new drug with some awful side effects but which would also advance him on the list of waiting recipients. He would have a far better chance of getting a heart before time ran out.

Soon after he was admitted, I went for a visit. I sat on his bed as he showed me a picture book about the Yankees. He turned the pages slowly, one by one, and I found myself growing impatient. What had this to do with me, with our friendship? I needed to talk about us right then; I needed to hear that I had been important to him. But he continued to show me photos of Babe Ruth, Joltin' Joe, and Mickey Mantle. His face was a boy's, eyes lit up. On a photo of Yankee stadium from the late 1930s, he touched the image of his childhood apartment building. The gout had flared up, and his skeletal hands were gnarled with knobs. One joint was so inflamed, it looked as if several grapes were under the skin. I raised his hand to my mouth and kissed it. I surprised him. The talk grew free associative, about his early life, about how hard everything had been, about how grateful he was to Sue, to his daughter, to his friends. I realized it was another form of goodbye, to make me a kind of repository of the story of his life. Did he know then that I would write about him later? I listened hard, trying to remember everything, but mostly drowning in feeling this was the last talk.

"I don't believe in heaven," he said. "I think this is all there is." We'd had this conversation several times, and he knew I would answer that, since we can't know for certain, we may as well believe in something that gives us comfort and confidence. "I wish I had your faith," he always said. At one point, I crawled onto the bed and hugged him, held him next to me. I think it gave him some comfort. He was like a bag of sharp bones.

A week after the operation, I dropped by. He was angry, raging, furious. The nurse could do nothing right. His voice was hoarse and he was trying to yell at her. When an intern came in, Sam calmed down somewhat and tried to engage him in conversation. But the intern was in a hurry and left. Sam's jaw clenched and his dark eyes were aflame. I told the nurse I would stay with him and she looked relieved. I tried to stroke his arm. He wouldn't let me. So I rubbed his scalp. He glared. He was unreachable. I told him soothing things; the operation had gone well; some people had called to ask how he was. He only had to lie there and relax, not worry. His obdurate rage filled the room. I stayed, sometimes silent, sometimes talking. After an hour, he began to loosen up, to respond, and I left, drained and angry myself, when he fell asleep.

The last time I stopped by, orderlies were crowded around his bed. I caught a glimpse of bony mottled legs. He was naked and his catheter was being changed. I backed out of the room before he saw me and stood by the doorway listening. He was miserable — almost hysterical. It was not going well and would take a long time. So I left.

I meant to visit again. I was going away for a month to an arts colony — I felt indulgent and selfish to be leaving. With all the preparations and packing, one thing and another came up, and suddenly we were in the car riding across the George Washington Bridge on our way to Chicago. As we were crossing the bridge, we gathered speed and the shadows of the suspension cables blinked faster and faster. I turned to look back at the hospital's sandstone towers that rise on the east bank of the Hudson River.

Two weeks later, Lee Walter, Sam's personal manager, left a message that Sam had taken a turn for the worse. The next day he called to tell me Sam was dead.

A couple of years later, I asked Itzhak how he was managing the loss. He said he had prepared himself in advance of Sam's death by imagining life without him. But, he said, he thought about Sam all the time.

And it's the same for me. I no longer see Sam's ghost on the street. But as I listened to his recordings, talked to his friends, read his papers, and thought about his life, I came to understand something else about a life hereafter. In the here and now, we continue to live in another's memory. At his fiftieth birthday party, Sam had said, "This is so great! I never thought I would live to see thirty. Or forty. And here I am at fifty. It's so amazing that I'm still here."

ANITA LAHEY

Confessions of a Eulogist

Let death and exile and every other thing which appears dreadful be daily before your eyes; but most of all death: and you will never think of anything mean nor will you desire anything extravagantly.
— Epictetus, *The Encheiridion*

SHE GREW UP ON A FARM IN SOUTHERN ONTARIO, learned to drive on a tractor, and always described the killing of chickens with horror and relish. She didn't like my father when they first met; loved to tell us he was boring, dry, an utter nerd. At the drive-in on their first date, she ate, to his astonishment, a hot dog, a bag of popcorn, pop, peanuts, and a bag of chips. On their second date, he asked what religion she was. "Thank God I answered Catholic," she always said of her response. "Otherwise he probably would have stopped the car and let me out." She loved the sun but hated mornings. She gave birth to four children and never let any one of them forget the pain she endured — while giving birth, but also during all the anguish-filled parenting years that followed. She kicked smoking for twelve or thirteen years, then picked it up again in some sort of undefined rebellion. She was weepy, might have carried some gene responsible for the unlimited production of tears.

She was Polish but hated making cabbage rolls, preferring a casserole that contained all the same ingredients, layered rather than tediously rolled. "It tastes the same. What's the difference?" she'd say, leaning into the counter, one hip raised, her milk-chocolate eyes flattering you, daring you to call her lazy.

I am walking on a paved path along the Ottawa River as these thoughts whirl. It's early June, a muggy evening. People bike, jog, and rollerblade past me. This is the sort of normal, summery thing I imagine the people around me are doing: admiring nature, absorbing heat and sunlight. Nothing more complicated than moving or being still. I, meanwhile, have been composing a eulogy for my mother.

She is not dead. In fact, she's only fifty-one years old and relatively healthy. I'm beginning to think I am ill, however, caught in morbid fantasy: If Mom died, when Mom dies, what might I say about her at the funeral?

And it's not just Mom. One of my not-so-rare daydreams involves the death of someone close to me, and the oratorical role I might play in marking his or her departure. My one living grandparent, my father, my siblings, and a number of close friends have all been victimized on my morning jogs, in the dentist's chair, as I finger peaches at the local farmer's market, and at those foggy, early-morning moments when I lie on my back in bed, not yet ready to rise.

Some days I think this may be grounds for some serious psychological excavation. We live in a society where death is hardly top of mind. Am I suffering from some affliction? A pathological desire to perform at funerals? I try to see it in more benign terms. There are people who can be counted on for certain things in times of mourning. The aunts and neighbours who bring casseroles. Those women in church basements everywhere, cutting up the tuna sandwiches to offer after the service. People who sing at the graveside, who bear the coffin, who listen intently and empathetically to out-pourings of grief. People who pray. Food, muscles, hugs, fresh Kleenex — these are all gifts people proffer to help their dear ones (and themselves) wrestle death. I am a eulogist. I bring words.

Eulogy One: The Friend

It's my twenty-second birthday. My friend Joana Fraser and I have been napping in my snowed-in basement apartment in Toronto. We now sit, still somewhat groggy, in the dark living room, discussing where we should go for supper. I have the Yellow Pages open to the restaurant section.

Joana has been my closest friend since we met waiting for the school bus in the nearby suburb of Burlington during our first week of Grade 9. She was the cheerful redhead who seemed to know everyone and who had already, somehow, made her school uniform appear personalized. (We went to a Catholic high school.) I was the quiet one with slouching shoulders and dull, brown, wretchedly winged hair. We both wore glasses for distance, and this somehow solidified things. That, or she was in need of a faithful listener. Within a week, I was in the living room of her mother's townhouse, being led through the pages of her parents' wedding album. (They were now divorced.) She introduced me to Billy Joel, Mr. Noodles with melted cheddar cheese, horoscopes, the delicate art of popping zits, and good old fashioned spontaneity, from dancing wildly in the living room to trying on all the clothes in your closet, in different combinations.

We have been inseparable ever since, through high school, university, and her six-year ordeal with cancer. Well, until four months ago anyway, when in September 1993 she moved to Vancouver to be with her boyfriend. This is our first visit since then, and I am try-ing not to notice how thin she is. She has always been beautiful but now seems translucent, lit from within. Her cheekbones, once masked beneath the roundness of her face, are delicate sculptures. Her navy eyes float above them like planets on a mobile. I could spin them around.

I can't think about supper. We talk about the treatment she's taking to augment chemotherapy, an extract from mistletoe that she injects to stimulate fighting cells against the hard tumours sprouting just beneath the skin all over her body. I can't believe she's giving herself needles. Remember, I prod, how afraid you used to be of swallowing pills? That ridiculous ordeal with the spoons and the juice?

"Yeah, that," she says. There's a pause. "It's come back, you know. I can't do it anymore. Well, I mean. I think I have a lump in my throat."

She looks at me and I look at her. I make a lame joke about hanging her from the ceiling so people can stand beneath her stomach to kiss. She laughs weakly.

I remember the fat phone book in my lap but can't bring myself to move it. Joana straightens her back and says something about elephants in the living room, how she needs to be able to talk about this stuff, and I say OK, not knowing or wanting to know what I'm agreeing to. Then it happens. Her funeral, she instructs, should not be a depressing affair, because she hasn't had a depressing life. It's been good and full, and she does not feel cheated. So there. No black. Spring flowers, she is saying. Tulips. Daisies. And that nice hymn, she thinks, about the sea and the sky. I know the one she means. And, Anita, I'd like you to write something for me. She slips it in. Somewhere around the tulips and the hymn. You don't have to read it yourself, if you don't think you can, but would you write it?

"Of course. Of course, I'll read it myself."

"Well, you don't know, you might not —"

"I will."

I do not think to ask her any questions. I am too intent on making sure she understands I'm unfazed. Maybe I am shaken, but I don't stop to try to figure this out. I focus on not stopping to figure at all. Therefore, I don't learn a thing. For example: What would she like me to say? Or not say? Why me?

This is how I come to be standing at the pulpit in St. Raphael's Catholic Church in Burlington, Ontario, before four hundred and fifty people on the evening of May 4, 1994, six days after Joana's death, on the verge of delivering my first eulogy.

I have had little exposure to eulogies, or funerals for that matter. My uncle died when I was seven; I remember touching his cold, dead cheek, but of his funeral I recall nothing. My grandfather died last fall. His funeral was a high Catholic mass, said in Polish. I didn't understand a word of it. The only eulogy I've ever heard was for a boy I used to play with across the street who was hit by a car. The idea that someone other than the priest or minister would address the gathered in church flabbergasted and impressed me. But I remember nothing of what was said.

One of the first things I think when her father calls to tell me the news is OK, Anita, it's time to do that thing she asked. I buy myself a new notebook, a nicer, more expensive one than I've ever owned, a black spiral with thick pages and a wine-red textured cover. I make notes. I am single-minded, dogged, sure. If anyone can write about her, it is me.

I spend the days approaching the memorial in an underwater state, with moments of clarity and stillness occurring while I write, as though gripping a pen in my hand means I've come up for air. The motif for my speech: all the things I "learned" being friends with Joana. I don't know how I chose this theme, but it seems to work: appropriate anecdotes emerge into my thoughts frequently and send me reaching — or running — for my notebook.

I know too little about this business to be daunted, am too green to be aware of what might go wrong, to consider jealousies, politics, and family conflicts, and all the people I might neglect or offend. When the moment at the memorial comes, I approach the podium and heed some long-ago remembered instruction about public speaking: Look slightly over the heads of your listeners, never at their faces, and never, ever into an eye, no matter how tempting.

I open my mouth and the words sound, splashing through the church, one on top of the other. It's easy. Easier than it should be.

Almost instantly I have people laughing, about Joana's obsessive admiration of Anne of Green Gables, her lack of organizational skills, her vanity, her ability to embrace her "geeky" side, even her specific instructions on how we should mark her death. I speak of her gumption and spirit, describe her exploding into dance on a crowded sidewalk, her refusal to let a nurse pronounce her name wrong. In what I will later see as a creepy manifestation of denial, I insist on speaking of her in the present tense, an affectation I explain with one of those jokes meant to soften the edges: I know she's here, I say. This is Joana we're talking about. As if she'd miss a party that's all about her.

I quote from her last journal entries. (She had urged me to read them.) In one of the entries, she describes "the most important thing in life," which, not earth shatteringly, is rooted in love. She expresses her epiphany toward this understanding by referencing, without irony, a line from the movie *City Slickers:* "It's that one thing that Billy Crystal refers to — 'that one thing on the end of your finger that's the most important thing in life.' I remember watching that video and being perplexed. What could it be?"

I look up at the congregation and close with the following words: "I just want to say that of all the people in all the world, only my friend Joana could take the most important thing she's learned in life and put it in the context of a blockbuster Hollywood film about some middle-aged men and some cows."

With that I step away. I have just spent several minutes talking about my best friend behind her back — or in front of her ghost, depending what you believe — to nearly every person she's ever known. I have praised her and poked fun at her. There is nothing left to do. Halfway to the pew, I break into gut-wrenching sobs. They smack against the walls of the silent church.

Eulogy Hazard Number One: Fresh-Squeezed Grief

Seven years pass after Joana's death. I am living in Ottawa, a twenty-nine-year-old journalist trying to transform herself into a poet and playwright. I have weathered other losses, recently delivered another eulogy — for my grandmother — and suspect the next funeral is not far off, for a middle-aged friend beginning to weaken in that now-familiar duel with cancer.

I realize that while those around me approach funerals with dread and the gritting of teeth, I can't hate them. I find them fascinating, have to consciously subdue my interest in the proceedings. It's the gash they tear into our everyday existence that I appreciate, this being forced out of complacency, routine. But it is more than this. I have borne losses through which funerals have helped me, and I think I know why. What are the patterns, pieces of a funeral? There is music, of course, sometimes heady but often disappointing. There are prayers — in which I can't believe, try as I might. Then there are the usual Bible readings to do with, ho-hum, God's mercy, his promises to the righteous and faithful. But if the funeral includes a eulogy, there is story. Story, for me, is a thing to revel in, even when it ends in sadness. Even when it's made of your own pain.

When attending a funeral, it's the eulogy for which I wait, and the lack of one that leaves me grasping. I begin to think that long-ago tribute to Joana whet my appetite, that she accidentally pinpointed my skill in mourning. Once I allow myself to indulge this theory, I find myself in the throes of discovering a new literary form — new to me, that is. And wildly, thrillingly different from any other I've tried.

The writing, giving — and consuming, which I begin to do voraciously of any printed examples I can find — of eulogies seems a questionable pastime, particularly for a writer. The eulogy's definition alone — "speech or writing *in praise of* a person" — renders it suspect. Compare it to some more highly regarded forms of literature. A poem is a polished jewel, and it feels that way, rubbed and loved. A story is meticulously chipped into fine definition, like an aging profile from a blank-faced stone. A eulogy is a blurt. Sappy, incomplete, and awkward, dripping love and exaggeration.

Though we all listen intently when a eulogy is being read, outside the funeral's insular circle of shock and grief, the eulogy is held in popular disdain, slotted into that dangerous realm of touchy-feeliness. You won't find a Norton's anthology of eulogies, nor a category for the eulogy in a broader volume. Death scholars either ignore it or abhor it. Typical is *The Funeral: Vestige or Value,* in which author Paul Irion mercilessly dissects American funeral customs, without neglecting the smallest detail. Except, that is, for eulogies. He mentions them only when he must, and then with desperate caution. He speaks of the "perfectly legitimate desire to avoid the pitfalls of lavish eulogies." After asserting that a funeral offers the chance to honour the deceased and his or her contributions, Irion quickly covers himself: "This does not necessarily require a glowing eulogy."

But Irion must suspect he's indirectly making a case for eulogies. Why else would he keep trying to convince us — and himself — that he's not? Irion tells us that according to anthropologists, there are three basic rites that must be carried out after a death: the rite of separation, the rite of transition, and the rite of incorporation. There is no handy *History of the Eulogy* to tell us how, or how long ago, this particular mourning ritual began. Anthropologists and scholars have been far more concerned with what we do to a corpse — cremate, mummify, bury, dance around — than what we say to or about it. But I submit that, aside from being clearly rooted in the ancient practice of storytelling — one of the earliest ways we humans tried to make sense of our existence — the eulogy shows remarkable potential to serve each of Irion's rites, indeed stems from these necessary acts.

Separation is the cruel, initial jolt. This person was here and is suddenly, irrevocably gone. But on some level, particularly at first, this absence is not so different from that created when a person departs the room where some gathering has taken place — say, Thanksgiving dinner. The turkey is eaten; the table cleared. Aunt Martha says her goodbyes. Those who remain are now free to analyze Martha's contribution to the evening. If her impact was dramatic — perhaps even if it wasn't — we might do this out loud, together. We will say we were impressed by some witticism she uttered, alarmed at her treatment of Cousin Jeff, or once again shocked by her greedy consumption of stuffing. She made us laugh; made us boil. Confused us, bored us, taught us something lovely.

This is what we do. We assess. We grope for our reactions to people when their presence is no longer here to weigh us down with vulnerability. The process is no different when a person dies, merely more urgent and utterly final. When the eulogist stands up to speak, it's as if she's saying, formally, officially: "It's OK, she's gone. We can talk now. Just us."

Once we begin speaking to one another in this way, we embark on the next rite: transition. Relationships change as we feel our way around this gap in our midst, explaining to one another what the life that once filled it meant to us. Our sentences stretch across the emptiness, fill it with new moments and shared thoughts. Like it or not, we adjust.

After Joana's memorial service, her father came to me, wrapped his big bear arms around me, and said, "You're my new daughter now." These were words of uncorrupted grief, not entirely meaning what they said. Joana's father and I had a new reality to navigate, and we found, at first, that speaking about Joana was the easiest way to do this. As the years passed, when we saw one another, we spoke more about ourselves, less about Joana. Our relationship evolved to the point where she became not an absence between us but a silent presence, solid and sure, made whole but unobtrusive by the earlier work we'd done.

Which leads us to the third rite: incorporation. That is, as Irion describes it, "incorporating the deceased into a new form of existence." This is not the business of the afterlife as some religions see it; this is memory work. I once heard the earnest and intelligent minister Brian Kopke, of the First Unitarian Church of Ottawa, eloquently describe, while presiding over a funeral, "our duty to memory." Our purpose here, said Kopke, rubbing his cropped beard, is to "build and solidify our memories so we can take them with us into our new lives" and in that way grant our friend a form of immortality. This may sound a degree too pat. And Kopke's voice does bear some of that suspicious breathlessness of the late-night, mush-hour, radio DJ. But his words made plain, psychological sense. Learning to replace a life force with memories, to live with this diminishment, is no easy task. Yet we must use memory — for we have nothing else — to transplant this person from physical space into our minds.

Such work is fraught with danger, for we become impatient. We think our memories, when they don't flow fast enough, have abandoned us. We also manipulate them into truths we prefer. After Joana died, I raged at myself for not being able to recall a single conversation with her. I saw scenes in my head, dozens of fragmented scenes: It's her sixteenth birthday, and we sit in a cool, damp crevice in the Niagara Escarpment. We are eighteen, standing in a dingy student co-op in downtown Toronto, surveying the dreary room we will share during our first year at university. We are in a wind at a railing, riding the ferry to Toronto's Centre Island for a rare afternoon in the park. These are painfully, infuriatingly silent scenes, in which I know we spoke — deeply, earnestly. In the days and months after her death, the temptation to fill in the blanks was nearly overwhelming.

It's no wonder that an intellectual like Irion, trained in measured, passionless prose, would be wary of the eulogy. It gallops into our loneliness bearing on its back all the statements of comfort we could ask, all the fumbling admiration we might hold up to our lost companion. I shudder to think what Irion might have thought of Justin Trudeau's eulogy for his father after the former prime minister's death in the fall of 2000. Justin revealed to us, with a theatrical flourish, that his dad was a looming figure, a force to negotiate. He described himself and his siblings as "the luckiest kids in the world," with a father who "loved us with the passion and the devotion that encompassed his life."

Ugh! Cringe. Puke.

I loved it. The eulogy was not remarkably cohesive or beautifully written. It wasn't tempered with references to Pierre Trudeau's failings, of which there were many. (He was arrogant, a know-it-all, likely a workaholic, and so on.) It was emotionally naked, nothing more or less than a gift, an expression of love — minus inhibition, hesitation, checks, balances, or buts. You knew it was true, in that deeper sense — the soul's truth — by the way Justin dissolved into sobs when it was over, as if something had been removed from his centre, and he knew, finally, there was no getting it back.

For me, in the throes of such loss, the eulogy's more reserved cousins won't cut it. Consider the obituary: the chronicling of a life, anchored by educated but tempered guesses at its impact on some field of study or profession. It is not even this much for the supposedly average among us; for most, the obit these days will simply list the date and manner of death, surviving family, and the place and time of the funeral. Perfectly practical, bland. The epitaph — pithy, sorrowful, sometimes witty, always carved in stone — wins hands down in the dignity department. But its brevity and habit of quoting literature and scripture can seem defensive, a holding back. The elegy, a verse of lament, is arguably as personal and unreserved as the eulogy — it might even achieve decent wallowing. But an elegy is a poem, as is its musical twin, the blues song — a status that somehow lends these tributes credence and respect.

The eulogy is not after respect, and neither are freshly skinned mourners. We are raw, and raw is what you get. This can result in beauty: thick, haunting, heavy. The sort that will bruise you.

Phyllis Theroux, a writer of magazine columns and children's books, is a rare public appreciator of the eulogy. In 1997, she edited *The Book of Eulogies,* an unabashed homage to the form. One of her more remarkable finds is by a John Conrad Sr. about his son, who died at fourteen, having lived with a difficult disease called tuberous sclerosis. In opening, Conrad asks, "How do you find any redeeming value to the life of a retarded boy who suffered from severe bizarre emotional problems?"

When Conrad does uncover something redeeming in his son's life, you buy it and rejoice, because he took the hard way to find it. "In the end," he says, "we got nothing that we wanted in our child John and everything that we could ever have needed." You wonder to what extent Conrad wrote his way to this redemption.

Other gems: William Makepeace Thackeray rhapsodizing over Charlotte Brontë: "I remember the trembling little frame, the little hand, the great honest eyes." Philosopher Hannah Arendt lamenting poet W. H. Auden's demons, admitting she "found it difficult to understand fully what made him so miserable, so unable to do anything about the absurd circumstances that made everyday life so unbearable for him." Mark Twain wrestles with the loss of his daughter, and former slave Frederick Douglas lauds Abraham Lincoln (after taking him down a peg or two). Among these, many lesser-knowns are sketched by spouses, parents, children, and friends. Revealed are broken hearts, failures, betrayals, swift but indelible moments, acts of red-eyed courage. Reading them gives a sense of the grand continuum, that fleeting taste of the greatness of life, and at its fringes the niggling, relentless reality of death. Author Richard Selzer writes of his mother, Gertrude: "When it came, that last breath, it was as though a lamp in whose circle I had lived all my life had been extinguished. Now I was free to live anywhere. In the dark."

Writing a eulogy is the real thing, honest-to-God "blast-it-out-sucky," a mantra a group of writers I meet with developed to describe our goal of not hedging on the first draft of a work. The idea is not to edit as you compose, but to squeeze words from the elbow, the shin, the skull — dump it all on the page. You never know what might emerge. The eulogy forces this sort of honesty. No danger of your internal editor getting in the way — she's on shock holiday as you process this loss. And what time is there for revision? They've booked the venue, published the time and place in the newspaper.

There's bravado to this, a conscious choice to give yourself over unexamined, unsieved. That's one of Theroux's guilty delights in the form: "Eulogies are always double portraits … We are aware as much of the eulogist as the eulogized … we are given glimpses into the recesses of their minds and hearts that under ordinary circumstances are concealed."

After Joana's memorial service, I reprinted my eulogy on purple paper and pasted it into the fancy red journal. I didn't dare scan it. I feared almost immediately that rereading would reveal some syrupy crap that I had been blind to in the after-death shock.

I still avoid it, still fear what it may reveal. For rawness can also sting, like a scraped knee.

Three years before Justin Trudeau's tour de force, I rose very early one morning to watch the televised funeral of Princess Diana.

I still can't shake the image of her brother, Earl Spencer, speaking so bitterly of the royal family, the media, and the photographers who plagued his sister. He described the princess as "the most hunted person of the modern age," vowing to protect the souls of her sons from being "simply immersed by duty and tradition" and not permitted to "sing openly as you had planned." At the time I thought, better if he'd not spoken at all. Anger in grief I can accept, but what good does it do to spew it to the world?

Yet a part of me understood his need to blast — in all directions — his rage at having lost his sister. And I've spoken to people who admired his outpouring. Good show, they said, finally let those royals and the predatory media have it. Much of the world, for better or worse, mourned — or thought it mourned — Diana's death. If Earl Spencer ever evolves beyond his anger, he may recoil at the acidity of his words. And yet there may be something of value in the way he seethed. It certainly said more about human nature than most sociology textbooks. One hopes it was the beginning of letting go.

In the introduction to her anthology, Theroux raises what I've called a "blurt" to near glory. "The eulogist," she intones, "is the first person to step forward, in a formal way, to hold a lantern above the loss." And that little speech he or she offers, dangling above our stunned selves, "has a natural majesty."

"As a powerful container for human feeling, it may not be surpassed."

No one promises that the eulogy will be pleasant to listen to. Nor that it might be illuminating, articulate, transcendent, or even interesting. This is death we're talking about, and, while death is the only truly reliable thing about our existence, it is seldom tidy, never predictable in the way it stomps through, nudging and knocking us about.

When the eulogist — me, for example — steps up to the lectern in the church, or wherever a funeral or memorial service is being held, the congregation sits stunned, eyes puffy, fists gripping balled tissues. They (I imagine) are thinking to themselves, "What can she possibly say that could mean a bloody thing in the face of this?" They are thinking: "Look how small and red-cheeked she is. Surely she's going to break down. That's the *last* thing I need to see right now."

Mostly they are thinking: "What on earth will come out of this one's mouth?" And why not, I ask myself, add suspense to the proceedings? Give us some uncertainty to steal our attention for a few thankful moments away from the biggest certainty of all.

Eulogy Two: The Grandmother

Six years after Joana's death, my grandmother, Beatrice Lahey — known to all as Beat — succumbed to breast cancer. She was seventy-five years old, a timid, wiry creature no taller than a nine-year-old girl. She lived in Cape Breton, and I had grown particularly fond of her throughout my twenties, visiting several times from my home in Ottawa and relishing early mornings in the kitchen with her, drinking tea, and flipping through the flimsy *Cape Breton Post*.

After she died, I travelled once more to the fishing village where she had lived. For three days, I hovered as my father and his seven siblings wrestled with all the marginal decisions necessitated by death — details that seem to grip the forearm and twist the punishment of loss all the more tightly: who would sing which hymns, what rings would or wouldn't be buried with her, which grandsons had agreed to act as pallbearers, who else should be approached, and so on.

The absence of something (other than the familiar bemused exclamations of Beat) nagged. Halfway through the second day I understood. There had been, to my knowledge, no mention of a tribute of any kind, by anyone. I took my father aside. Eulogies, he told me, just weren't part of the norm around here. A funeral consisted of a mass (Catholic), followed by interment. Any thoughts to be expressed would emanate from the mouth of the priest.

This was long before I'd begun to examine the nature of the eulogy and my attraction to it. I was operating on instinct, troubled by the likelihood of my grandmother being sent off without a word to distinguish her life from the multitudes that pass each year, without some account of her own trials and triumphs, and, most of all, her idiosyncrasies. But I was also keenly aware of my status here, as a usually absent Ontario relative. This woman had eight children who were, with dignity and restraint, orchestrating her send-off. Who was I to step in and suggest the traditional Catholic service wasn't enough? And yet, as the hours passed I was seized more strongly by the feeling that a failure to properly eulogize my grandmother would constitute a larger failure, not just against her but against life itself, these lives already extinguished as well as the mad pulsing that persists all around. It would be an act of neglect, that quaint Catholic concept known as a "sin of omission." And it would be mine. For by the end of my period of dilemma, I understood that not only did I desire an oral tribute to my grandmother, but if there was to be one, I would write and deliver it.

My assumption of the eulogist's role was not just a matter of sensing that even if they felt it right and proper to include such a speech in the service, no one else would want the job. There was a palpable conceit in it; I believed that this was my role, that I would perform it admirably — indeed might have hesitated to trust another in my place.

After Joana's memorial, people — ranging from complete strangers to my mother — had told me I was "so strong" for having delivered a eulogy. I was wary of this assumption. I did not feel strong; I was normal but for the fact of my grieving, having been abandoned by my dearest friend. (I was still young enough to think loss the exception in life.) And I did not think of myself as anything other than a person who had simply, in faithfulness, fulfilled the wish of a friend.

But now here I was thinking perhaps I ought to do another, this time for a person who hadn't asked me to step forward and star in her show — and to a group of mourners who didn't think it necessary; in fact, who hadn't thought of it at all.

Would my aunts, uncles, and cousins (not to mention my own father) think I was claiming some right to Nan, trying to turn her event into my own? If one of them had made such an accusation, I couldn't have said with assurance that they were wrong. How far would I have to plunge to uncover my motives? There was no time for such serious excavation; Nan would be buried in two days.

I decided the impulse ran deeper than the doubts. An exchange with my aunt, the wife of my father's brother, made some difference as I balanced and weighed. A friendly, polite woman, she is not one to speak her piece in a crowd. When we were out of earshot of the ever-present crowd in the kitchen, she smiled, gently whispering her reservations: "You do know it's going to make it sadder for everyone, don't you?"

At first I thought yes, she's right; this is an imposition. And then I thought: Yes. It *will* make it sadder. And I nodded to myself. We should not, I decided, be left to wade through this moment untouched. If it be sadness that must gather for this woman, this death, then bring it on.

We say our goodbyes to Beat in a small wooden church facing the ocean. After the service the pallbearers will carry her body across the street to the narrow plot next to my grandfather's, at the back of the cemetery, on a moist, grassy lip overlooking the salty bay.

I sit gripping my folded speech, printed out from my cousin's computer just this morning. This one was difficult to write, perhaps because I agonized over my right to do it. Perhaps because I feared I didn't know her deeply. She wasn't my wisdom-sharing elder, and we'd never had any truly heart- or mind-revealing talks. I asked myself whether I was embellishing when I wrote certain things, such as "Beat was one of the few adults I had known when I was growing up who didn't talk to me like I was a child — and whose presence didn't require censorship of the sometimes daring banter of youth." Did I really remember her this way, or did I just want to?

But as I culled my memory and strung together anecdotes, a theme began to emerge that felt true, of a woman of habit and determination, who took comfort in small rituals and who had her own peculiar ways of doing things, from how she killed flies — addressing the pest before swatting it with satisfaction — to how she drank her tea (with Carnation condensed milk, the spoon always in the cup). Moments came to mind as I wrote, most not destined for the eulogy, from the times she'd shared her bed with me (she did not move at all in her sleep) to the times I'd seen her angry, worried, or frightened. In many respects, she had been frank about her feelings and her fears. I knew her more than I had thought.

Having learned this much, I almost feel, sitting in church as the funeral begins, as though my work — at least, the part of it that concerns me — is over. The reading aloud of the result will be something of an epilogue. At least, I think so until I stand up.

I falter somewhere on the first page, in the section about how, as a child, I'd come into the kitchen and she'd say good morning "just as if I was completely grown up." This is pathetic and sweet. The tears well and I must stop. I lower my head, press my eyelids with a thumb and forefinger, shake it off. I get through the part about her love of solitaire (and the many varieties she taught me) and how meticulously she would scratch her cherished Bingo lottery cards. But then I start talking about how small she was and yet still able to give a proper dressing-down to each of her seemingly gigantic adult sons. This story is meant to be funny, and people do laugh, but she's down there in the coffin in front of me, never to be teased for being short again, never again to be crouched down to for a hug. I have to stop, breathe, squish my voice back into some stable shape.

And so it goes. It strikes full force, with every characteristic and quirk I describe, every anecdote I share, that these are things of the past.

There is nothing shocking about losing your elderly grand-mother. Yet I'm breathless with the notion that this woman's life is over. She no longer resides in that little house on the hill, to which we will soon return. This can't be! It simply can't. She was so real, so Beat, even a few days ago when I spoke to her on the phone.

I finish the speech but deliver the final lines in a thin voice. This is what I get for wishing to force this death down people's throats. It is thoroughly lodged in mine.

Eulogy Hazard Number Two: The Audience

I don't mean the audience itself is dangerous. It's the eulogist's response to having one that's more likely cause for concern. A eulogy is an oral form, after all. And not everyone is good with oral.

As Theroux fondly remarks, eulogies are often delivered by "rank amateurs." These people are not accustomed to standing at a podium, opening their mouths to a room full of attentive faces. The prospect may terrify them. That's no fun to watch. Nor is uncontrolled sobbing. Many priests and ministers regard this possibility as they might a plague of locusts after God has promised one: They expect it — smugly, but with dread.

For her 1990 study, "The Acceptable Face of Human Grieving? The Clergy's Role in Managing Emotional Expression during Funerals," British sociologist Jenny Hockey found that British clergy, though they expressed a desire to lead funerals that offered some therapeutic value to mourners, greatly feared uncontrolled outpourings of emotion. One minister fretted over eulogists who cry, introducing "an upsetting thing in the service." Another described eulogists who "break down" as "embarrassing" for all.

Thank God I didn't know this before delivering those two eulogies. Was the priest, each time, back there wringing his hands while I spoke? As I wavered? Hard enough to deal with my own worries, let alone those of the man who's supposed to be lending some spiritual serenity to the proceedings.

Worse than nervous Nellies, in my opinion, are people with issues. People with issues are emboldened by microphones and audiences. They spend their lives waiting for such opportunities. I'm not knocking Mark Antony here. So his eulogy to Julius Caesar was a call to arms, an exploitation of his podium, of the vulnerability that death leaves in its wake. It was true. And it was breathtaking in that familiar but never ordinary Shakespearean way —

My heart is in the coffin there with Caesar,
And I must pause till it come back to me.

Everything — pain, love, our bizarre, futile existence — is crammed into that "pause." It heaves and breathes like a giant bear.

I once, as a reporter, attended the funeral of a man in Ottawa who had been chased by police and had, in his attempt to escape, drowned in the Rideau River. Wayne Johnson was black, the details surrounding the incident were foggy, and his death had followed other, similarly tragic incidents involving black men and local police. Much of the community was outraged, and the main speech at Johnson's funeral focused on that rage. I don't blame the man who spoke; perhaps his words were unavoidable, necessary, even welcome. But it seemed to me Johnson had died twice: first in rushing waters amid horrible circumstances, then once more, by his absence at his own funeral.

The hijacking of eulogies with political rhetoric is nothing new. African American activist Amiri Baraka published an entire volume of eulogies a few years ago. In his foreword, Baraka describes the collection, which spans thirty years, as "a summing up of a period of history." But it is more than this. It is one attempt after another to summon the anger and energy of a people against injustice. Perhaps Baraka is wise; perhaps he knows the aftermath of a death is the best time to seed change. But his words seethe and boil, and his subjects drown beneath them: "Once again, we come together to mourn one of our fallen children. Today, another man-child slaughtered by imperialism. Again, a wanton bleeding of all of us, through our babies. These same babies we swore to transform the world to save!"

At least Baraka's preoccupation is about something larger than himself. Let's whip back to 10 B.C., to meet Roman senator Quintus Lucretius. Lucretius is believed to be the man behind the famous — in classical scholarship, anyway — "Funeral Eulogy of Turia," in which he hardly gives his poor dead wife the chance to jump into his watery prose, never mind drown.

Lucretius speaks of his wife's character, but only from the perspective of how she fulfilled her duties to him. "Why should I mention your domestic virtues: your loyalty, obedience, affability, reasonableness, industry in working wool ..." Soon his speech is all Quintus: "You provided abundantly for my needs during my flight ... showing great ingenuity in deceiving the guards posted by our adversaries ... [Y]ou pronounced the words of the edict in a loud voice, so that it should be known who was the cause of my deadly perils ..." Reading this two millennia later is to sense Lucretius's relief — a palpable, bright yellow relief — at uttering these words. The eulogy has nothing to do with his wife and everything to do with having an audience to whom he can set the record straight about how he has been treated.

One longs for Turia to interrupt her husband: "No, no, you've got it all wrong." But the dead, of course, are speechless. And not listening. Somewhere beneath our sorrow — or other, less congenial emotions — we know this. And so we are graced with such liberties as those found in the "character sketch" written upon the death of Queen Anne by her childhood friend, Sarah, Duchess of Marlboro. It begins: "Queen Anne had a person and appearance not at all ungraceful, till she grew exceeding gross and corpulent." By line four, we encounter her "gloominess of soul" and "cloudiness of disposition."

I am not concerned about turning vicious or political on my dead; my passions lie elsewhere. I sometimes fear weeping before the crowd — as I came close to doing during my grandmother's eulogy — but this is not so bad an event as Hockey's clergy might suppose. Some mourners might take comfort to see they aren't alone with their sniffles and tight cheeks and that welling, that awful, tidal welling in the chest.

What I do fear is inappropriate enjoyment of the audience.

The life of a writer can be simplified as follows: pound keyboard in solitude, struggling over meaning and language, eventually (barely) meeting deadline. Enjoy brief respite, perhaps some praise from editor. Begin again. In between, attempt to convince some family member or casual acquaintance that days are spent in real toil, not lying on the couch sucking candies.

Seldom does this type of writer encounter a person who has read what she's written. Rarely does a writer witness the immediate reactions another may have to her words. She doesn't expect recognition. It was her choice to live this way. Yet she feels the absence of her readers like a black hole in her side.

Enter the eulogy, rare literature of the masses, heard by anyone and everyone, from bankers to bums, lawyers to jocks. Enter attentive listeners, criers, laughers. Here is intoxication, a room of people responding to your voice. Here is your chance to show them what you can do, to prove that you can be more articulate than you may appear in real life, to assure them (and yourself) that words do matter. Here are people who may seldom buy books, who have perhaps never seen a literary magazine. Here may be members of your family, seeing that, yes, Anita does do something with her time. Something useful. At last, it shows.

At last, too, the writer who must make her living at less-than-honourable tasks — composing, for example, less-than-illuminating journalism — is thrust into a situation of urgency. She is looked to for wisdom and respite. For compassion and humour. For some glimmer of the ghost of a lost friend, spouse, or child. How can she turn away from this naked need? How can she not be proud of her ability to meet it? Disgusted — yes — by her uncanny ability to use the death of a person she loved to make herself feel special, necessary, talented?

Alive.

Eulogy Three: The Teacher

April 19, 2001. I walk through the neighbourhood thinking — in that familiar, dangerous way — of a friend who has, till now, been spared my morbidity. Her name is Diana Brebner, and she is at what increasingly seems like the end of a ten-year relationship with cancer — the wrong end.

She lives nearby, on the eighth floor of an apartment building, with a view of what used to be a hospital and is now a demolition site. I slept at her apartment recently, a companion during a rough night. In the morning, as we sat by the window drinking coffee and eating toast with orange marmalade, she pointed to the half-destroyed building and described the meticulous process she'd been witnessing, of the piecing apart of this structure. Where most would see a godawful mess, Diana saw order and mastery. She liked to be in awe of things.

I met Diana two years ago, when her cancer was in remission. I had enrolled in her poetry workshop at our local bookstore. She became a mentor, then a friend. I could feel her that morning playing teacher again, guiding my gaze to those heaps of rubble.

She was forty-four years old, had written three books, and raised two daughters. She gave a first impression of being proper, almost soft, but she was demanding, precise, fearless, unforgiving. Once, in a wild, poetry-inspired act, she left a mangled shopping cart on my lawn. Another time, in a moment I can only describe as transcendent, she sat in her winged-back chair wrapped in a white woollen blanket and told me that, through writing, she'd experienced something like "heaven on earth." How did she describe it? "Wow!" — a statement she used her entire face to pronounce: nose, eyes, lips, and cheeks, all layered gracefully around that one syllable.

I "eulogized" my mother on a dusk-walk. Though unsettling, you might put this down to the waning of the day: an imaginative, introspective woman can loosen the hold on herself in fatigue, or when the light passes by on an angle, revealing gaps between bricks and foliage, causing odd shadows. But this time it's morning and I'm not walking by the river, giving myself over to the rush of water. I'm on Wellington Street, my busy neighbourhood strip, as I construct Diana's eulogy, among buildings, traffic, noise, dust. The sun is not sinking; it blares. I pause at the demolition site, peer through the holes in the fence, try to see what she sees.

Nine days later, I am in a hospital room ringed with people, all of us looking wide-eyed at Diana. She is dead. I am not arrogant enough to think I've brought this on myself. I knew she was dying, or likely dying, well before "composing" her eulogy. But I didn't know it the way you know you're hungry or know you've stubbed your toe. I knew it somewhere within that fluffy cloud we create for ourselves when we know death is imminent but are still, as Kubler-Ross stresses about all the dying and their loved ones, holding out for a miracle. Something in me shrinks from what I've done. I can say I was playing regarding my mother's "eulogy," since — barring a sudden accident — she seems a good, long road from her final days. But to let my mind go at such a delicate time, when a drop of juice, a cracker, a tear, might upset the balance between here and there? This shows a lack of diligence — a failing the high-minded Diana would disdain. What it feels like is betrayal.

Two days later is a meeting with the ministers, for friends and family, in someone's backyard. We are to tell stories, plan the service. The call goes out for participants, and the two Unitarian ministers, a bearded, soft-edged man and quiet, birdlike woman, glance around the table. I avoid their eyes. I have the feeling of pressing down an urge, but my friend's daughter speaks up. Good for her, I think. It's her place to do this, not mine. Besides, I am growing weary of the pattern that seems to be emerging. It's as though I'm now going to reach this point of decision — to speak or not to speak — every time a person I love dies. I can let this woman depart without my two cents. Without having to consciously tell myself, "No. Keep it zipped."

This is not so tough a choice considering how impressed I am with this little meeting the ministers have called. Here they sit, pens poised over notebooks, scribbling as we talk. For three hours we talk. She was this; she was that. She said this; she said that. She did this, and can you believe she did that? Of course, there is laughing and crying. Also, snickers, nose wrinkling, elbowed ribs, meaningful glances, the crunching of chips and carrot sticks. It's a cementing of bonds forged in recent days, as we sit vigil together, many of us having never met before.

People share stories when friends die. It's natural, instinctive. To do so with not only permission but urging, from people you'd describe as spiritual leaders — well, that's something. That's grand, top o' the world. I walk home that night smiling inside, thinking, yes, this is how it's done.

By all of us, together. Not just me.

Eulogy Hazards Numbers Three and Four: False Gods and Forever

In her anthology *Readings for Remembrance,* Eleanor Munro writes, "Why human beings come together at all to mourn their dead is a deep unknown."

If you ask me, it's only a mystery most of the time. There are days and moments when such puzzles snap into clarity. In that blessed smidgen of time — before the monster of the cosmos, with a cough of foggy breath, blows the pieces back into a jumble — it all makes quiet sense.

I can point to one such moment in my life, a morning in late May 2000, less than a month after Beat's funeral, about one year before Diana's.

I stand among multitudes in the one grand square in Ottawa, at the top of Elgin Street, staring up at the nation's haunting war memorial with its massive archway, beneath which horses gallop and soldiers trudge. The event is the interment of Canada's Unknown Soldier, whose remains have recently been shipped back from France.

Governor General Adrienne Clarkson is, in her regal manner, eulogizing this boy. She begins unremarkably, lamenting his early death, evoking the noble notion of dying for freedom. But she raises the bar, quoting Herodotus: "In peace, sons bury their fathers; in war, fathers bury their sons." There are spirits among us now: ancient writers, slain soldiers, broken fathers. She launches into a list of all the things we can't know about the life that once inhabited

328

this body: "We do not know if he was a MacPherson or a Chartrand. He could have been a Kaminski or a Swiftarrow. We do not know if he was a father. We do not know if his mother or wife received that telegram —"Was he a Prairie boy? Did he have brown eyes? Read poetry? I am nearly swooning. The speech is shamelessly patriotic. She — or, more likely, her speech writer — has patched in references to canoes, whales, the Rocky Mountains, even hockey. But underneath the carefully inclusive language thrums a scolding, a bald horror at the disappearance of this life. In itemizing our ignorance so particularly, Clarkson evokes every boy and girl, every thrashing vulnerability and failing of humanity. She breathes life into death, and — spectacularly, chillingly — inserts death into life.

It's this perfect marriage of the two eternally opposed truths of our existence that a mourning ritual ought to accomplish. You'd think we'd get it right more often. We've been struggling with it long enough.

More and more, I think getting it right is a matter of — as Clarkson magnificently managed to do with this anonymous casualty of war — honouring that one, weird, pimply, bruised, struggling, aquamarine existence; the lone life that has passed. In so doing, we honour them all. But most of the time, this is not what we're trying to do. We are sorry, flailing creatures; we aim lower. We make the requisite appearances at funerals, share a few hugs and memories, and turn away, back to work, back to "ordinary" life, temporarily shaken: It could have been *my* mother, *my* husband, *my* child. If the death is not too close, we try not to think on it too hard. The life — and its end — retreats into shadow.

What's worse is when the death *is* a direct hit. Now we aim higher. We're out for glory.

Neanderthals, as far back as 50,000 B.C., buried their dead with provisions: food, weapons, and other objects they might "need." The belief that something in us survives death — must continue to have needs — also seems intrinsic to humanity. There are doctrines and anti-doctrines that contend death means annihilation, but even their proponents follow rituals when a death occurs; even they vow to cultivate in memory something of the life that has past.

There is narcissism in this, a deep-seated need not just for immortality — for this will hardly suffice. We want to live forever, yes, but to be special while we're at it. One of the most heartbreaking books to mess about in this quicksand of desire is American writer Annie Dillard's *For the Time Being.* True to form, Dillard spares us nothing, laying the brutal facts across the page like indictments. For example: "There are 1,198,500,000 people alive now in China. To get a feel for what this means, simply take yourself — in all your singularity, importance, complexity, and love — and multiply by 1,198,500,000. See? Nothing to it." Worse than the lives are the deaths: 164,000 a day, she reports, around the world. "Off they go," writes Dillard, "these many great and beloved people, as death subtracts them one by one …"

Dillard winds me with magnitude, the crushing honesty of numbers. I take comfort, oddly, in Irion, Mr. Anti-Eulogy himself. It's a thrill to find him describing death, in *Vestige or Value,* as "an intensely personal thing … as distinctly individual and personal as life." The eulogy may prod our memories, our relationships with fellow mourners. It may even offer insights into our own lives. But what matters is whether it accomplishes that separation from the crowd of lives and deaths that threatens to suffocate, render insignificant, this one — this one that matters to us.

Does this mean we must make this life out to be better than the other 163,999 that have ended today?

It is only in death that one can become flawless. The temptation to cast a glow of saintliness on a dead person is sometimes irresistible, a hold-over of superstition — we don't want no ghosts shaking their misty fists at *us* — or a desire in ourselves not to be bad-mouthed after *we're* gone. There may also be an instinctive kindness at play. Is it fair to criticize a person who's beyond encountering any opportunity to improve or change? Once you're dead, as far as the living are concerned you're a finished product. What's the point of complaining about you now? You're not bothering us anymore. But it's more than all of this. We often need to elevate this lost person to something greater than your average human being. We told ourselves incessantly after Joana died that she had crammed more life into two decades than many are capable of in seven. What, other than her untimely death, gave us the right to believe this? But seven years later, I still can't shake the conviction. Nor will I allow that my grandmother was in any way typical. She didn't bake cookies, didn't force food down our throats, didn't pinch our cheeks, I reported in my eulogy. She was different. This was my implication: She was more.

It matters, in the face of death, to tell ourselves we've had something more. Make something bigger, better, and maybe it's easier to hang onto. And yet this desire can ring false with the insistence and strength of a bell tower. It gets embarrassing. I have a hardback called *Soldier of Conscience,* a slim, faded, grey volume containing a biography of and funeral addresses for an Edward Perkins Clark. Clark died in 1903. His widow had published this vanity memorial within the year. He was a Brooklynite and — if you believe the solemn eulogies preserved here — a highly esteemed editorial writer for the *New York Evening Post.* The Reverend Joseph Dunn Burrell tells us Clark was a man who'd achieved "perfect sincerity" and that "whatever he wrote had upon it the mark of an authority." By the time Burrell thanks God for the "privilege of knowing a man so upright, unselfish and loyal," I am looking for the catch. Perhaps he ate like a pig. Patronized his wife. Put too much pressure on his kids — or hardly knew them. I imagine these poor dears huddled in a pew, being force-fed all this praise about an indifferent father.

But I am also tempted to lift some of the quotes — particularly those relating to his prowess as a writer — to pass on to my spouse for possible inclusion in my own eulogy.

No wonder the form is greeted with so much suspicion. The worst can happen when people get up to speak: uncomfortable revelation, bitterness, lies, amateur preaching, and long, unbearable speeches that have little to say about the person who's died. To allow it, if you are presiding over a service, is to surrender control. Roman Catholics do so begrudgingly, fearing length, inappropriate content, and the eulogy's usurping of the real purpose of the funeral mass: to focus on a hope for resurrection. Muslims don't eulogize their dead; they recite prayers meant to ease the passage of the soul. Romans are not even supposed to utter the name of the person who's died, for fear of summoning the ghost. The book *In Memoriam: A Practical Guide to Planning a Memorial Service,* by Amanda Bennett and Terence Foley, describes various religious services marking death. The Eastern Orthodox priest quoted within is unforgiving regarding any method of personalizing a death: "A memorial service isn't simply allowing the bereaved to do whatever they like. The event needs solemnity and mystery." The implication: If people weren't so spiritually lazy, so weak, they wouldn't need to harp on this person's life. They could let the dead go in peace.

French social historian Phillipe Ariès says we once managed exactly this, as a matter of course. He tracks, in the small 1973 volume *Western Attitudes toward Death: From the Middle Ages to the Present,* how we have turned mortality into a personal thing. Before the eleventh century, he describes, death was "both familiar and near, evoking no great fear or awe." This is Ariès's favourite period. By the later Middle Ages, people were beginning to believe their fate at the Last Judgment would link back to how they lived their lives. Death has been touched by the singular existence, and Ariès's tone has begun to sour. By the sixteenth and seventeenth centuries, this growing individualism manifests in a resurgence of grave-marking, and by the nineteenth century, Ariès is aghast at the emergence of what he calls a "cult of memory," which has "conferred upon the dead a sort of immortality." It's a cult, he writes, that grows like gangbusters throughout the twentieth century: "Those who no longer go to church still go to the cemetery ... They meditate there, that is to say they evoke the dead person ..."

Ariès emerges through his recounting of this evolution as a plagued soul, likely pacing through long nights, fretting over the way we've forgotten how to die. I wonder what sort of epilogue he might write today, for, as individualistic baby boomers age and as Western society in general takes less comfort in religious notions of afterlife, we have raised the personalization of death to an extreme. Funeral homes market themselves on their ability to accommodate whatever quirky wishes people might have. Homemade mourning rituals are almost *de rigueur*. It is not uncommon to hear Elvis and Mick Jagger crooning in funeral parlours. Bristol-board (or digital) photo essays at wakes are a matter of course. And libraries are stocked with recently published guides on how to stage "creative" services. These guides inevitably include tips, or entire chapters, on eulogies, for the eulogy is key to the individualization of death. It is "likely the place you want to spend most energy," writes Carolyn Pogue in *Language of the Heart: Rituals, Stories and Information about Death*. As Vancouver Anglican reverend Donald Grayston told the Canadian Press in an article in 1996: "To say someone is resting in Abraham's bosom, you can hear the little voices in people's heads saying, 'Oh yeah, does he believe that?' But the common experiences that people share with the departed are something we can all agree on."

Well, maybe not always. As Theroux argues, "If the eulogist is wrong about the deceased, he or she can be quite right about a larger truth." With all respect to Ariès, there *is* a narrative of growth here. In spooking ourselves so profoundly, we have learned to appreciate every life that touches our own — to distill the moments that create and define who we are; to assert that each of the lives behind that evolution was important.

Of course, the working out of our memory muscles, making them bulge with the juices of the lives that have gone before us, can also constitute denial. Which is winning out, growth or fear? There is no place more apt for examining such questions than the Internet, our handy storm sewer for the modern psyche. "Google" the word "eulogy," and pages of links arise, many leading to sites where the texts of eulogies for famous people have been posted, including William Shakespeare and William Gilbert (of Gilbert and Sullivan). Mostly, personal home pages appear at which loved ones — hardly so famous while living — are given tribute. I visit the site memorializing Paul Dean Koontz, created by his daughter, Dianne Evans, which contains the eulogy she read at her father's funeral. Reading it, I learn that this man — an ordinary American who lived in El Dorado, Kansas — fought in World War II, made his living as a geologist, volunteered for the Boy Scouts, and bribed his softball-playing daughter with the promise of one silver dollar for each home run she hit.

On other Web sites I become acquainted with the "elf woman" Margaret Nygard, who died in 1975 and apparently single-handed-ly saved the Eno River in central North Carolina from unchecked development; Dr. Anthony Dipple, whose son remembers asking him for an explanation of "the Coriolis effect" and receiving a long lesson that somehow connected to Einstein's Theory of Relativity; and Garry Yablans, who jogged twenty-five thousand miles over a twenty-year period. I am partial to Bucky Walker, who, orphaned as a teenager, "struggled to make some sense of life," sometimes suc-ceeding and sometimes failing. He "loved to hunt, but didn't have the heart to kill anything." He died at forty-two.

Most of these on-line eulogies are neither profound nor well written. Many are as empty as a Hallmark card. But I have to force myself to stop clicking. For in enough of them to keep me coming back for more, some detail leaps out, wearing the badge of a personality, hinting at that fascinating string of events — which can never be duplicated — that make up a life.

Yet I worry. To what extent are these tributes changing the nature of the eulogy? A eulogy, traditionally, is a moment in time. What matters is the speaking of the words aloud at a designated event. On the Internet, this event — and that initial unwillingness to let go — can go on, and on, and on.

The sheer number of on-line souls is unsettling. At the Virtual Memorial Garden *(catless.ncl.ac.uk/VMG/)* mourners can, for no cost, post eulogies and messages to dead loved ones. At forevernetwork.com, run by the Hollywood Cemetery in California, more elaborate tribute pages can be purchased. The "Diamond Biography," for example, at $995 U.S. contains twenty-five photos, twenty-five recorded audio descriptions, two videos, an "interactive media scrapbook," and a six-hundred-word biography. The Web site promises "permanent preservation" (suggesting the company will never fold, change its business plan, or remove your husband from its archives once you are too dead to notice). Speech-writers.com, meanwhile, sells stock eulogies for twenty-five dollars, offering a "selection of suitable" texts for children, mothers, fathers, colleagues, siblings, grandparents, or "friends and neighbours." For $275 and the time it takes to fill out a questionnaire, you can buy a "personalized" eulogy, running about three minutes. "What connection do you have with the deceased and why are you speaking?" "Name a particular habit of the deceased, i.e., he/she was a great amateur actor/dancer." Buyers are warned to remember that "it is content rather than length that is important."

I shouldn't wrinkle my nose; we're not all comfortable with our writing skills, particularly in the wake of a death. But this is not fast food, or hotel management, where some argument can be made for uniform quality. There's no getting away from the fact that a eulogy is written in haste, by someone in the grip of unfiltered emotions. This is part of its charm and its intrinsic value. Even when it fails, even when it sanctifies. How else can we see who we are, what we must try to overcome?

Not all is lost, for there are also promising changes in the way we eulogize. Along the way, we have begun to learn the power of honest portrayal. Not: He was good or he was bad. Simply: He was like this.

A piece in the *L.A. Times* a few years ago concluded that the best eulogies don't shy away from darkness. It quoted sportscaster Bob Costas, who refused to offer praise alone when "eulogizing" Mickey Mantle, who had been a reformed alcoholic. "I felt that if I didn't in some way acknowledge the complexity of his character — the flaws as well as the more appealing parts of him — then the appreciation would sound just like hero worship. The facts of his life did not render untrue what was magnificent about him. If anything, they made it more poignant."

Costas alluded to Mantle's "flaws." He didn't run down the list. He didn't name one. This, to my mind, was enough. It was also a relief. Nobody's perfect, and we ought to acknowledge that, or a eulogy may grate. But I rail against the warts-and-all philosophy. Who are we to judge these people, deciding which faults we ought to scrutinize alongside their virtues — indeed, deciding which are faults or virtues? We are well aware we're all imperfect. Must a eulogy drive this home? Why not let a person's few most remarkable — or weird or interesting or funny — qualities shine, untarnished, just this once?

A friend of mine, Rod Charles, who recently eulogized his father — himself a United Church minister who'd eulogized hundreds — shared with me his philosophy, learned from his dad, of honouring the dead. "You focus on the one attribute this person had that everyone would know, would have felt. Find that one telling thing, the thing they did better than anyone. There is always something to admire and appreciate." Rod compared his eulogy to his father to a practice he had taken of laying blankets over him in the hospital when he was ill. "It's nothing really, I just wanted to do something for the guy. That's what it was. It was the last thing I would say to him; a warm blanket I was putting over him in the church."

Was this wimpy? His father was dead, gone. He had no more need of blankets. But that's not the point. In *Giving Sorrow Words: How to Cope with Grief and Get on with Your Life,* by Candy Lightner (founder of Mothers Against Drunk Driving) and Nancy Hathaway, a woman explains why she spoke at her niece's funeral. It was a simple eulogy. She shared how they became friends "over a box of crayons," how the girl liked gruesome movies, and she described some time they had spent together. What mattered was saying anything at all. "I was glad I spoke because most of the time nobody wants to hear you talk about someone who's dead. It was a relief to say this is why I loved her; this is why I'm going to miss her so much."

There must be something to respect here. Not all religions are sour on eulogies. Baptists, unless ultra-conservative, allow eulogies, as do Mormons and Methodists. Unitarians build the entire funeral service around memorializing the deceased: religious messages are out. Some Buddhists believe proper remembrance aids the soul's rebirth. And Judaism, bless it, doesn't just allow eulogizing; it is a prescribed part of the funeral. If a Jewish funeral took place without a eulogy, one rabbi tells me, "the people attending the service would be amazed."

Eulogy Three, Take Two

She had short brown hair and rosy cheeks. Grew up in the suburbs: a bookworm, a ballplayer, and a clumsy, earnest child. She loved to swim, dreamt of living by the ocean, in dense fog. She thought too much, analyzed her impulses and actions to death. Friends and family counted on her, considered her reliable, steady. The responsible one. She absorbed this impression of herself, tried to live up to it. When she failed, she would lie awake nights, replaying situations in her mind, asking herself why she'd made the decision she did. Why she'd faltered.

Chickened out.

The service for Diana, two nights after our wonderful, uplifting meeting with the ministers, is difficult to sit through. Her daughter has decided she's not able to speak — perfectly understandable. But because nobody else volunteered, the main eulogy is delivered by one of the ministers. She puts forth a valiant effort to relate our sentiments and anecdotes, weaving them around a loose biographical sketch, including all the facets she can of this woman's life and character. But the thing echoes flat and empty. Because this is a Unitarian memorial service, containing no mass nor any religious content, we are left with little, certainly nothing with the power to draw us in, rub us against the brutal truth of Diana's death. I leave the church thinking I would have welcomed "Be Not Afraid" or some equally maudlin, but appropriately soul-piercing hymn.

Not long after, on a visit to Toronto, I talk with writer Rick Salutin, who has given many eulogies, and who also dutifully writes about deceased friends in his *Globe and Mail* column. This might seem touching, but Salutin is hardly some huggable rag doll. When I ask what he thinks a eulogy should accomplish, he glares from beneath his columnist's slouch. "It's bullshit, really. You try to say something intelligent and insightful. There's no way it can be comprehensive. Anybody who thinks they can sum up the essence of another person … I don't think there is any such thing. It's completely about you. It's what strikes you about this person."

That's what was missing. The minister was faithful to everything she was told, and that was the problem. What she did was try to sum up — and Salutin is right, this is impossible. I'm reminded of how Theroux describes eulogies as "double portraits." What I begin to think they are, at least the way I do them, is a window into a relationship. And it's through staring down that relationship that those listening might begin to understand or at least examine their own relationship with the person who's died. For it's not just a person we mourn, it's that particular thing they were to us.

Things crystallize back in Ottawa, when I meet with Susan Brown, a funeral director for Tubman Funeral Homes. Brown wears her brown hair straight and, on her face, a perpetual expression of concern. She folds her hands on the table as we talk. I ask this woman, who's witnessed scores of funerals, what eulogists have in common. I am hoping for characteristics. Perhaps, she will say, eulogists are people who tend to observe more than interact. They are not afraid to talk about death. They are, by definition, witnesses. Storytellers. People seeking answers. I recall a habit I developed in high school of keeping a notebook that contained brief character sketches of all my friends. Just what did this portend?

But Brown is a practical woman in a navy suit who sees a lot of death, doesn't just daydream about it. More important than character traits, she guesses, is a person's relationship to the deceased: "Individuals who are able to get up and speak are very clear on what their emotions and thoughts are toward this individual."

Brown is less worried about who says the eulogy than what good ones tend to accomplish. For starters, they give people something to talk about. "We realize nobody wants to be here. It's one of the saddest occasions and one of the most stressful of our lives. And everyone's afraid of saying the wrong thing. It opens that door for people to step forward and say, 'You know, I really appreciated what Bob said about Bill. It was so true and it made me remember a story about …' It opens up those gates."

That's no small feat. Brown describes grief as a thing of shifting balance: it begins in overpowering sadness, with emotion that is gradually balanced by pleasant memory (an idealized summary, but there seems some basic truth to it). "At the time of the service," she explains, "the weight of grief is physically on everybody's shoulders and heart. The eulogy is like a hook coming out of the sky, hooking into some of that grief and starting to alleviate some of the weight."

That is all a eulogy is. A hook. A hook that you fashion out of your experience. It might be heavy or light or sharp or barbed or rusted or packed with bait. I have been afraid of reducing people, lives that have affected me deeply, to words, forgetting that words are nothing more than a tool. They can't take over a life, merely tattoo it.

And what of these false eulogies I compose, for the living? Am I really "practising" for their deaths? It's not so bald as that. These are pop quizzes I spring on myself, demanding answers: Am I paying enough attention? Am I really seeing this person I care for — appreciating and absorbing her with all the scrutiny and openness she deserves? If she were gone, what might I tell you about her? What could I tell myself?

I open my wine-red journal and read my eulogy to Joana. It is shamelessly enthusiastic but not so bad as I feared: playful and honest, neither sappy nor mean. What strikes me more than the eulogy itself are two comments I wrote outside of it. The first, in glaring red ink and circled amid rough notes for the speech, reads: "Maybe it should be what I've learned, so everyone can leave thinking about what Joana taught them." The other was written four days after the service, addressed directly to Joana: "I need to thank you for asking me to write something for your memorial. It was a task that kept me up and positive and close to you last week."

So. It's for them. And it's for me. And it's for her. And it seems to work. Why be stingy with any of us at a time like this?

I sit down to write. There will be a second service for Diana, a public memorial, in just a few days. I see this as a second chance. This time I will blast out my admiration and affection for her, scatter it beneath the light for people to examine, to catch in their palms, to consider and question, and compare with their own.

Eulogy Four: The Listener

I am not the only one who decides to speak at Diana's memorial service. We do it the way it ought to be done, telling tales about her as a teacher, a friend, a mother — sharing the now-precious thoughts and moments she left us with. For that brief hour we feel her among us. We return to our lives rejuvenated, braced for her absence.

About a month later I receive a devastating phone call. For several moments I stand motionless, saying into the receiver, "Oh my God, I can't believe it. I can't believe it." For a friend is telling me that Diana's younger daughter, Anya, sixteen years old, has been struck by a bolt of lightning. She is dead, leaving her father and sister, a family cut by half in the space of eight weeks — leaving all of us gasping, reeling, unable to voice that unanswerable question: Why?

Again, as in some surreal sitcom rerun, we enact the motions of funeral preparation, meeting with the same ministers, in the same backyard of the same friend. I didn't know Anya well enough to puzzle over my role. I am here to lend what meagre support I can to her father, sister, and those close to me who watched her grow up, saw her as one of their own. My job is clear: not, this time, to bring my own words, but to listen to theirs. It's a relief to see that I do know my place — the only relief to be had in these blinding days.

One morning shortly after Anya's funeral I am on the phone with my younger brother, Matt. He is twenty, bulky, and manly, but not so different to me from the uncommonly wise four-year-old I used to ferry to the park every day after school. He speaks softly. He too is mourning a friend, a victim of one of those crimes we helplessly call a "random act" of violence.

Death, I feel, is coming at us from all sides — it will do this; it is ever-present. But rarely does it hit the same targets so consistently. Matt and I compare notes on the funerals, the only tangible things we have on which to dwell.

Anya, like her mother, was Unitarian. Her service was bookended with music she liked, involved a vegetable plant exchange (she preferred "practical" plants to flowers), and was packed with tributes and eulogies: one by the minister (who knew her well), one by her father, another by her sister, and many remembrances shared by friends during something of an open-mic session. I listened, entranced, as the pieces of her person, the various translations and interpretations of her life, melded together into a whole being — not exactly her, but pretty darn close. Her wit was biting and inventive (yes, I had experienced this). Her favourite spot in the house was the back roof over the kitchen. She would absorb any new situation fully, at her leisure, before engaging. (This made her appear timid, which she was not.) She had recently written a precocious note to herself about how to live life as a work of art.

My brother's friend, meanwhile, was sent off with an old-fashioned Catholic mass, containing neither a eulogy nor any other representation of his character. Matt has little to say on the subject except "It's like they're trying to make them all the same."

What could be more diminishing to the life that has ended, more demoralizing to those that trudge on? What could be more false?

Sadly, but also magically, I knew Anya better after her death. This was the power of words, a mystery I was grateful to absorb, for we were superbly fragile that day. Nothing but story — our own narratives — could keep us intact. I was buoyed to see what we are capable of in sorrow, what simple eulogies can achieve: that gentle nudging, massaging — even removal — of the raw, outer layers of grief. How words can keep a soul aloft, hovering above the multitudes, long enough for us all to have that last, blurry, merciful look.

Contributors

Katherine Ashenburg says she has a ten-year attention span when it comes to careers. She was by turns an academic, a CBC Radio producer, and an editor at the *Globe and Mail*. Her first book, *Going to Town: Architectural Walking Tours in Southern Ontario* (Macfarlane Walter & Ross 1996), won the Ontario History Society Prize. Her second, *The Mourner's Dance: What We Do When People Die* (Macfarlane Walter & Ross 2002), was a finalist for the Pearson non-fiction prize. She is *Toronto Life's* design columnist and writes often for the *New York Times* travel section.

Douglas Bell's first book, *Run Over: A Boy, His Mother and An Accident,* was published by Random House in June 2001 and subsequently shortlisted for the 2002 City of Toronto Book Prize. The piece appearing in this volume is the basis for that book. Currently writing for and acting in the CBC television series *The Newsroom,* Bell is a frequent contributor to Canadian newspapers and magazines including the *Globe and Mail, National Post, Saturday Night,* and *Lola.* He lives in Toronto with dogs, cats, children, and a variety of other associates.

Ted Bishop rides a Ducati and teaches English at the University of Alberta in Edmonton. He has published articles on James Joyce and modernist publishing, authored or edited books on Virginia Woolf and the Bloomsbury group, and written motorcycling articles for *Rider* magazine and *Cycle Canada,* two of which were nominated for National Magazine Awards.

A-A Farman-Farmaian is a writer and artist who lives and works in Amirania.

Moira Farr is an award-winning writer and editor whose essays, reviews, feature articles, and editorial work have appeared in numerous publications, including the *Globe and Mail, National Post, This Magazine, Toronto Life, Chatelaine,* and several writing anthologies. Her first book, *After Daniel: A Suicide Survivor's Tale* (HarperFlamingo 1999), was shortlisted for a number of prestigious awards and was also the *Edmonton Journal*'s top pick for non-fiction. She is contributing editor for the *Ryerson Review of Journalism* and teaches magazine writing at Carleton University.

Alyse Frampton is a Toronto-based writer. Her articles have appeared in *Saturday Night, Smithsonian, Equinox,* and many other magazines and newspapers.

Camilla Gibb is the author of two novels, numerous short stories, articles, and reviews. Her novels, *Mouthing the Words* (Pedlar 1999) and *The Petty Details of So-and-So's Life* (Doubleday 2002), were both selected by the *Globe and Mail* as best books of the year and have been published in fourteen countries. She was the winner of the CBC Canadian Literary Award for short stories in 2001.

Matthew Hart began his career at the *Ottawa Citizen,* became a CBC reporter and producer, then turned freelance. He has written for the *Atlantic Monthly, Saturday Night, W,* and many other magazines. He had a column in the *Globe and Mail*'s *Toronto* magazine, was a contributing editor of *Canadian Art,* and has written for television and film. Of his six books, the most recent, *Diamond: The History of a Cold-Blooded Love Affair* (Penguin Canada 2001) was translated into seven languages. He is now at work on a book about art theft.

Johanna Keller's essays on music and literature appear in the *New York Times, Los Angeles Times, London Evening Standard, Opera News, Symphony,* and *Musical America.* In 2002, she was a USC Annenberg Getty Arts Journalism Fellow in Los Angeles. For her *New York Times* essays she won the ASCAP–Deems Taylor Award and the New York Newswomen's Club Front Page Award. She has taught at Eugene Lang College, The New School University and is a visiting assistant professor at the S. I. Newhouse School of Public Communications at Syracuse University.

Chris Koentges lives in Calgary. He is the author of *Towards an Erratic State* (Fox Run Press 2003) and publisher of *The Jack Jackman Project (jackjackman.com/).* His documentary *Seeking the Urban Eldorado* was broadcast on CBC Radio's *Ideas* in March 2003. He writes the National Magazine Award–winning "Reluctant Nomad" column for *Outpost* magazine.

Anita Lahey's journalism has appeared in *Canadian Geographic, Cottage Life, Saturday Night, Canadian Business, Ottawa City, Chatelaine, Equinox, Vernissage,* and many other magazines. She has published poetry in *Arc, The New Quarterly, Pagitica,* and *The Malahat Review,* as well as on fabric and as a Delirium Press broadside. She is an art and creative writing tour guide at the National Gallery of Canada, and is writing a play.

Philip Marchand has been books columnist for the *Toronto Star* since 1989. His books include *Just Looking, Thank You* (Macmillan 1976), a collection of his magazine journalism; *Marshall McLuhan: The Medium and the Messenger* (Houghton Mifflin 1989); the crime novel *Deadly Spirits* (Stoddart 1994); *Ripostes: Reflections on Canadian Literature* (Porcupine's Quill 1998); and a revised and reissued edition of *Marshall McLuhan: The Medium and the Messenger* (MIT 1998). Marchand currently lives in Toronto with his wife.

Ian Pearson is a veteran Toronto writer, editor, and radio producer. He has worked as an editor at *Maclean's, Toronto* magazine, and *Saturday Night*. His articles have appeared in most major Canadian magazines, winning five National Magazine Award nominations. He was books producer for CBC Radio's *Morningside* for three seasons and was a contributing editor of *Saturday Night* during the 1990s. He is also a consulting producer for CBC Radio's *Writers and Company* and the proprietor of the Zedtone record label.

Alberto Ruy-Sánchez is a Mexican writer and editor and the author of seventeen books of fiction, non-fiction, and poetry. He earned his PhD from Jussieu University in Paris. His first novel, *Mogador* (City Lights 1993), was awarded the Xavier Villaurrutia Prize, the most prestigious literary recognition in Mexico. Since 1988, Ruy-Sánchez has been the publisher and founding editor of Latin America's leading arts magazine, *Artes de Mexico,* which has received numerous national and international awards. In 2000, Ruy-Sánchez was decorated by the French government as Officier de l'Ordre des Arts et des Lettres. He is the chair of the Creative Non-Fiction and Cultural Journalism Program at The Banff Centre.

Ellen Vanstone grew up in Winnipeg, worked briefly as a sports reporter in Vancouver, and is now a writer living in Toronto. The piece in this anthology is based on her stint as an arts editor at the *National Post*. Over the past twenty years, she has subsidized her freelance career with stints at various other publications, including the *Globe and Mail, TV Guide, Toronto Life, T.O. Magazine,* and *Canadian Art.*

Previously published essays include Katherine Ashenburg's "Doctor's Daughters: Helen, Sue, and Me" (*American Scholar,* Summer 2003), Douglas Bell's "The Accidental Course of My Illness" (which was the basis for *Run Over: A Boy, His Mother and An Accident,* Random House, 2001), an abridged version of Philip Marchand's "Lea and Me" (*Toronto Life,* 2002), an abridged version of Ted Bishop's "The Motorcycle and the Archive" (*Enroute* magazine, April 2003), and Ellen Vanstone's "*Post* Traumatic Stress" (*Toronto Life,* October 2001).